THE CHESS
COMPETITORS'
HANDBOOK

THE CHESS COMPETITORS' HANDBOOK

B. M. Kažić

With co-authors

D. Djaja
M. E. Morrison
A. Elo

ARCO PUBLISHING, INC.
New York

Published 1980 by Arco Publishing, Inc.
219 Park Avenue South, New York, N.Y. 10003

Copyright © 1979 by B.M. Kažić

Printed in Great Britain

Library of Congress Cataloguing in Publication Data

Kažić, B
    The chess competitors' handbook.
    Includes bibliographical references and index.
    1. Chess—Tournaments—Handbooks, manuals, etc.
    I. Title.
    GV1455.K265   794.1'57   80-11137

ISBN 0 668 04959 6
ISBN 0 668 04963 4 pbk.

Contents

Acknowledgements
and General Bibliography

Abramov, Lev, Zrazhevsky, Yuri and Karakhan, Yuri: *Organizatsia i sudeistvo shahmatnykh sovevnovanii*, Moscow, Fiskultura i sport, 1977.

Brinckman, A. and Rellstab, L.: *Turnier Taschenbuch* (4th edition), Berlin & New York, Walter de Gruyter, 1977.

Elo, Arpad E.: *Ratings of Chess Players, Past and Present, The*, London, B. T. Batsford Ltd, 1978.

Garkunov, L. and Zrazhevsky, Y.: *Sudeistvo Shahmatnykh Sorevnovany*, Moscow, Fiskultura i Sport, 1959.

Harkness, Kenneth: *Official Chess Handbook*, New York, David McKay Inc., 1967.

Karakhan, Yuri: *Osnovy Sudeistva v Shahmatah*, Moscow, Sovetskaya Rossia, 1974.

Kažić, Božidar and Djaja, Dragutin: *Šahovski piručnik*, Belgrade, Šahovski savez Jugoslavije, 1966.

Kažić, Božidar: *Pravila šahovske igre sa komentarima* (2nd edition), Belgrade, Sportska Knjiga, 1977.

L'Italia Scacchistica: *Regolamenti FSI - FIDE*, Milan, 1975.

Minutes of FIDE Congresses (1950-79).

Morrison, Martin E.: *Official Rules of Chess* (with official FIDE Interpretations), New York, David McKay Inc., 1977.

Reuben, Stewart and Morrish, Peter: *London Chess Association Swiss Pairing Rules*, London, 1979.

Siegfried Engelhardt Verlag: *Streitfälle aus der Turnier-Praxis*, Berlin, 1963.

United States Chess Federation: *Catalog of Chess Books and Equipment*, New Windsor, 1978.

Yurchomanski, N., Todorov, G. and Stanchev, Z.: *Shamaten Kodeks*, Sofia, Medicina i fiskultura, 1973.

Foreword

By the former President of FIDE

Many questions are regularly asked by national and local chess federations, clubs, players, organizers, chess developing countries and other interested persons concerning regulations, conditions, instructions and anything else in the field of chess. FIDE has an information index, a coded system which helps us in finding the answers to such questions, but FIDE is not so well equipped that it can answer all questions from everywhere in the world. FIDE sometimes tries to do so, but mostly it has to limit itself to references or simply answer: ask your own federation, which has received in proper time all regulations and other documents.

Therefore the publication of this Chess Handbook is a service of immense value not only for FIDE, but also for all chess federations, and especially for developing chess countries. Many efforts have been made recently to open the 'third world' to chess, to teach its players, to give them practice in tournaments etc. But teaching the organizers of the 'third world' countries is a most important job which scarcely has been done so far. This book goes a long way towards solving this problem.

Those who are interested in promoting chess in a developing country now have a reliable guide to start. The beginning is often the most difficult part of the work. There is no doubt that the Handbook, as well as assisting FIDE and national federations, will be a life saver for chess communities far away, and will make its tour round the world in the hundred and more countries where chess is either flourishing or has just started or still finds itself in an embryonic stage.

The Handbook fills an urgent need of the whole chess world and I recommend it heartily and with full conviction.

Dr. Max Euwe,
President of Fide 1970-78

Introduction

This unique book offers an 'international anthology' of the best procedures developed throughout the world for organising and controlling chess competitions. We have tried to compile a book useful to everyone – organizers, arbiters and players – by making use of experience, knowledge and reference to handbooks from many countries.

We hope the result is an international handbook which will not be limited by national boundaries. The focus has been on what we consider to be of general importance and away from problems of purely local relevance. The needs of organizers in developed environments as well as those of countries where chess is only just beginning to develop is borne in mind.

The large number of tournaments being organized in the world today, the general expansion of chess, many changes in the Laws of Chess and in FIDE regulations, the Elo System, and many innovations in world chess, make such a book topical. We hope that it will help clubs, arbiters, organizers and chessplayers in general to promote the organization of chess competitions. 'Competition', as former world champion Botvinnik states, 'is the common concern of players and organizers, and arbiters are collaborators in creating the art of chess, in educating and in fostering the game of chess.'

B. M. Kažić
Belgrade, March 1979.

1 Types of Chess Competition

Chess competitions greatly vary in terms of their structure, character, selection of contestants, purpose, etc., and they can be divided into several groups.

Competitions may be *team* or *individual* (depending on how the attained results are calculated), *official* or *off-hand*, (depending on the purpose and character of the competition), *senior, junior, ladies*, etc., *national* or *international* etc. We can divide all chess events in terms of their internal structure into several general groups: matches and tournaments, exhibitions, chess composition and other events.

Types of Chess Games

We may distinguish between tournament, off-hand and lightning games; games which are played by post, radio, telex, telegraph and telephone; and, finally, simultaneous displays, consultation games and blindfold games.

Tournament games are played with a chess clock at a pre-determined move rate, with the moves being recorded. Each player is given a certain amount of time on his clock for a given number of moves, say two hours for the first 40 moves and one hour for every 20 subsequent moves.

The off-hand 'skittle', casual or *'friendly' game* is a feature of home, club and coffee house chess, usually played at a quicker rate than competitive chess and mostly without a chess clock. The length of off-hand games depends on the agreement and understanding reached by the players.

The lightning game is played extremely rapidly, and the rate of play is determined in one of the two following ways:
a) each player has a set time, e.g. 5 minutes, for the entire game.
b) the time is prescribed for each move, e.g. 10 seconds.

A bell or buzzer is set to ring every 5, 7 or 10 seconds (depending on the rate of play): the player who has the move must execute it precisely at the sound of the bell. Other regulations on the playing of lightning games can be adapted from the FIDE Regulations for lightning chess competitions (see p. 8).

Lightning games, given their dynamic and often unexpected turns, are extremely popular with the broader chess public. They are important for the contestants because they serve to improve their speed and reflexes, elements which are of significance for tournament games, especially when under time-pressure.

Correspondence games, using the post (mail), can last several months, a year or even more. Against one opponent, two or more games are often contested simultaneously. There are many organisations for conducting postal competitions which are played according to special regulations.

Since the players have considerable time (e.g. 48 hours) to make each move, correspondence chess games are of great importance for the qualitative development of chess, especially in terms of opening theory. Moreover, they allow thousands of chessplayers from non-chess centres, from small and remote places, to compete without leaving their places of employment. Many renowned grandmasters enjoy playing in correspondence chess competitions.

Chess games may also be played over the radio, or by telegraph, telephone, or telex.

Blindfold games are played without looking at the chess board and pieces. Several hundred years ago, blindfold games were a tremendous attraction, but today, practically any average player can play a blindfold game.

The playing of one or more blindfold games, provided that the number of games remains within reason, is of value to players for, more than in 'ordinary' chess, this form develops memory and strengthens the power of concentration.

Consultation games are played on one board with two groups of players vying against each other. These games are organized so that groups of players play in one room, and the others in another. Each group notifies the other as to its executed move through the arbiter. These games are also usually played with a chess clock and the moves are recorded.

Consultation games are most useful, for several players exchange views on a given position and thereby improve their own knowledge.

A master can play a consultation game alone against an entire group of players.

Similar to the consultation game is the *alternating consultation game* in which two players play against another two, without consultation, and with all four alternating in the execution of moves.

Matches and Tournaments

Strictly speaking, any competition which embraces more than two players could be called a tournament, while a match is a competition of several games between two players (or two teams). Match-tournaments consist of a small number of players who play two, three or more games against each other.

Various tournament systems exist for determining the pairings, colour of the pieces and ultimate ranking of the players. These systems are explained in a separate chapter of this book. Here, we should just like to mention special kinds of tournaments which are sometimes organized.

Many clubs hold what are called *ladder (or permanent) tournaments*. After the club's championship tournament, the players are ranked and each is given a number. The player with the lower number has the right to challenge the one above him to a match. If the former wins the match he switches places with the defeated player. If he loses or the match is a tie, then the players retain their standings in the ranking. Challenges to a match may be addressed through the club's management which rules on the request, decides on the number of games, the date and other details, so that these matches have an official character. In all uneven games, the white pieces go to the player who has been challenged. These matches are called permanent or 'ladder' tournaments.

Theme tournaments are organized so that all contestants must play an opening which has been prescribed in advance, i.e. a certain number of initial moves prescribed by the tournament regulations. The importance of such tournaments lies in the fact that currently unclear variations are prescribed for the mandatory openings so that they may be theoretically elaborated and investigated. If some gambit is chosen as the compulsory opening, then the tournament is called a gambit tournament.

Handicap tournaments are another special kind of tournament: here the stronger players make some concession to the weaker players e.g. a piece or pawn and move.

Exhibition displays

This group of chess events includes simultaneous displays, clock simuls and blindfold displays.

Simultaneous displays are competitions in which a strong player plays simultaneously against several players. These are always popular among chess fans and are of great importance in terms of publicity.

It is extremely simple to organize simultaneous displays. The tables with the chess sets are set up next to each other in the shape of a horseshoe or rectangle. The contestants sit on the outside and behind them are the spectators, while the master moves around the closed area in a circle so that he moves directly from the last player in line to the first, etc.

The rules which apply to simultaneous displays are simple and can be termed as follows:

1. The master plays with the white pieces in all games. This rule can be overlooked if the master so agrees.

2. The player (the contestant in the display) executes a move only when the master comes up to his board. Even if he has already thought of a move, the player must wait for the master to reach his board and only then execute that move in front of him.

3. If the player does not execute a move when the master reaches his board, then the master may declare that game in his own favour.

4. The player may, when the master reaches his board, occasionally execute the following and more moves while the master is there, provided that he can immediately reply to the master's moves.

5. In exceptional cases, the player may postpone executing his move for the next round, but only with the master's consent.

6. While the master is at the other boards, the contestant in the simultaneous display must not move a piece on his board. If the master sees that the position on the board has been changed, i.e. that the player has rearranged the pieces by himself, he has the right to call the arbiter who will register the game in favour of the master.

7. The contestant in a simultaneous display may not change the move he has executed. For the master conducting the session, however, a move is considered played only when the master has moved away from that board and played a move on the next board.

8. All contestants in the display are advised to write down their games.

Alternating simultaneous displays are organized in the same way, except that two masters play simultaneously, one after the other, which means that they alternate in executing the moves. The masters must try not to be directly behind each other, but rather at an equal distance, so that the contestants have enough time to contemplate the move before the second master reaches them. This is an extremely interesting kind of simultaneous display because both masters must penetrate not only into the plans and combinations of their opponents, but also into those of one another. Consequently, this type of simultaneous competition can be played well by masters who are similar in strength and in playing style.

Clock simuls or handicap matches differ from simultaneous displays in that a much smaller number of players takes part, usually 6 to 12, but these are usually selected, highly skilled players.

The participants in a handicap match are usually players who are two categories below that of the player conducting the session. The matches are played with chess clocks and are serious chess events of significance for the training of a team and for the training of the person conducting the session. In these displays, the master does not go from one player to another in order, as in simultaneous displays, but rather must wait for a player to execute a move. The problem as far as the master is concerned is that several opponents may execute a move at the same time, so that his clock is running on several boards. The rate of play is usually as at tournaments, i.e. 40 moves for the first two-and-a-half hours, or 40 moves in two hours.

Since a fewer number of players compete in these matches, the tables are placed next to each other in a straight line. The clocks should be placed to face the middle table, so that the master may have the best possible view of the time on the clocks. In contrast to simultaneous displays, in the handicap match the master plays with the white pieces in half of the games, and with the black in the other half.

Blindfold displays were known in ancient times, and they thrill the audience. With his back turned to his opponents, the master dictates the moves and knows at every moment the exact position on all the chessboards. It is difficult and exhausting to play blindfold games, especially if several such games are played simultaneously. Many players who tried to set a record in the number of blindfold games, have, in the process, seriously injured their health. Hence, some countries (e.g. the USSR) do not hold such displays.

The oldest record of blindfold games dates back to the year 970. This was the Greek Joseph Chelebi who demonstrated his skills across India, Persia, Arabia and Tripoli. Three hundred years elapsed until the next chess artist who played 'blindfold'. In 1266, Saracen Bizzerca played three games simultaneously in Florence: one normally and two blindfold. He awed the world, for his oponents were the three strongest players in Italy. Bizzerca won two and drew one game.

In 1790, the simultaneous playing of two blindfold games was still an attraction, as can be seen from the French *Encyclopedia* of that year: 'We had a young man in Paris who played two games simultaneously without looking at the boards or pieces, and he won both games. Both his opponents were first class players, but the young man was even able to give both players the odds of a knight. This young man was named Philidor, the son of the famous musician; he, too, is an accomplished musician. His achievement ranks as an unusual example of the power of memory and performance'.

In 1793, as a 67-year-old in London, Philidor played another blindfold display against two players, winning both games, but he won world-wide fame in 1788 in London when he played three games simultaneously, giving each of his opponents the odds of one move, as well as a pawn to the third. Philidor won all three games.

Since then the number of games played blindfold and simultaneously by masters has steadily risen, and in the past 90 years it has attained undreamt-of proportions.

Competitions in Solving Problems and Studies

These competitions can be organized in a chess room or in the form of special tournaments which are announced in individual papers and journals. The competitions held in a room are short in duration (usually 2 hours) and are held in one of two ways, depending on the technical possibilities of the organizers. Both ways are equally suitable and guarantee the objectivity of the attained standing, provided the necessary order and discipline prevails in the room.

In the first, each contestant is given a separate paper with several problems and studies (usually six), which have to be solved within a given period of time. A certain number of points, prescribed in advance according to the difficulty of the individual task, is won for solving each problem and study. Usually a two-move problem brings 2 points, three-move 3, and four-move 4 points. The number of points for multi-move problems and studies depends on the difficulty of the task. Every partial solution with proof of insolvability brings the same number of points as a solution. Every contestant solves the problem at his table, independently of the others, and writes down the solution: in two-move problems, it is enough to write in the first move, while with other problems and studies the main variants have to be included in the solution. The standings in the competition are determined by the number of points scored, and if two or more have the same number of points, then their order is established according to the time they spent.

When the rate of the competition is accelerated, or when the organizers lack funds to print up diagrams, then the problems are put up one after the other on the demonstration board, and the contestants solve them at their tables. The custom is for two-move problems to be solved in 10 minutes and for the solution of each problem to be adjourned when half the contestants announce the exact solution to the arbiters. Upon submitting their answers, the contestants leave the room. The first contestant to solve the problem is given as many points as half the total number of the contestants. For instance, if there are 20 contestants, the first to solve a problem receives 10 points, and the tenth, 1 point. The contestants then return to the room and the competition is resumed along the same principle. When the last problem is solved, all the points are added up and the standings are determined. This method is especially suitable for massive problem competitions.

In contests organized by newspapers and journals, the solutions are sent within a given period of time to the editors of the problem column or journal. The table of solvers is drawn up on the basis of the number of compiled points.

Composition Contests

Composition contests are announced by individual newspapers and journals or are organized by chess organizations in conjunction with jubilee celebrations and other important events. These contests may be informal or thematic.

Informal contests embrace all original problems which have been published in the newspaper or journal within a certain period of time (usually over a one-year period). They are judged and the best problems are presented awards, honourary tributes, etc.

In thematic tournaments, the contestants send in their problems by a prescribed date to a neutral person, who turns them over to the judge without designating the name of the author. The judge eliminates works which have missed the theme of the tournament, and awards the best compositions.

2 Time Limits

Howard Staunton advocated the use of time devices in the middle of the nineteenth century, as at that time players sometimes took hours over a single move.

The 'modern' chess clock, in which the device which stopped one clock automatically started the other, was designed by Thomas Bright Wilson (1842-1915), a Lancashire (England) organizer, and used successfully in the big London 1883 Tournament.

Each player is given a set amount of time on his clock for a prescribed number of moves e.g. 2 hours for his first 40 moves and 1 hour for each subsequent 20 moves.

At the end of the two hours, and later at the end of each hour on each clock, there is a time-control at which it is verified whether the player has executed the prescribed number of moves within the given time. Time not used is carried forward to subsequent time controls.

Games in many competitions are adjourned at a set time and resumed later. The length of the subsequent sessions is also predetermined. In important tournaments, the first session usually lasts 4 or 5 hours and the sessions for adjourned games 2, 4 or 6 hours. Exceptionally, when all the games have to be completed, for instance the games of the last round or adjournments prior to the last round, the length of the sessions is unlimited.

The usual rate of play at tournaments is one of the following:

a) 40 moves for the first 2½ hours and 16 moves for every subsequent hour (the length of the first session is 5 hours);

b) 45 moves for the first 2½ hours and 18 moves for every subsequent hour (the session lasts 5 hours);

c) 36 moves for the first 2 hours and 18 moves for every subsequent hour (the session lasts 4 hours);

d) 40 moves for the first 2 hours and 20 moves for every subsequent hour (the session lasts 4 hours);

e) 50 moves for the first two-and-a-half hours and 20 moves for every subsequent hour (the session lasts 5 hours).

Here it should be noted that the first session for games which are adjourned usually lasts somewhat longer than the time indicated in the above table. This occurs when the players have executed the prescribed number of moves (or more) and have used up all their time, so that the player who is sealing the move extends the session by spending the time for the second time-control on the sealed move. The duration of subsequent adjournment sessions, however, remains as prescribed.

The Reykjavik System

This system was first instigated in the International Tournament at Reykjavik in 1978. As usual the playing session was 5 hours but the rate of play was 30 moves in 1½ hours and 20 moves per hour thereafter. Thus the players had to complete 50 moves (instead of the normal 40) before a game could be adjourned.

The organisers believed that this arrangement would lead to more vigorous play and in many cases eliminate the need for adjournments. The new system also produced a benefit for the spectators with a lot of excitement coming after less than three hours.

Accelerated Finishes

For tournaments with a limited time for finishing games e.g. weekend tournaments, a popular system is to give the players a fixed time each for completing the remaining moves of the game after the main time-control has been reached. An example is where players make 48 moves in 2 hours and then are given, for example, 15, 30 or 60 minutes to complete all the moves.

The procedure is that when Black has made the last time control move (e.g. move 48), both clocks are stopped, their times noted, and the clocks are reset by the stipulated time so that the final time control is on an hour.

London Chess Association use the following rules:

1. For any query necessitating the presence of a Controller, *the clocks may be stopped.*

2. All Laws of Chess apply, except where specifically amended by these rules.

3. The clock will be placed, except in special circumstances, at the LEFT hand of the player of the white pieces.

4. Players must keep a game score up to date until less than TEN minutes remain on their clock.

5. The clock button MUST be pressed by the hand which makes the move. *Note: gentle pressing is more efficient than banging. Any player using undue force, may, after warning by a Controller, be penalised by the loss of that game.*

6. To win the game on time, a player must have mating material.

7. If the controller is satisfied that a player is making no effort to win the game by normal means, or that it is not possible to win by normal means, then he may declare the game drawn. This may still apply even though one player's flag has fallen.

8. Any *appeal* against a Controller's decision must be made immediately, and accompanied by a deposit. The Appeal will be referred forthwith to an independent 3 man committee.

Rules for Five-Minute Lightning Chess

Approved by the 1977 Central Committee Meeting. To be applied in FIDE-tournaments and strongly recommended to be used in all other international five-minute lightning tournaments.

Duration of the game

1. Each player must make all his moves within five minutes on his clock.

The clock

2. All the clocks must have a special device, usually a 'flag', marking the end of the time-control period.

3. Before play begins the players should inspect the position of the pieces and the setting of the clock. If they have omitted to do this, no claim shall be accepted after each player has made his first move.

4. Each player must handle the clock with the same hand with which he handles his pieces. Exception: It is permitted to perform the castling move by using both hands.

5. The arbiter should stipulate at the beginning of the tournament the direction the clocks are to face, and the player with the black pieces decides on which side of the board he will sit.

6. No player is permitted to cover more or less permanently the button of his own clock with one of his fingers.

7. During the game the clock must not be picked up by either player.

The won game

8. A game is won by the player–
   - (a) who has mated his opponent's king;
   - (b) whose opponent declares that he resigns;
   - (c) whose opponent completes an illegal move, which includes leaving his king in check or moving his king into check, but only if the player claims the win before he himself touches a piece (see rule 17) or captures that king as valid proof;
   - (d) whose opponent's flag falls first, at any time before the game is otherwise ended.

9. A player must claim a win himself by immediately stopping both clocks and notifying the arbiter. To claim a win under rule 8d, the player's flag must be up and his opponent's flag must be down after the clocks have been stopped.

If both flags are down, the game is declared a draw (see rule 10c).

The drawn game

10. A game is drawn –
   - (a) if one of the kings is stalemated;
   - (b) by agreement between the players during the game, not before or after the game;
   - (c) if the flag of one player falls after the flag of the other player has already fallen and a win has not been claimed;
   - (d) if a player demonstrates a perpetual check or a forced repetition of position under the conditions of Article 18.2 of the Laws of Chess;
   - (e) if both players have insufficient material for a possible check-mate (only king vs. king, king and bishop vs. king, king and knight vs.

king, king and bishop vs. king and bishop on diagonals of the same colour);

(f) if one player has insufficient material for a possible check-mate as described in rule 10e and his opponent's flag falls first.

11. The player having the white pieces must notify the arbiter of a drawn game.

Miscellaneous

12. If a player accidentally displaces one or more pieces, he shall replace them on his own time. If it is necessary, his opponent may start the player's clock without making a move in order to make sure that the player replaces the displaced pieces on his own time.

13. Play shall be governed by the FIDE Laws of Chess and the FIDE Interpretations of these Laws, in all cases to which they apply and in which they are not inconsistent with these rules. In particular, Article 8 ('The Touched Piece') remains in full force.

If a player first touches one piece and then moves another, his opponent should restart the player's clock, if it is necessary, and inform him that he must complete the move in accordance with Article 8.

14. In case of a dispute, either player may stop the clocks while the arbiter is being summoned. All of these rules are subject to interpretation by the arbiter, whose decisions are final.

15. Spectators and participants in another game are not to speak or otherwise to interfere in another game. If a spectator interferes in any way, such as by calling attention to a flag-fall or an illegal move, the arbiter may cancel the game and rule that a new game be played in its stead, as well as expel the offending party from the playing room. The arbiter too, must refrain from calling attention to a flag-fall or an illegal move, as this is entirely the responsibility of the players themselves.

16. The arbiter shall not handle the clock except in the case of a dispute or when both players ask him to do so.

17. A move is completed as soon as the player's hand has released a piece in accordance with Article 7 of the Laws of Chess.

18. Illegal moves unnoticed by both players cannot be corrected afterwards, nor can they afterwards lead to a claim of a won game under rule 8c.

19. Before a five-minute lightning tournament, the organizers should hand out a copy of these rules to each participant, or, if this is not possible, see that a sufficient number of copies of these rules are posted in the playing room at least half an hour before the tournament is to begin.

3 Systems for Individual Matches

A match is a competition between two players (an individual match) or between two teams (see Chapter 4), the latter being essentially a sum of individual matches.

Matches are certainly the oldest form of chess competition. A large match played in London in 1834 (it actually consisted of 6 individual matches) between L. Ch. de la Bourdonnais and A. Macdonnell marked the beginning of a 'golden age' of chess matches, and the first 'modern' international tournament (London 1851) was in the form of a series of knock-out matches. In the first round 16 players drew lots and were divided into eight pairs. The winner of each of these mini-matches was the player who scored two wins out of three games, draws not counting, the loser dropping out of further competition.

Matches are a more direct test of strength between two opponents, as compared to tournaments in which results against 'third' players also affect the ultimate standing. Since in a match the two players directly determine which of the two is stronger without the influence of third parties, the match system has been retained in the Candidates' Matches for the world championship and in the direct duel for the world championship title. Today's Candidates' Matches, which start off with eight players, are a knock-out series of matches.

The colour of the pieces in the first game of a match is usually decided by drawing lots, and is subsequently alternated.

Various systems have been tested in the history of matches, especially in matches for the world championship title. Basically, however, there have been only two ways to determine the winner of the match and the actual length of the match: a match of a given number of games, or a match for a given number of wins with no restriction on the number of games. Other combinations of these two systems and other possible variations, however, also exist.

1. The match with a restricted number of games

The number of games is established beforehand by the rules of the match, and the winner is that player who is the first to score half a point or a point above 50% of the possible points which a player can score in the match. In a match of 24 games, for instance, the winner will be the player who is the first to score 12.5 points. The match is usually terminated as soon as one of the players fulfills the required score. The regulations prescribe what should be done in the eventuality of a tie in points, usually either supplementary games after a new drawing of lots for colour or until the first win (again after having drawn lots for colour); occasionally lots decide the winner. World title matches usually follow the rule that the world champion retains his title in the case of a tied score.

Whatever the case may be, these matters should be determined beforehand by the regulations.

2. A match for a given number of wins

The first player to win a given number of games is the winner (e.g. six in the Alekhine–Capablanca match, ten in the Steinitz–Zukertort match). Draws are not counted in the result, but are counted in alternating the colour of the pieces. The number of games in the match cannot be envisaged beforehand.

3. A match for a given number of wins, but with a limited number of games

One must start off by saying that these two criteria do not logically go together. FIDE's General Assembly in Nice in 1974 planned for the 1975 world title match between Fischer and Karpov to be played for ten wins, but the number of the games was to be no more than 36. This is not a good 'combination', because the limitation excludes the demand for the match to be played until a given number of wins.

4. A match for a given number of wins, with a set of minimum of games

In this system, one can provide for the winner, for instance, to be the player who scores the highest number of points in 30 games, provided that he has scored six wins.

Advocates of matches for a given number of wins stress that this helps to reduce the number of draws, for the player who, in a match with a limit on the games, gains the advantage early on, tries to retain it throughout the rest of the match by drawing the remaining games. Such tactics cannot be used in a match for a given number of wins. Opponents of this idea stress, however, that a match with no limits on the number of games can be played 'ad infinitum' and that what then becomes important is the player's physical stamina rather than his chess-playing ability. The bone of contention in the dispute over the Fischer–Karpov match, however, was the provision concerning an even score. Fischer asked that in the case of a score of 9:9 in wins, the match be declared a tie, and the champion retain his title, which the other side interpreted as meaning that the challenger would have to win the match with at least a two-point difference.

A match can also be played for a set number of *decisive* games. Fischer's demand for the match with Karpov could be put as follows: the match is played for the majority of 18 decisive games, and in the eventuality of a 9:9 score, the world champion retains the title.

4 Systems for Team Matches

Team matches may be played over any number of boards. At chess olympiads, for instance, the teams consist of four players and two reserves. The European Team Championship is played over eight boards. Inter-state matches are usually played over ten boards, and some matches are played over a thousand boards, etc. They may also be single or double round.

The rule for the majority of team matches played today is that the players should be placed in board order according to their chess strength; furthermore, the basic make-up of the team, which is announced at the beginning of the competition, remains the same until the end of the competition. Substitutes are included on the last (or next-to-the-last) board, and all the other players move up accordingly. In some competitions, substitutes play in the place of a player who is resting, as for example in competitions held according to the Scheveningen system. For typical result forms see p. 219 & 221.

Matches between teams can be league competitions, inter-club, international, inter-state, etc. In terms of their make-up, the matches can be for seniors, juniors, ladies, or mixed.

If the match between two teams is to determine which is to qualify for further competition, then the regulations should include a clause on the criteria to be used if the overall result is a tie. The first criterion usually used in matches between two teams is which did better on the first half of the boards. If the score here, too, is the same, then priority is given to the team which did better on the next board and so down the line.

Team matches can be organized also as tournaments, according to the round-robin system (i.e. when each team plays against all the other teams); according to the cup system (in which the team which loses a match or a certain number of match-points is eliminated); according to the Swiss System (the score is calculated according to the total number of points compiled by a team, or on the basis of the number of match points); or according to a mixed system (preliminaries, for instance, according to the Swiss or some other system, and the finals according to a round robin system).

Before the competition begins, numbers are drawn, as in individual tournaments. In the Berger System, this automatically also establishes the colour of the pieces in all the matches and on all boards; the first team to be called has white on the odd boards and black on the even boards. In competitions played according to the Scheveningen System, numbers are drawn for each participant of each team.

The winner of a team competition is the team which compiles the highest number of points. The overall score compiled by a team in a match against another team is registered on the scoreboard (for instance 7:3, etc.). Two or more teams may score the same number of points, and if a differentiation in the standings must be made, then this should be determined in the regulations.

In chess olympaids, when two or more teams have the same number of points, the advantage is given to the team with the larger number of match points, a won match counting 2 points and a draw 1 point. Other criteria, which can be used when teams score the same number of points and match points, are the score of the encounter between the teams in question, the Sonneborn–Berger tie-break, etc.

The regulations should stipulate whether adjourned games will be resumed or adjudicated. The former is better, since adjudication can sometimes be lengthy. In the 1968 Moscow–Leningrad match, for example, the game between A. Volovich and V. Lyavdanski could not immediately be adjudicated, and the decision on that complicated position was finally made only a year and a half later!

In team competitions each team has a captain, who may also be a player in the team. He represents the players before the arbiters, announces the board order of the team, and all announcements made to the captain are considered to have been made to the entire team. The captain, however, may not interfere in the play of his players, nor may he give them advice or comment on the position in the game. The captain usually may advise his player to accept or reject an offered draw, but he must not comment on the given position. The Laws of Chess discuss the duties and rights of the captain, and these stipulations should also be included in the regulations of the competition.

It should be stressed that more arbiters are required for team matches than for tournaments. The usual criterion used is one arbiter to every four boards. There should also, of course, be the main arbiter and possibly a number of deputies, depending on the size of the competition.

The arbiter should keep a scorecard on each match with the scores for individual games and other data. National federations usually have scorecards for this purpose. Many countries hold, apart from individual, team championships as well, and have special regulations for them. The Team Championship of Yugoslavia, for instance, is played annually in two leagues with ten teams in each. Teams consist of ten members, with seniors playing on the top six boards, juniors (up to 20 years of age) on the next two and ladies on the bottom two. This combination is meant to compel clubs to focus their attention on developing chess among young people and women. There is also a huge cup competition for teams of four, with some one thousand teams taking part. Also, in England, the Sunday Times schools competition attracts over 800 teams.

Scheveningen System

Match between two teams

It is an unwritten law that the criterion used in weighing the playing strength of two clubs, two towns, two countries, etc., is the score of a match played on a given number of boards, where one team's first board player meets the first board player of the other team, its second board player meets the second board player of the other team, etc. The scores of such matches, however, show a true result only if both teams are arranged in order of playing strength.

Let us look at a match between team A, whose players, A_1, A_2, A_3 and A_4 are lined up in order of playing strength, and team B, with players B_1, B_2, B_3

and B_4, lined up along the same principle. Now, let us assume that A_1 is equal in strength to his opponent B_1, and that he is so much better than the other members of the opposing team that he can defeat B_2, B_3 and B_4. Let us again assume that A_2 is so good that he can defeat B_3 and B_4, and is equal in strength to B_2, while A_3 can defeat B_4 and is equal in strength to B_3, and A_4 and B_4 are equal in strength.

Now let us see what the results of the matches played between these teams should be.

If team A has a line-up of A_1, A_2, A_3, A_4, and team B has a line-up of B_1, B_2, B_3, B_4, then the result of the match should be a $2:2$ tie (all games ending in a draw).

If we change the line-up of the teams' players, however, we get a different score: A (A_4, A_1, A_2, A_3) vs. B (B_1, B_2, B_3, B_4) = $3:1$, because A_4 loses to B_1, while A_1, A_2 and A_3 defeat their opponents B_2, B_3 and B_4 since they are stronger players.

A different line-up can provide yet a different score, for instance, A(A_1, A_2, A_3, A_4) vs. B (B_1, B_4, B_2, B_3) = $1.5:2.5$ (individual scores: A_1–B_1 $0.5:0.5$, A_2–B_4 $1:0$, A_3–B_2 $0:1$, A_4–B_3 $0:1$).

One observes that the score of the match greatly depends on the line-up of the teams' players, which means that it is not sound as a criterion. Naturally, this is not something which is so blatant in actual practice, since the difference in the strength of the players at individual boards is not as great as we presumed in our illustration for the purpose of clarity. Nonetheless, albeit not always visible, this aspect does exist.

In order to reduce the result's dependence on the line-up of the players, a provision was adopted according to which the line-up of players in teams must be established according to categories. This has considerably restricted the captains free choice in putting the team together, and has also diminished the possibility of 'resorting to tactics'. But tactics can still be used among players in the same categories, and we know that there are players who are considerably stronger than others with higher categories. Even if the composition of both teams were to be ideally aligned in terms of playing strength, the result of such a match would still not represent, in absolute terms, the balance of forces between the two teams; this would merely be the sum total of a given number of individual scores.

In practice, however, such a result is recognized in virtually all competitions. We can get the real balance of forces between two teams only if we add up the scores of all their mutual encounters which have been played so that one team rotates its line-up in each ensuing encounter while the other team plays with an unchanged line-up. The Scheveningen system offers us this possibility.

Definition and principles of the Scheveningen system
The Scheveningen system is a competition between two teams in which each player on one team plays each player on the other.

The system acquired its name after the 1923 international tournament in Scheveningen (Holland), when 10 Dutch chessplayers played against the same number of guests.

Two variations exist for determining the pairs in given rounds in this system: the classical and the modern (Master Djaja).

The ideal variation of this system would be one which would meet the following conditions, in order of importance:

1. that both teams have the white and black pieces an equal number of times in the entire competition.

2. that each player on each team has the white and black pieces an equal number of times.

3. that both teams have the white and the black pieces an equal number of times in each round.

4. that from round to round the colour of the individual players' pieces alternates.

Competitions according to the Scheveningen system are played on an even number of boards, since the alternative would obviously not allow any of the first three conditions to be met. There is no variation which completely meets all the aforementioned conditions with an even number of boards, either, but the classical variation completely complies with the first, second and fourth conditions, while the modern variation, which is better, fulfills the most important conditions, the first, second and third, and largely the fourth as well.

In the Scheveningen system, the number of rounds is equal to the number of boards in the competition.

Classical variation

Before the competition begins, lots are drawn to determine which team will be the first – team A, and which the second – team B. Then both teams' players draw tournament numbers from 1 to n (n is the number of boards in the match). This determines each player's order of play with his opponents, as well as the colour of the pieces, according to the tables which apply to this system.

With $n = 6$, for instance, the competition follows the following pattern (Diagram 1), in which the horizontals refer to team A's members, and the verticals to team B's. The number of the round in which a player from team A meets a player from team B can be found at the point where his horizontal crosses the respective vertical. The colour of the pieces used by the player of team A is given by the colour of that square.

B\A	B_1	B_2	B_3	B_4	B_5	B_6
A_1	1	2	3	4	5	6
A_2	6	1	2	3	4	5
A_3	5	6	1	2	3	4
A_4	4	5	6	1	2	3
A_5	3	4	5	6	1	2
A_6	2	3	4	5	6	1

Diagram 1

B\A	B_1	B_2	B_3	B_4	B_5	B_6
A_1	·					
A_2		·				
A_3			·			
A_4				·		
A_5					·	
A_6						·

Diagram 2

On the basis of Diagram 1 one can write out the line-up of the pairs for all the rounds in a competition played on 6 boards:

round 1	round 2	round 3	round 4	round 5	round 6
$A_1 - B_1$	$B_2 - A_1$	$A_1 - B_3$	$B_4 - A_1$	$A_1 - B_5$	$B_6 - A_1$
$A_2 - B_2$	$B_3 - A_2$	$A_2 - B_4$	$B_5 - A_2$	$A_2 - B_6$	$B_1 - A_2$
$A_3 - B_3$	$B_4 - A_3$	$A_3 - B_5$	$B_6 - A_3$	$A_3 - B_1$	$B_2 - A_3$
$A_4 - B_4$	$B_5 - A_4$	$A_4 - B_6$	$B_1 - A_4$	$A_4 - B_2$	$B_3 - A_4$
$A_5 - B_5$	$B_6 - A_5$	$A_5 - B_1$	$B_2 - A_5$	$A_5 - B_3$	$B_4 - A_5$
$A_6 - B_6$	$B_1 - A_6$	$A_6 - B_2$	$B_3 - A_6$	$A_6 - B_4$	$B_5 - A_6$

Diagram 1 shows how the table has been drawn up: numbers one to six are written out in each horizontal, starting with the square on the main diagonal (marked by dots on Diagram 2) in natural sequence. When the end of the horizontal is reached, the numbers are again written in from the beginning of that horizontal, again from left to right. Consequently, all numbers from 1 to 6 will be inscribed in each horizontal. The squares are alternately coloured like squares on a chess board.

The tables are drawn up in the same way for a match based on the Scheveningen system on any number of boards.

This method is also suitable for and most often used in lightning chess competitions, because it is technically easy and rapid to execute; the players on team A always sit at their boards, while the players on team B move up one place in each round (the first board player always moves to the last). In the first round all players on team A have white, as in all odd rounds, while in all even rounds the players of team A play with the black pieces.

This system of playing matches according to the classical variation, however, has a serious drawback, since in individual rounds the team with white always has the advantage over the other. Hence, the scores for each individual round do not reflect the real balance of strength.

The modern variation (Master Djaja's)
The modern variation is used to avoid the above situation, i.e. that in given rounds an entire team has white for all the games. This modern variation enables the teams to play the same number of games with white and black in each round. The system was used for the first time in the Yugoslavia – USSR match Belgrade, 1956.

If all the players on a team play with the same colour of pieces in each round (as in the classical variation), then conditions 1, 2 and 4 are fulfilled, but condition 3 is not. Conditions 3 and 4, however, cannot be fulfilled simultaneously. If we accept that condition 3 has priority, then we must find a system which will not only fulfill conditions 1 and 2, but also condition 3 and as far as possible condition 4.

For Full Tables for the Scheveningen System see Appendix, p. 214.

If these tables are not to hand, it is not difficult to remember the principle used in drawing them up for a number of boards which can be divided by 4. This is done in the following way: in the first round the pairs are determined by natural sequence, so that they go: 1-1, 2-2, 3-3, etc., with the first half of the players on a team having the white pieces, and the second half of the same team playing with the black pieces. Now the entire match should be regarded as a separate match between the first half of the players on team A_I and team B_I, and a separate match between the second half of the players on team A_{II} and team B_{II}. Both matches are played according to the classical variation of the Scheveningen system. When these matches are completed, then the first half of the players on team B (i.e. B_I), play the second half of the players on team A (i.e. A_{II}), while team B_{II} plays team A_I, again according to the classical variation. The entire competition is over when these matches, too, are completed.

Consequently, according to Master Djaja's variation of the Scheveningen system, a competition on a number of boards which is divisible by 4 would follow this pattern:

First half of the competition: A_I-B_I B_{II}-A_{II}
Second half of the competition: A_{II}-B_I B_{II}-A_I

As one can see, the entire competition consists of 4 matches played according to the classical variation, with both halves played at the same time.

In holding a competition according to the Scheveningen system, one must not only keep a record of each round, but also a table of the match scores according to rounds and a table of individual results, according to the following pattern (this example is for a match on 6 boards):

Table for the results of individual matches

Belgrade, 1975	1.	2.	3.	4.	5.	6.	total points	match points
Yugoslavia								
Hungary								

Table of individual results

Belgrade, 1975	1. Szabo	2. Vadasz	3. Sax	4. Portisch	5. Barcza	6. Forintos	Yugoslav players points	%
1. Gligorić								
2. Ivkov								
3. Velimirović								
4. Parma								
5. Ljubojević								
6. Matanović								
Hung. players points								
%								

If there are reserves, the rule is that reserves play on the board of the player they are replacing. The disadvantage of allowing reserves is that one reserve may play several times with the same player, and may have the white or the black pieces several times in succession.

The winner of a match according to the Scheveningen system is the team which at the end of the competition has the highest number of points. In the case of a tie the regulations should prescribe that the match points of individual rounds determine the outcome.

The Scheveningen system with three teams

It is more awkward if three teams take part in a competition, and that for two reasons: first, because one team is free in each round, which means that the time is not rationally utilized, the second, because the teams are placed in an inequitable position – the team which is free in the last round is in the worst position, because the other two teams know the number of points of the third team, and, hence, are in a privileged position. As a result, a three-way match is usually avoided in competition systems. A modified version of the Scheveningen system, however, offers the possibility of eliminating these drawbacks, provided that the number of boards is even, which is usually the case.

Let us say that teams A, B and C take part in a competition and that the matches are played on 6 boards. We shall divide each team into two equal parts (this is why the number of boards must be even): $A = A_1 + A_2$, $B = B_1 + B_2$, and $C = C_1 + C_2$. The first half of the team, designated by $index_1$ encompasses players 1, 2 and 3, and the second half, designated by $index_2$ — players 4, 5 and 6. Now all these groups (except groups of the same team), play matches according to the classical variation of the Scheveningen system, along the following lines:

first quarter (rounds 1, 2, 3)	second quarter (rounds 4, 5, 6)	third quarter (rounds 7, 8, 9)	fourth quarter (rounds 10, 11, 12)
$A_1 - B_1$	$A_1 - B_2$	$C_1 - A_1$	$C_2 - A_1$
$C_1 - A_2$	$C_2 - A_2$	$A_2 - B_2$	$A_2 - B_1$
$B_2 - C_2$	$B_1 - C_1$	$B_1 - C_2$	$B_2 - C_1$

Each player on one team has played with each player on the other two teams, making it a total of 12 games in 12 rounds.

The advantages of this system are evident:
a) competition involves the least possible number of rounds.
b) there are no free teams or free players in any of the rounds.
c) in each round the teams have the white and the black pieces the same number of times.
d) the scores of all the teams can be equally followed in each round of the competition.

This system can also be played in competitions with three clubs, each of which has two teams, where the teams of the same club do not play against each other.

Application of the Scheveningen system to individual competitions
A match between two teams played according to the Scheveningen system can also serve as a reliable criterion for comparing individual achievements. In view of the fact that all players on one team play all players on the other, the team match can be observed from the viewpoint of an individual tournament of players on one team and an individual tournament of players on the other, in which each player has played against the same opponents in one of these tournaments. Consequently, the individual standings of the players on one team will be determined by the number of points they have. This kind of comparison becomes all the more feasible if the players play a large number of games.

Individual preliminary tournaments can be played on this basis. They are played, according to this system, in two groups of equal number and, if possible, equal playing strength. The groups play a match according to the Scheveningen system between each other. If the groups are equal in playing strength, then, ideally, the outcome of the match will be a tie. In such a case, an equal number of players from each group would qualify for the final tournament. If the match result is not a tie, then the playing strength of the groups is reflected in the proportional number of points compiled, i.e. in the result of the match.

This can be used for corrections in preliminary groups in the number qualifying for the finals. When the competition is played according to the Berger system this is not possible.

We can express this proportion mathematically. Let f represent the total number of finalists, out of whom f_1 qualified from the first, and f_2 from the second group. Let us assume that the first group scored p_1 and the second p_2 points out of a total of p possible points in a match played on n boards. Then:

$$f_1 : f = p_1 : n^2 \quad \text{and} \quad f_2 : f = p_2 : n^2$$

whereby

$$f_1 = \frac{f}{n^2} p_1 \qquad f_2 = \frac{f}{n^2} p_2$$

For instance, if the outcome of the match (with 12 players in each group) is $96 : 48$, and we allow a total of 6 players into the finals, the above formula gives us the number of players to be advanced from one and the other group:

$$f_1 = \frac{6}{12^2} \cdot 96 = 4 \qquad f_2 = \frac{6}{12^2} \cdot 48 = 2$$

In making these calculations one does not usually get whole numbers so one must, of necessity, round them off. For instance, if the number of players is 16, and we are to advance a total of 10 into the finals ($f = 10$) with the score $150 : 106$, we get: $f_1 = 5.84$ and $f_2 = 4.16$, which, when rounded off, gives us: $f_1 = 6$ and $f_2 = 4$.

The Hutton Cross Pairing System for 3 or more teams
This is a method of pairing 3 or more teams as fairly as possible where only one or two rounds are available. It is essential that teams be placed in order of strength with the strongest player on Board 1.

For the full tables see Appendix, p. 215.

5 Tournaments: Introduction & Knock-out Systems

Tournaments are the most widely spread form of competition and they serve to weigh playing strength between several players at the same time, or between several teams.

As we have already noted, matches are the oldest form of chess competition and they probably date back to the origin of chess itself. Tournaments are of a much later date. Chess historians record that it was only in 1575 that a competition was held in Madrid at the court of King Philip II of Spain which differed from the then customary match. The first international tournament in the modern sense was held in London in 1851, according to the cup system.

The drawback of the tournament as a system of competition, when compared to matches, is that the standing of two players at a tournament, if abstracted, is not the result of their mutual battle; it is the result of their struggle with other contestants, and hence it only indirectly weighs playing strength, for other players need not always play with equal strength against these two players. The advantage of the tournament, however, is that it offers a larger number of players the opportunity of competing at the same time, and this transcends the aforementioned shortcomings, so that today, tournaments are used as the best means for acquiring qualifications, titles, ratings, etc. Priority is given to matches only in the final stages of the battle for the world championship.

Various *tournament systems* exist to determine which contestants are to meet in various rounds, the colours of the pieces, etc. All these systems can basically be divided into five main groups: *elimination*, *Round robin*, *Swiss*, *Scheveningen* and *combined systems*. The most popular of them all are the Round robin and Swiss systems.

The Knock-out System

The knock-out system may be applied both in team and in individual competitions, and it is especially suitable for competitions with a large number of players or teams which are to be played in the shortest possible period of time.

The drawback of this system is that only a small number of contestants are given a realistic standing; for instance, stronger players (or teams) who play against each other may drop out, while during this time weaker players (or teams), in encounters with weaker counterparts, forge on ahead. Consequently, this system is rarely used in competitions today.

Two kinds of these systems are known.

The Single Life System

In the single life system, the player who loses a game, or the team which loses the match, is eliminated. The tournament regulations prescribe what occurs in the case of a tie: In individual competitions, a new game is usually played with the colour of the pieces reversed. If it, too, ends in a tie, then lots are drawn to decide the winner. In team competitions, a new match is avoided, because it substantially increases the costs of the competition. Here, other clauses are applied, for instance, that the best score on the first half of the boards decides, and if this too is a tie, then the next board decides, etc.

Since the number of contestants competing for first place is always cut by half at the end of each round, the number of contestants must be to the power of the number two (4, 8, 16, 32, etc.).

Before the beginning of competition, numbers are drawn which automatically pair the contestants for the entire competition and which determine the colour of the pieces according to the following diagram (the example is for 8 players, or teams).

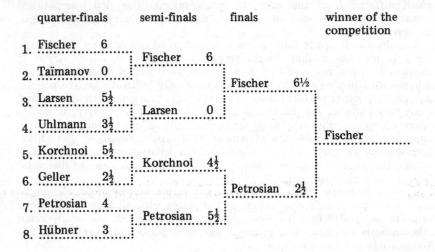

This means that pairs 1-2, 3-4, 5-6, 7-8 meet in the first round. The player who has the lower number plays with the white pieces in the first round, and if it is a team competition, then the team with the lower number plays in the first round with the white pieces on an odd number of boards, and plays the match at home (as the host) unless the entire competition is being played in the same place.

In the following rounds, the white pieces go to the player who played white a fewer number of times than the opponent he is playing, and if both players have had the white pieces the same number of times, then they go to the player with the lower ordinal number. The same rule applies to team competitions with respect to the colour of the pieces on odd boards and with respect to the venue.

These rules for pairing and determining the colour of the pieces are entirely automatic. In order to avoid having the stronger players (or teams) eliminated in the early rounds, one can make a 'skeleton' of the tournament for the first few rounds: players are divided into two groups, a stronger and a weaker, and they are paired by having each player in the stronger group draw lots for his opponent from the weaker group. Lots also determine the colour of the pieces.

If the number of contestants is not to the power of 2, then the competition can be held along cup system principles by applying one of two variants.

Variation 1

An elimination round may be used before the real cup system begins. If, for instance, we have 34 participants, the number should be cut down to 32. This means that two contestants should be eliminated, by determining two pairs to play an elimination match, with the winners joining the other contestants. The number of participants in the elimination round is calculated by subtracting from the number of participants at the tournament the nearest lower number to the power of two, and then multiplying the total by two. For 70 contestants, for instance, the number who should play in the preliminaries is 12, since $(70 - 64) \times 2 = 12$.

Variation 2

All participants who have not yet been eliminated are paired. If the number of participants in a given round is an odd one, then one player is free. Lots are drawn to determine which player will be free in a given round and what the pairings will be, but no contestant may be free more than once. According to this variation, a cup competition with, say, 70 contestants would look as follows: Round I - 35 pairs, Round II - 17 pairs with one player free, Round III - 9 pairs, Round IV - 4 pairs and 1 player free, Round V - 2 pairs and 1 player free, Round VI - one pair and 1 player free, Round VII (Finals) - one pair.

Either variation may be applied in any competition where the number of participants is not to the power of 2. Which of the variations is more suitable, however, depends primarily on the number of contestants. Variation 1, for instance, is better suited for a tournament with 70 players, because variation 2, as we have seen, leaves us with 1 player free in the final part of the competition, and this should be avoided at all costs. If, however, the number of participants at the beginning of a tournament is, say, 60, the situation changes. Here, the second variation is better because a fewer number of players would be given the bye during the tournament - only one and that in the first part of the competition, as compared to the first variation in which 4 players would be given the bye.

The Belgrade Elimination System (Two-Life System)

This is a more interesting system than the above. The player does not drop out after having lost a game, but only after having lost two or three points, depending on the tournament regulations (two draws are counted as one defeat). The competition is played until only one player is left in the tournament (or none at all if only two players are left, and both drop out after their game has ended in a draw). That player is declared the winner of the tournament. One of two alternatives may be used in pairing the players in this system.

a) *Pairings by lot.* The colour of the pieces in the first round is also allocated by lot, while in the ensuing rounds the white pieces go to the player who has played white fewer times than his opponent, unless he is playing him for the second time and in his first encounter already had the white pieces. In this case he automatically plays black. If both players have played white an equal number of times the colour is allocated by lot. The participants' standings are based on the number of points they have at the end of the competition. The Buchholtz System can be used for evaluating the position of all players. See Chapter 12.

The weakness of this system is that the same opponents can play each other several times and that luck decides whether someone will get a weaker or a stronger opponent, white or black pieces. Another shortcoming of this system is that one cannot foretell with exactitude how long the competition will last.

b) *Pairings by lot among players with the same or approximately the same number of points.* Here, one avoids as much as possible matching up players who have already met in an earlier round. The colours of the pieces are allocated along the same principles as in variation a).

6 Introduction to the Swiss System

The Swiss System Tournament by Martin E. Morrison
(Former Executive Direction, US Chess Federation
FIDE Permanent Rules Commission)

History of the Swiss System

The Swiss System, far from being a modern invention, was first used at Zurich in 1895 and is credited to Dr. J. Muller, of Brugg. Use of the system in its basic form continued into the twentieth century in Switzerland, where four- or five-round tournaments were played in two days.

Outside Switzerland the system was not widely used until introduced into the United States by George Koltanowski at the 1943 Pennsylvania Championship. The US Open Championship, at which Swiss-System preliminaries had been used in 1946, was converted to the Swiss-System format in toto the following year and has remained a completely Swiss event ever since, reaching a peak in 1973 of 775 players competing over twelve rounds. Today, the US Chess Federation runs seven of its national tournaments as Swisses (the US Open, American Open, National Open, US Amateur, National High School, US Team, and Pan-American Intercollegiate).

Although the United States leads the world in conducting Swiss tournaments, both in frequency and in size, the advantages of the system have brought about its increased use throughout the world, even in the most important national and international competitions. The system is used particularly extensively in Canada, Great Britain (where it has been used for the final stages of the British Championship since 1949), and Continental Europe.

Recognition of the Swiss System for World Chess Federation (FIDE) events has come more recently, although the system was used occasionally in earlier years, as in 1937 at the Ladies Championship. In 1972 FIDE adopted recommended procedures for applying the Swiss System to FIDE tournaments. In 1973 FIDE adopted new regulations for the World Junior Championship, which called for Swiss-System preliminaries to the final round-robin sections. Finally, in 1974 FIDE took the momentous step of deciding to try out the Swiss System at the 1976 Olympiad for Men's Teams (having rejected a similar step in 1967). After the 1976 Olympiad a definite decision is to be made concerning the system under which the Olympiad will be played in the future.

Appeal of the Swiss System

As long as chess tournaments were conducted primarily under the round-robin (all-play-all) system, the extension of organized chess competition to larger and larger numbers of chess players was hampered by the problem of handling a large number of participants in a limited time. The Swiss System solves this problem, and as a result the opportunity to participate in organized chess has been opened to all chess players.

Organized chess before the advent of the Swiss System was restricted for the most part to those who could engage in lengthy round-robin competition at a chess club or who had the time to participate in tournaments lasting a week or more. As a round robin can successfully handle only a small number of players, participants have to be invited or have to qualify from preliminary sections which eliminate all but the very top players from the main final section. A tournament of thirty players might necessitate two weeks to complete preliminaries and finals.

The Swiss System, on the other hand, allows for a competition of many players to be completed in one open section within as little as four or five rounds over a Saturday and Sunday. In the United States, for example, the open weekend Swiss tournament is the most popular form of competition. Many important state and regional championships are played over a three-day holiday weekend in six or seven rounds. All in all, over 2,000 US Swiss-System tournaments were played on weekends and at chess clubs in 1974, about 100 of these having drawn over 100 players. The result has been a popularization of organized chess competition, a general increase in knowledge and study of the game, and a heightened public awareness of chess.

General Principles of the Swiss System

The fundamental laws of the Swiss System are that in each round players with equal scores must be paired if it is possible to do so; that if it is impossible to pair all players with equal scores, every player who is not paired with an opponent whose score is the same as his own must be paired with an opponent whose score is as close to his own as possible; and that a player must not be paired with any other player more than once.

Consequently, the system consistently works to reduce the number of players with perfect or high scores. Round by round, the field is narrowed down to (a) the leading contenders in the high score-groups, (b) the players near the tournament average in the middle groups, and (c) the least skilful players in the low score-groups.

In the first round, all the players have equal scores of zero and play together in one group. Then, in the second round, the players are divided into three groups: (a) the first-round winners, (b) the players who drew their games, and (c) the first-round losers. The players in each group are paired.

The same system of grouping is continued throughout the tournament. Thus, in the fourth round, those who scored 3–0 in the first three rounds are paired, those who scored $2\frac{1}{2}$ –$\frac{1}{2}$ are paired, etc., down to the group that scored 0–3 (using the usual scoring of one point for a win, one-half point for each player for a draw, zero for a loss in each round).

Within these general principles of the system, there are several variables. A Swiss System may be controlled by the use of ratings for the players when the pairings are made, or may be noncontrolled. It may be accelerated when the players-to-rounds ratio exceeds the maximum, or non-accelerated. Refinements may be prescribed for dealing with byes (which arise when there is an odd number of players), games unfinished when pairings must be made for the next round, allocation of colours, odd men in a score-group (when a player must be removed to another group), and other specific occurrences.

Objectives of the Swiss System

The basic objective of the Swiss System is to produce a clear winner in as few rounds as possible. This winner should have met strong enough competition to prove his right to the top place in the tournament. Depending upon the form used (non-controlled, controlled, accelerated, etc.) and the players-to-rounds ratio, the Swiss System may determine an additional number of places below the top place.

Basically, the Swiss System is a concealed knockout tournament, the difference being that the losers, instead of being 'knocked out' of further competition, are paired with other losers (with the resulting popularization of tournament chess this feature affords). It has been said, therefore, that the Swiss System represents a combination of the best features of the knockout with the framework of the round robin. This configuration gives the Swiss System its maximum players-to-rounds ratio (four rounds for 16 players, five rounds for 32 players, six rounds for 64 players, etc.), as the top of the field is theoretically halved after each round as some players win and others lose. However, the existence of the drawn result in chess and the continuing possibility of interplay (as no player is eliminated) affect this theoretical concept.

Most Swisses fall into two stages. In the first stage, the players are sorted out round by round into an ever-increasing number of score-groups. During this stage the top score-group diminishes in size since more and more players drop from that group as the competition becomes stronger. Finally, only one player may remain in the top score-group. This player, however, may be a 'false winner' since at this point he has generally not met the strongest competition in the tournament. Such a false winner would normally be produced before the proper players-to-rounds ratio had been achieved (e.g., after only four rounds of play in a tournament of 16 players, after only five rounds of play in a tournament of 32 players, etc.), particularly if the top score-group has been diminished by drawn games. If the tournament ends at this point, the first stage may never be passed, especially in a non-controlled tournament or one which exceeds the maximum players-to-rounds ratio.

In the second stage the leading player begins to meet stronger competition from players in the top score-groups. The longer the second stage is, the more accurate the top placings and the determination of the true winner will be.

In short, the great organizational advantage of the Swiss System – accommodation of large numbers of players in a short period of time – is balanced by varying degrees of accuracy in the final standings. If the form used is one of the most accurate (e.g. the controlled form), and if the players-to-rounds ratio is highly favourable (e.g. seven or more rounds for a 32 player tournament), the final standings will assure a true winner and additional accurate placings.

Limitations of the Swiss System

Theoretically, the round robin (or better, the double round robin, in which a player plays twice against each opponent, once as White and once as Black) is the best system of competition, as all players are judged according to the same field of opponents. Two practical considerations, however, limit the round robin's use. First, the competition is lengthened for every added player who participates. (International round-robin tournaments, for instance, take about three weeks to accommodate sixteen players.) Second, when there is a surfeit of players or some disparity in the playing strength of the players, a method of qualification into final sections on the basis of results in preliminary sections is generally resorted to. Aside from a further lengthening of the competition, such a qualification system leads to the danger that a strong player may be unduly penalized by an early loss in a strong preliminary section, whereas a weaker player may reach the finals because of a weak preliminary section.

By far the most common criticism one hears about the Swiss System is that pairings are too dependent upon chance to be suitable for important championships. Actually, under the general term 'Swiss System', there is a great degree of variation in specific form, from the noncontrolled to the controlled and even accelerated forms. The highly accurate and elaborated systems which have evolved over the last two decades are a far cry from the rough version used in nineteenth-century Switzerland.

Basically, it is a question of efficiency. Even a noncontrolled Swiss will eventually produce a true winner if enough rounds are played in relation to the number of players. On the other hand, a controlled Swiss will produce more efficient and more consistent pairings, in the early rounds particularly, as the strong players are quickly advanced to the top score-groups, whereas the weak players will be eliminated from these groups. The element of chance in pairing is greatly reduced by the use of the highly-developed controlled methods and can be virtually eliminated by increasing the number of rounds in relation to the number of players.

Of course, any tournament system, when pushed beyond its practical capabilities, will produce inferior results. Consider, for example, the case of a fifty-player round-robin tournament. The consequent length of the tournament (49 rounds) would make such an event a virtual impossibility. Even if held, it would not provide an accurate measure, as the number of withdrawals likely over the period would greatly affect the final standings.

Just so, a fifty-player swiss tournament to be completed in four rounds (when six rounds are the theoretical minimum) will not ensure that a single winner will be produced or that the winner will have met the strongest competition. Though such a tournament could be held (and often is because of limited time available for the tournament), its efficiency would be dependent upon the form (non-controlled, controlled, accelerated, etc.) and the players-to-rounds ratio.

In this context, the basic purpose of the Swiss System must be kept in mind, that is, to produce a clear winner who has met strong enough competition to prove his right to the top place in the tournament. Although in recent years, with the growing size of Swiss tournaments around the world, the system has been used to award prizes not only to the first few overall winners but also to the top finishers in designated rating classes, the Swiss is not intended to make such fine distinctions at these lower levels. It is far better to divide the players into sections from the beginning according to rating class and to conduct each section as a separate Swiss.

Thus, although it is only an imperfect approximation of a round robin, the Swiss System has practical advantages which outweigh the variability introduced by the system into the pairings.

Capacity of the Swiss System

In order to assure a true winner, it is necessary to observe a maximum players-to-rounds ratio. Theoretically, a clear winner will be produced in the same number of rounds as required by a knockout tournament for the number of players involved, indicated in the following table:

No. of players	No. of Rounds Required
5–8	3
9–16	4
17–32	5
33–64	6
65–128	7
129–256	8
257–512	9
513–1024	10

Two additional rounds are required to determine each additional placing desired.

Two complimentary formulae can thus be established.

(1) To determine the minimum number of rounds for a given number of players and placings,

$$R + 2A$$

where R is the number of rounds required for a knockout tournament to accommodate the number of players involved and A is the number of placings desired in addition to first.

Example: For a tournament of 32 players, in which the first four placings are desired: $5 + (2 \times 3) = 11$ rounds.

(2) To determine the maximum number of players who may be admitted to ensure a given number of placings in a given number of rounds,

$$2^{(N - 2A)}$$

where N is the number of rounds and A is the number of placings desired in addition to the first.

Example: For a tournament of nine rounds in which three placings are desired: $2^{(9 - [2 \times 2])}$, or $2^{(9-4)}$, or 2^5, or $2 \times 2 \times 2 \times 2 \times 2$, or 32.

If the maximum players-to-rounds ratio is exceeded, a true winner cannot be assured. However, playing more than the minimum number of rounds or admitting fewer than the maximum number of players will increase the accuracy of the system.

Role of the Director

Some time has gone by since the principles and operation of the Swiss System were understood only in an elementary way. In the early period, when controlled forms and specific procedures were as yet undeveloped, the director was often called upon to use a good deal of subjective judgment to produce workable pairings.

The situation today is quite different. With specific forms of the Swiss System having been carefully developed and standardized, the director is called upon less for his subjective judgment than for spelling out clearly and definitely in advance his pairing procedures and for following those procedures precisely.

Grandmaster Larry Evans has ably epitomized the characteristics proper to the modern director of a Swiss System tournament: 'His pairings are impartial and automatic, thus making it possible for any competitor to predict his opponent in the next round. Everyone knows where he stands and what to expect.' A worthy goal indeed for the director.

References

Acknowledgement is made of the assistance provided by the following publications in the writing of this and the following chapters.

British Chess Federation: *Rules for Swiss Tournaments at B. C. F. Congresses*, Gerrards Cross, England; By FIDE, s.d. p.64–67.

FIDE (World Chess Federation): *Application of the Swiss System to FIDE Tournaments* (Simplified Edition). *FIDE Congress of 1973*, Vol. II, Amsterdam; By FIDE, s.d. pp.29–31.

Harkness, Kenneth: *The Swiss System Tournament. The Official Blue Book and Encyclopedia of Chess.* New York; David McKay, c.1956. p.135–196.

Harkness, Kenneth: *Official Chess Handbook.* New York: David McKay, c.1967. p.118–143.

Harkness, Kenneth, and Haley, Philip G.: *Application of the Swiss System to FIDE Tournaments. FIDE Congress of 1972*, Vol. II. Amsterdam; By FIDE, s.d. p.33–44.

Kühnle-Woods, Walter: 'Swiss System/Schweizer System'. *Chess Express/ Schach Express*, 1973:6, p.114–118.

Morrison, Martin E., ed.: *Official Rules of Chess.* New York; David McKay, c.1875. p.79–96.

Morry, W. Ritson: *How to Run a Chess Tournament. Year Book of Chess 1965–66.* St. Leonards-on-Sea; British Chess Magazine, s.d. p.341–354.

7 Swiss: Ratings Controlled (USCF Form)

Swiss-System tournaments in which players' ratings (international, national, or other) are used to rank the players for pairing are called 'ratings-controlled', as distinguished from non-controlled forms. The difference is one of efficiency. As the pairings should enable the strong players to rise to the top score-groups and should prevent the weak players from attaining these groups, the more rapidly the players are sorted out, the more efficient the pairings are.

In the ratings-controlled form, the top half of the field plays the bottom half in as close to consecutive order as possible. Since the top half is more likely to win the games, the differentiation between strong and weak players – particularly important in the early rounds, when there are few score-groups into which the players can be sorted – is more rapidly achieved than under the noncontrolled form. The winners are not a mixture of strong and weak players (as noncontrolled pairings would match strong with strong and weak with weak, as well as strong with weak, in each score group), but are for the most part the players with the high ratings (as controlled pairings would match only strong with weak in each score-group), who should advance rapidly to the top score-groups.

In 1952 Kenneth Harkness first proposed using ratings to rank players for pairing Swiss tournaments to the US Chess Federation, which two years before had established a national rating system. Harkness incorporated a modification of his proposal into the USCF's first set of Tournament Rules in 1956, and from that time on, the USCF's ratings-controlled form of the Swiss System has regularly been modified to include the most proven methods of Swiss pairing – first in 1967 by Harkness himself and then in 1974 by a USCF committee chaired by the author. In 1972 the ratings-controlled form of the Swiss System was accepted by FIDE in a study of the application of the Swiss System to Fide tournaments.

The following rules are taken from those of the US Chess Federation published in 1974. This is currently the most elaborated set of rules for ratings-controlled Swiss tournaments and closely parallels the FIDE recommendations of 1972. (The references to USCF ratings are easily converted to any other national or the international rating system.)

Pairing Rules of the US Chess Federation for Ratings-Controlled Individual Swiss-System Tournaments

Pairing Cards
1. A pairing card is made out for each entrant on which the director records for each round the color of the player's pieces, the opponent's name and

identification number, the player's score in the game, and the player's cumulative tournament score (see Rule No. 6).

Ratings of Players

2. The rating entered on a player's card is his last-published USCF rating (unless use of a given Rating List or Supplement was specified in the advance publicity). A foreign entrant without a USCF rating may be given his most recent FIDE international rating, or, if he has none, his national rating. Entrants without any official ratings may be given estimated ratings based on whatever information the director wishes to use. On pairing cards and wall charts, U with or without an estimated rating following (based on a player's statement of the number of games he has played in USCF-rated events and the scores he has made) indicates an unrated player who has played in a rated event before. An N similarly indicated a new player who has never played in a rated event before.

Identification Numbers

3. After the entry list is closed, all the cards are arranged in the order of the players' ratings, the cards of entrants without even estimated ratings being placed at the bottom.
    VARIATION. Unrated players, for their actual strength to be reflected more accurately in the pairings, may be arranged –
    (a) just below the average rating of the tournament or section, or
    (b) approximately one-fifth of the way up from the bottom.
Players with identical ratings and players without even estimated ratings are arranged by lot. Then the identification numbers of all players are entered on the pairing cards, starting with the highest-rated player as No. 1. These identification numbers generally remain unchanged throughout the tournament.

Late Entrants

4. The director may, at his discretion, accept and pair entries after the announced closing time, but a late entrant defaults any round he has missed for which it is inconvenient or too late for the director to pair the entrant for play. The director may also assign a 'pairing score', to be used only for the purpose of pairing the entrant, if the director feels that pairing each defaulted game as a loss would be unfair to the other players.
    The identification numbers of late entrants follow in sequence the last number assigned before the entry list was closed, but, in pairing, late entrants are arranged in the order described in Rule No. 3 regardless of their identification numbers.

Byes

5. If the total number of players in any round of a tournament or section of a tournament is uneven, one player is given a bye. A player must not be given a bye more than once, nor is a bye to be given simply because a player enters late. In the first round the bye is given to the player with the lowest last-published USCF rating, in subsequent rounds to the lowest-ranked eligible player, rank in this case being determined first by score, then by official rating (estimated ratings should not be used for awarding byes). If all players eligible for the bye are without official ratings, the bye is awarded by lot.

Scoring
6. The scoring is one point for a win, one-half point for each player for a draw, zero for a loss. A bye is scored as one point for the byed player. Any game defaulted because of a player's failure to appear within one hour after the starting time (FIDE Article 17.2) is scored as one point for the winner and zero for the loser, and the defaulting player is not paired for the succeeding rounds without an excuse acceptable to the director. Defaulted games (as those of a late entrant or of a player who is excused from being paired in a round after the director has been notified in advance that the player will be unable to play) are scored as zero. The remaining games of a player who is excused, withdrawn because of a default without notice, or expelled from the tournament are scored as zero. The scores of unplayed games are circled on the pairing cards and wall chart. Each player's final position is determined by the total of his score.

VARIATION. A bye may be scored as one-half point for the byed player.

Unfinished Games
7. A game that is not finished before it is time to draw the next round is temporarily scored as a draw for pairing purposes. When an unfinished game is completed, the correct results and cumulative scores are entered on the players' cards.

Basic Swiss-System Laws
8. All Pairing Rules are subject to the following basic Swiss-System laws.
   (a) A player must not be paired with any other player more than once.
   (b) Players with equal scores must be paired if it is possible to do so.
   (c) If it is impossible to pair all players with equal scores, every player who is not paired with an opponent whose score is the same as his own must be paired with an opponent whose score is as close to his own as possible.

Pairing the First Round
9. After the bye, if any, is given, the pairing cards are arranged in the order described in Rule No. 3 and are divided into two equal groups. The players in the top half are paired in consecutive order with those in the bottom half. For example, if there are forty players, No. 1 is paired with No. 21, No. 2 with No. 22, etc.

VARIATION. If specifically requested by the players involved, minor transpositions may be made in the first two rounds of a tournament at the director's discretion in order to avoid pairing players from the same region, county, club team, family, etc., *but only to the extent that the results of the tournament as a whole are not substantially affected by this procedure.*

Pairing Subsequent Rounds

Score Groups and Rank
10. In these rules the expression 'score group', or simply 'group', is used in reference to a group of players having the same score. Sometimes a group may consist of only one player whose score is unequaled by any other player.

Individual 'rank' is determined first by score, then by rating, in the order described in Rule No. 3.

Order of Pairing Groups

11. In general, the order of pairing is from the group with the highest score down to the group with the lowest score. Occasionally, in the late rounds, the pairing of the lowerscore groups may have to be adjusted to conform to the basic Swiss-System laws (Rule No. 8), if many of the players in those groups have met before.

Method of Pairing Each Score Group

12. In the second and as many of the subsequent rounds as possible, the players are paired as follows.

   (a) Any odd men are paired first as described in Rules Nos. 13–15.
   (b) Within each score group, after the odd man, if any, has been removed, the cards of the remaining players are arranged in the order described in Rule No. 3 and divided into two equal sections. The players in the top half (with the higher ratings) are paired with those in the bottom half (with the lower ratings) in as close to consecutive order as possible. Transpositions in the bottom half of a group are made to make the pairings conform to the basic Swiss-System laws (Rule No. 8) and to give as many players as possible their due colors (Rule Nos. 19–21). If it is impossible to meet the two requirement just mentioned, one or two players in the top half may be interchanged with one or two in the bottom half. Every effort should be made, however, to observe the principle of pairing the higher-rated against the lower-rated players in as close to consecutive order as possible [but see Rule No. 21 – *Variation*]. *Note.* Directors differ somewhat in their exact methods for implementing this procedure, but any reasonable method, followed consistently, is acceptable.

Rules on Odd Men

13. If there is an odd number of players in a score group, the lowest-ranked player is ordinarily treated as the odd man. However, the pairings in the group must accord with the basic Swiss-System laws (Rule No. 8). Sometimes two players who have met in a previous round must be treated as odd men because there is no possible way in which either of them can be paired in their original group.

Method of Pairing One Odd Man

14. The odd man is paired with the highest-ranked player he has not met in the next-lower group.

   VARIATION 1. The odd man may be paired with the highest-ranked player whom he has not met in the next-lower group and who is due the opposite color.

   VARIATION 2. Except in the last quarter of a tournament, a player should not be treated as an odd man or paired with an odd man more than once unless such a pairing cannot be avoided. To implement this variation, an indication should be made on the card of a player who has been treated as an odd man or paired with an odd man. In the last quarter of a tournament, a player may be treated as an odd man or paired with an odd man as many times as necessary.

Method of Pairing More Than One Odd Man
15. If there are two odd men to be paired, the order in which they are paired is determined by their rank according to Rule No. 10. If both cannot be paired, rank determines which is paired and which is removed to another group.

Pairing Players with Unfinished Games
16. Players with unfinished games (Rule No. 7) should not usually be treated as odd men if it is possible to avoid doing so.

Color Allocation

General Principles
17. The director assigns colors to all players. His primary objective in a tournament with an even number of rounds is to give white and black the same number of times to as many players as possible, and, in a tournament with an odd number of rounds, to give white and black the same number of times to every player, plus one extra white or black. After the first round the director attempts to give as many players as possible their due colors, round by round (Rule Nos. 19–21).

First-Round Colors
18. In the first round, when the top half of the ranked field plays the bottom half, the color assigned to all the odd-numbered players in the top half is chosen by lot, and the opposite color is given to all the even-numbered players in the top half. Opposite colors are assigned to the opponents in the bottom half of the field as the pairings are made. (Once the first-round colors are thus chosen by lot, Rule Nos. 19–21 preserve equitable color allocation, and no further lots are necessary.)

Due Colors in Succeeding Rounds
19. As many players as possible are given their due colors as described in Rule Nos. 20 and 21, so long as the pairings conform to the basic Swiss-System laws (Rule No. 8). Equalization of colors takes priority over alternation of colors.

Equalization of Colors
20. As many players as possible are given the color that equalizes the number of times they have played with the white and black pieces. When it is necessary to pair any two players who are due to be given the same equalizing color, the higher-ranked player has priority in getting the equalizing color, whether white or black.

Alternation of Colors
21. After colors have been equalized in a round, as many players as possible should be given, in the next round, the color each received in the first round of the tournament, the purpose being to continue alternation of colors. When it is necessary to pair any two players who are due to be given the same alternating color, the higher-ranked player has priority in getting the alternating color, whether white or black. However, if another pairing can be

made in accordance with the basic Swiss-System laws (Rule No. 8), a player should not be assigned the same color three times in a row. Interchanges between the top and bottom halves should not be made simply to preserve alternation of colors.

VARIATION. Neither transpositions nor interchanges, as described in Rule No. 12b, should be made simply to preserve alternation of colors. If both players are due for the same color, the higher-ranked player has priority in getting his due color, whether white or black.

Color for Unplayed Games
22. Unplayed games (including byed games) do not count for color.

The rest of this chapter explains some other experimental forms of the ratings-controlled system which have been used.

Accelerated Form: Quarter-Pairing

Because of the practical necessities in the organization of some tournaments, the maximum players-to-rounds ratio is exceeded, e.g., in the case of a tournament with fifty players which must be completed in four rounds (sixteen players being the theoretical maximum for such a tournament). Since the Swiss System is surprisingly flexible, the ratings-controlled form should handle reasonably well even such an excess of players, the main consequence being possibly (but not inevitably) a tie for first-place.

Some directors do not view this consequence as grave, arguing that cash for the tied-for places can be split among the tied winners, whereas titles, qualifying places, or trophies tied for may be determined by tie-breaking points. Furthermore, many directors in recent years are coming to believe that the best way to handle an excessive number of players is to modify the organization of the tournament by dividing the field into sections by rating. In this way, each section would more closely approximate a good player-to-round ratio.

Some directors, however, still prefer to compromise to a degree the standard ratings-controlled form by 'accelerating' the pairings in the hope of producing a single winner. One common accelerated form is that of 'quarter-pairing', so called because each score-group is divided into four parts for pairing, rather than the usual two. This accelerated form is supposed to produce more drawn games and make it less likely that two players will finish with perfect scores.

Accelerated Form of Pairing Early Rounds
Variation 1: Quarter-Pairing

In the first round, after the bye, if any, is issued and the pairing cards are arranged inthe order described in Rule No. 3, the cards are divided into *four* sections, and the first quarter of the field is paired against the second quarter, then the third quarter against the fourth quarter.

In the second and possibly later rounds, if the number of players with perfect scores exceeds the optimum for the number of rounds remaining, the cards of the players with perfect scores are arranged in the order described in Rule No. 3, and the first quarter is paired against the second quarter, the third quarter against the fourth quarter. The cards of the players in the score-group just below are arranged and paired similarly. Players in the other score-groups are paired according to the basic system.

Accelerated Form: Rank-Point Pairing (Haley)

A newer variation in the realm of accelerated pairings is championed by Philip G. Haley. In this form of acceleration, the actual scores of different segments of the field as initially ranked are weighted by the addition of imaginary 'rank points' for pairing purposes only. The assumption is that the results for the first round of a standard ratings-controlled Swiss are a foregone conclusion and that the hypothetical results of these rounds can be entered without play for pairing purposes only.

The pairings of the accelerated first round would be the pairings of the second round of a standard ratings-controlled tournament in which all the higher-rated players defeated their opponents, with no drawn games and no upsets. The result claimed is that the strong players will meet strong opposition from the first and that the winner will have met a higher percentage of stronger opponents than is otherwise possible, with the result that better differentiation is provided for in fewer rounds.

On the other hand, this form does technically violate one of the basic laws of the Swiss System, as players with equal (real) scores are not paired. For example, as a result of the addition of the rank points, high-rated losers are paired with low-rated winners in the second round.

Accelerated Form of Pairing Early Rounds
Variation 2: Rank-Point Pairing (Haley)

In the first round, after the bye, if any, is issued, the pairing cards are arranged in the order described in Rule No. 3. Then the field is divided from top to bottom into four groups (A, B, C, D) as close to the same size as possible.

For pairing purposes only, each player in groups A and B is credited with one 'rank point'. The first round is then paired as follows:

(a) In one section, the players in group A are paired against the players in group B in consecutive order.

(b) In a second section, the players in group C are paired against the players in group D in consecutive order. In each section, colors are assigned according to Rule No. 18.

For the second-round pairings, the rank point of each player in section (a) above is added to his actual game score in the first round, so that he enters the second round with a *pairing* score of two, one and one-half, or one, depending on whether he won, drew, or lost his game. The players in section (b) have no rank points, so they enter the second round with scores of one, one-half, or zero.

The players in each *pairing* score group are then paired from top to bottom, starting with the group having pairing scores of two points and ending with the group having pairing scores of zero. The one-point group

NO.	PLAYER'S FULL NAME — AS SHOWN ON MEMBERSHIP CARD —	IDENTIFI- CATION NO.	LAST RATING	ROUND 1 col.	ROUND 1 opp.	ROUND 2 col.	ROUND 2 opp.	ROUND 3 col.	ROUND 3 opp.	ROUND 4 col.	ROUND 4 opp.	ROUND 5 col.	ROUND 5 opp.	ROUND 6 col.	ROUND 6 opp.	ROUND 7 col.	ROUND 7 opp.	ROUND 8 col.	ROUND 8 opp.
1																			
2																			
3																			
4																			
5																			
6																			
7																			
8																			
9																			

— CUMULATIVE SCORES AFTER EACH ROUND —

includes players who *lost* in section (a) of the first round and players who *won* in section (b). In this way, the strong, high-rated losers are paired against the weak, low-rated winners of the first round.

In each second-round group, odd men are treated, colors are allocated, and players are paired as in the basic system.

For the third and all subsequent rounds of the tournament, the rank points used in the first two rounds are cancelled and the pairings made according to actual game scores as in the basic system.

The Swiss Pairing Card and Wallchart
Just as the director of a round-robin tournament has his International Table of Rounds, the director of a Swiss-System tournament has his practical aids, namely, his pairing cards and wallcharts. Examples of these supplies are displayed below and on page 38.

RATING _____   NO. _____

NAME _____

ROUND NO.	COLOR		OPPONENT NO.	SCORE		TIE-BREAK	
	W	B		GAME	TOTAL	A	B
1							
2							
3							
4							
5							
6							
7							
8							
9							
10							
11							
12							
			ADJUSTED				

Circle scores if unplayed game.

USCF SWISS PAIRING CARD

8 Swiss: Ratings Controlled (London Chess Association Form)

This is a synopsis of the rules and guide lines for seeded pairings in large Swiss System tournaments prepared for the London Chess Association during the 1970's based on the experiences of Stewart Reuben, I.J. and Peter Morrish, B.J.

Introduction

Players at Swiss system events should enjoy themselves as much as is reasonably possible. For instance, pairing together relatives, members of the same club or from the same distant area, or contestants with a difference of 300 Elo (about 40 BCF) rating points should be avoided. Also entrants generally prefer to play, rather than win by default.

A player's score should reflect his performance, e.g. similar scores should have similar sums of opponents' scores (see Buchholz tie-breaking, p.64), and similar rating results (i.e. inferior to that of a player on a higher score, etc.).

A Swiss system tournament can be an event coping with virtually any number of players or teams and any number of rounds. Basic rules are:
1. No player is to meet the same opponent twice.
2. In each round, players should be paired with opponents on as similar scores as possible.
3. After each round, players should have had as near equal number of whites and blacks as possible.

There is no *best* pairing system; one method may suit an event with few players and many rounds while another with many players and rather few rounds requires a completely different system. Pairing problems could be caused through the spread of competitors' abilities, or with the need to use unreliable ratings.

A *lottery* system should, according to the London C.A. organisers, have at least two rounds more than the number required by a K.O. system to reduce the entry to one winner.

The London Chess Association organisers strongly believe that a player should be able to pre-determine his or her opponent – at least in principle. The arbiter should not have any choice. This means that two separate arbiters would make a series of identical pairings. (Naturally some errors will creep in.)

It is possible for identical pairings to be made by using, in a pre-determined way, numbers allocated to every player.

Tournaments with large numbers of entrants can use a *seeded pairing* system, based on players ratings. This system is designed to create greater possibilities for competitors' scores to approximate to their strength after very few rounds. Procedure for such events is given in detail below.

Accelerated pairings systems are a further sophistication that have a number of advantages. An example of their use is the division of entrants into four groups according to ratings, and in round one pairing the highest group against the second group and the third group against the fourth. A further example, developed on this, is, in round two, the pairing of third and fourth group winners against first and second group losers. These systems should not be confused with the detailed *seeded pairings* system that follows.

The following table represents the maximum entry that a given number of rounds can cope with:

No. of rounds:	4	5	6	7	8	9	10
No. of players:							
K.O. system	16	32	64	128	256	512	1024
lottery system	10	20	42	86	172	344	688
seeded system	26	60	124	256	512	1024	2048
minimum accelerated	40	90	200	400	800	1500	2800

It is difficult to visualise the figures for a possible maximum accelerated system.

Special variations of the seeded pairing systems have been developed for international events where contestants are striving to achieve title norms. An example is the Reuben System which identifies potential FIDE norm candidates, and has the aim to make pairings without abusing the general structure of the Swiss system in such a way as **to create opportunities** for these candidates to play the required number of title-holders and foreigners and reach the required rating standard.

The two main problems in making pairings are:
1) When players have to meet opponents with different scores.
2) When players due for the same colour must be paired together.

Seeded Pairings Procedure

Charts and Cards

The following outlines the arbiters' procedure, for a seeded pairing tournament, such as used in London Chess Association events.

Before the tournament the arbiters prepare:
1. a **chart**, on which is written
   (a) the names in alphabetical order of all the entrants
   (b) entrant's chart number
   (c) entrant's rating
with spaces in which are entered round by round:
   (a) player's colour
   (b) opponent's chart number
   (c) progressive score (by adding 1, $\frac{1}{2}$ or 0 to the previous round's total).
2. a **pairing card** for each player, showing:
   (a) name
   (b) club, region or country . . .
   (c) chart number
   (d) rating

SAMPLE CARD

Rating	NAME	Chart Number	PROGRESSIVE SCORE ROUNDS						
			1	2	3	4	5	6	

and having spaces for:
  (a) round number
  (b) player's colour
  (c) opponent's chart number
  (d) player's result (1, $\frac{1}{2}$ or 0)
  (e) player's progressive score
and, as the cards are often used for post-tournament rating, a convenient space for:
  (f) opponent's rating.

Display Board
To display the pairings quickly Peter Morrish has developed a special pairings board, into which the pairing cards (which have the competitors' names in clear large printing on their backs) are slotted against a table number and in the appropriate colour column. Each board displays 20 pairings and is usually placed above 2 metres to enable the maximum viewing.

First Round Pairings
In order to make the first round pairings, sort the cards into rating order with the highest number on top.
    If there is an odd number of competitors give the bye to the *median* (the middle card of the pack). Then divide the pack of cards into two halves, higher rated all in one half. Pair the top card of each pack together, card by card, top half versus second half, and work down the pack until all cards are used. See *First Round Colours* for procedure of allotting whites and blacks.
    Enter player's colour and opponent's chart no. on cards and chart, using different colour pens for white or black.

Late Entrants
The names of late entrants are placed together at the foot of the chart. A special first round pairing, as if for another tournament is made between these.

Same Ratings
In sorting cards, players on the same rating are placed in chart number order except:
a) in round two, they are put in reverse chart number order, or
b) in any round, where it may be easier to arrange the pairings if the order is switched this should be done.

Median
The *median* is the middle card of an odd-numbered score group or colour sub-group, or if even-numbered the card one below the middle (e.g. 16 cards – No. 9).

If an alternative median is needed try firstly the card below, secondly card above, thirdly card below . . .

It is the median that is *floated* to another score-group (see *Floats*).

Byes
When in any round there is an odd number of competitors, one must be given a **bye**. The procedure is:
a) in round one, the bye is given to the **median** player.
b) in subsequent rounds, the bye is given to the lowest rated player who:
    1. is in the lowest score group, and its larger colour sub-group.
    2. has not already had the bye.
c) that for future colour allocation, the player receiving the bye is regarded as not having any colour in that round.
d) that for only third round pairings the player given the bye in round two is assumed to have scored a $\frac{1}{2}$ point.

Floats
Players **float** when they, not having the same score, are paired. This happens when there is an odd number of competitors within a particular score group, or when it is impossible to make pairings solely within the group.

Players floated down are placed as the highest graded in the next score group available.

Floats should be minimised for each player and should be given to those who have floated least. Such minimisation is carried out irrespective of the direction of previous floats; where it is necessary to choose between players who have previously floated, priority is given to equalising the direction of floats.

The direction of the float is indicated on the pairing card by upward and downward arrows for each $\frac{1}{2}$ point floated.

Colour Selection
Players' colours should alternate as much as possible.

When selecting which of two or more players should be chosen to change from their expected colour, previous colour patterns are compared by looking back first one round, then two, etc., until a difference is found.

Possible samples after 5 rounds:

1. WWBBB
2. WBWBB
3. BWWBB
4. WBBWB
5. BWBWB
6. BBWWB

7. WBBBW	9. BBWBW
8. BWBBW	10. BBBWW

The lower numbers are most deserving of white.

First Round Colours
Lottery decides whether the highest graded player has white or black in the first round. Then colours alternate down the list, e.g., for 64 players if the highest gets white, then pairings read, in grading sequence, 1-33, 34-2, 3-35, 36-4 . . . This is the only time there is a lottery. And it is for **one** pairing only.

Pairing Priorities
In pairing the second and subsequent rounds, apply priorities in this order:
1) Score
2) Equalising colours
3) Floats
4) Ratings
5) Alternating colours.
   Where difficulties arise, make pairings that cause the least disturbance. When an **error** is discovered too late to change many pairings, make the minimum number of amendments while trying to adhere to the pairing rules as closely as possible.

Second and Subsequent Rounds
In preparing to make the pairings for the second or subsequent rounds, first
a) Remove any cards for pre-arranged byes.
b) Sort the remaining cards into score groups.
c) Sort the score groups into colour sub-groups of those due for white or black.
d) Put each sub-group in rating order with highest on top.
   Pairings are made, either:
a) by starting at the top score group and working down to the lowest (floats goes downwards)
b) in large tournaments by starting simultaneously at the highest score group (floats downward) and at the lowest score group (floats upward) and finishing with the 50% score group.
   After sorting:
a) check the need for and allot the bye.
b) next, make each score group even-numbered by transferring (see *Median and Floats*) the minimum number of competitors from one score group to the next in a way to keep the number seeking each colour as near equal as possible. (If there is a sole leader, place as highest rated in the next lower score group available.)
   Next stages:
a) Pair the floats. If the median cannot be paired with one of the two highest rated in the score group below, choose an alternative median.
b) Within the score groups balance the colour sub-groups by transferring across those players least deserving of their expected colour. (To distinguish further between those being considered for the colour transfer, take the median and further cards according to the procedure for alternate medians. - Editor's modification.)

Check that colour sub-groups are equal and in rating order.

c) Split each colour sub-group into two piles; the white-seekers becoming Pile 1a – those above the median, and Pile 1b – the median and below; the black-seekers becoming Pile 2a – from the top of pile 1, the same number of cards as in Pile 1b, and Pile 2b – the remainder.

Pile 1a is placed to the left of Pile 2b.

Pile 1b is placed below and to the left of Pile 2a.

Pile 1a is then paired with 2b.

If a pairing is impossible due to players having already met, use the following rules in order until a pairing becomes possible.

1. Change the order of players of the same grade.

2. Take the next down on the right hand side.

3. Take the next further down on the right hand side (i.e. 3rd player from original)

4. Change the last completed pairing in that score group and re-pair the player on the left-hand side according to 1., 2. or 3. If this is impossible, return the completed pairing to its original form.

5. Repeat 2. down the 2b list until satisfied.

6. Break the completed last pairing as in 4. and re-pair the player on the left hand side according to 5.

7. Break the penultimate completed pairing and re-pair the highest player on the left hand side according to 5.

8. Continue this until satisfactory.

9. Change the player in 1a causing the problem, with the player of nearest grade from 1b. Continue changes until successful.

10. Change the 1a player with the player of nearest grading in Pile 2 who has been switched according to 8. Continue as necessary (no such players may exist of course).

11. Change the lowest player floated. Continue until solution.

12. Change the 1a player with the player from Pile 2a of closest grading. Continue until solved.

13. If there now results a player who cannot be paired, it is because two players both had only the same possible single opponent. The lower graded must be floated down together with the median.

Pile 1b is then paired with Pile 2a as above. Wherever 1a is mentioned change to 1b. Wherever 2b is mentioned change to 2a.

NOTE

Although this looks horribly complex, it is no more than the standard opponent-searching late in a small Swiss. In large tournaments it is never necessary to proceed further than 5.

Miscellaneous Points

Unrated Entrants

When there is no information on an entrant's strength or rating, assign a provisional rating (prefixed P) somewhat higher than the lowest rated player. Such provisional figures can be revised for later rounds.

Absentees

Absentees' opponents should be paired again, as close as possible to the original. Clock times will, of course, need readjusting.

Pre-Arranged Byes

In some tournaments a pre-arranged ½-point bye is given to competitors not wishing to play in a particular round. The Bye Rules apply, except that those allowed a ½-point bye in round one are placed in rating order to be allotted alternatively white and black in round 2 so as to best balance colours.

9 Swiss: Non-Rating Forms

Lottery Form

In the lottery form (a non-controlled variation), players are not ranked in any way within their score-groups for pairing purposes, the refinements of the controlled system giving place to determination by lot. The resulting form is simpler, though less efficient, and may be of some service when accurate ratings or other methods of ranking are unavailable for a large number of the players. Also, some directors argue that a completely free draw excludes any criticism that may be directed at any kind of steering, especially when there is a small number of players and the value of such steering is small.

The following rules are from a FIDE version.

Swiss System Rules (Simplified Edition)

Pairing Procedure

In order to facilitate the mechanics of the operation a pairing card is made out for each entrant. One side of the card, with the player's name and other details, serves as a registration form. The other side is used by the director to record for each round the player's board number, the colour of his pieces, the opponent's name and number, the result of the game and the player's progressive score.

For the first round the pairing cards of all the players are mixed together and cards drawn by lot to establish pairings and colours. At the end of each round the cards are sorted into groups of equal point scores. Cards of players in any one group who are due for white in the next round are paired by lot against players in the same group who are due for black in the next round. As the tournament progresses the director must be careful when making pairings to ensure that no two paired players have met before.

If the total number of players in any round is uneven, one player is given a bye. In the first round the bye should be given by lot to one of the weaker players in the tournament and this player is awarded one-half point. In succeeding rounds if the total number of players is uneven, the bye (and one-half point) is given by lot to one of the weaker players in the lowest score bracket of the tournament. Under no circumstance should the same player be given more than one bye.

If there is an uneven number of players in a score bracket one player is dropped and paired with a player in the score bracket immediately below. The player dropped should be one of the weaker players in the uneven bracket and at the same time one whose colour requirement will help or at least not harm the overall colour requirement of the group from which he is dropped.

Colours
The director assigns colours to all players. His primary objective, in a tournament with an even number of rounds, is to give white and black the same number of times to as many players as possible; and in a tournament with an odd number of rounds, to give white and black the same number of times to every player, plus one extra white or black.

The director also attempts to alternate, round by round, the assignment of white and black to individual players. When a player is given a bye it is customary to record the player's colour as white.

Scoring
The scoring is one point for a win, half a point to each player for a draw, and zero for loss. The unplayed game of a player who is given a bye is scored as one-half point. An unplayed game in which the players were paired is scored as one point to the winner and zero to the loser. The remaining games of a player who withdraws (or is expelled) from a tournament are scored as losses.

Each player's final position is determined by the total of his game points.

European Form

The form of the Swiss System most commonly used in Europe is a non-controlled form more highly developed than the lottery form. The rules (as those of the Swiss Chess Federation, which follow), are simple, relieving the director of making any selections and freeing him from any criticism, as the pairings are governed by a draw before the tournament starts in the manner of round-robin events. The rules provide also for color allocation and removal of odd-men from a score-group. Tie-breaking is, usually, by the Buchholz System, although it might equally be done by the standard system.

Swiss Tournament Rules of the Swiss Chess Federation

Tournament Form
1. The Swiss System is a shortened form of tournament whereby fewer rounds are played than are necessary for a round-robin event.

Draw
2. The draw (numbering of participants) is done as for a round-robin tournament.

Pairings
3. The pairings for the first round are 1-2, 3-4, 5-6, 7-8, etc. To achieve the best results the pairings should be made alternately from the top and from the bottom of the list. The director should take note that when pairing from the bottom, the highest number is paired with the second highest, etc.
4. In the subsequent rounds the players with equal points are paired in the order of their lot numbers and with alternating colors. No player plays twice against the same opponent. Pairings of players with equal points must be made even when no equality of colors occurs.
5. If the pairing of opponents with equal points is impossible because they have played with each other before, or if a single player is left over, players

of the next following group of points are paired, always subject to the provisions of point 4. The difference in points must be minimal.

Equalization of Colors
6. After each round the distribution of colors must be optimal, always subject to the provisions of points 4 and 5. At the close of the tournament, the distribution of colors to every player should not differ by more than one (or two when there is an even number of rounds).
7. If the distribution of colors is equal for both players, the player with the lower numbers gets white. The sequence of the colors has no importance.

Ranking
8. The final ranking of players with equal points is done by means of Buchholz points, i.e., the total of the points of all their opponents.

British Form

The 11 round British Championship has been run according to the Swiss System since 1949. Since that time the number of Swiss-System tournaments in Great Britain has multiplied rapidly.

The current rules of the British Chess Federation provide for a non-controlled form of the Swiss System (with the exception of the first round of the British Championship). These rules provide for the specifics of awarding the bye, dealing with odd-men in a score-group, and allocating colors.

Rules for Swiss Tournaments at B. C. F. Congresses

A. General
With the solitary exception of the application of the first part of rule C1(a) (dividing the British Championship competitors into two halves before deciding the first round pairings by lot), all competitors in all tournaments must be identified only by their tournament numbers and the rules must be applied only to the cumulated data on their tournament records. No consideration must be given to the names, playing potentials, personalities, etc., of the competitors.

B. Byes and Defaults
1. If in any tournament the number of players is odd or becomes odd (by a player withdrawing), then, for pairing purposes, an imaginary player termed 'Bye' is introduced whose colour is permanently black and whose score is permanently zero. In any round in which a real player is paired with Bye, that player is deemed to have white and score a win. Should the number of real players become even (by another player withdrawing), then Bye is also withdrawn; but should the number subsequently again become odd (by yet another player withdrawing), then Bye and its tournament record is re-introduced.
2. If in any round a player should default, then the pairing containing that player is cancelled. Instead, that player is deemed to have black and score a

loss against a blank opponent; and the partner of that player in the original pairing is demed to be paired with Bye, having white, and scoring a win. This rule applies whether or not (a) Bye has yet been introduced into the tournament, or (b) the player so favoured has been paired with Bye in a previous round, or (c) any other player is paired with Bye in the same round.

3. Except as provided in rule B2(b), no player shall be paired with Bye more than once.

C Pairings

1. First round
   (a) British Championship: The players are ranked on up-to-date grading figures supplied by the B.C.F. Grading Committee and the top half is paired against the bottom half, individual pairings being decided by lot.
   (b) All other tournaments: By lot.

2.–8. All other rounds, all tournaments: These rules are applied in their order of numbering.

2. All players are grouped according to their scores. The players in the top score level are the first to be considered for pairing, then the players in the bottom score level, then the players in the next-to-stop score level, then the players in the next-to-bottom score level, and so on until the process terminates with the players in the middle score level.

3. No two players who have once played each other shall again be paired together. (See also rule B3.)

4. At each score level, players shall as far as possible be paired inside that score level.

5. At each score level, if rule C4 cannot be fulfilled entirely, then the smallest possible number of players in that level shall be paired with players drawn from the next-nearest score level to be considered. Such players are termed floaters; in each pairing of floaters, the player with the lower score is said to have received a number of upward floats equal to twice the score difference between the floaters, and the player with the higher score the same number of downward floats.

6. If there is more than one arrangement which satisfies rule C5, then that arrangement is chosen which best satisfies rules D2–4.

7. If there is more than one arrangement which satisfies rule C6, then that arrangement is chosen which tends to reduce the largest disparities between the numbers of upward and downward floats of each player being considered (e.g. if three upward floaters are required to be chosen from four candidates, of whom one has had already three upward and two downward floats, the second has had one downward float, and the third and fourth no floats; and if the fourth has already played every player in the score level $\frac{1}{2}$ point higher, but the others have not; then the first choice is the second player, the second choice is the third player, and the third choice lies between the first and fourth players).

8. If there is more than one arrangement which satisfies rule C7, then decide by lot.

D Colours

1. First round, all tournaments: By lot.

2.-6. All other rounds, all tournaments: These rules are applied in the order of their numbering.

2. Bye, if present, always takes black. (Rule B1.)

3. For each real player, the colour should be such as to tend to equalise the total numbers of whites and of blacks.

4. (a) If rule D3 fails, then, for each real player, the colour should be such as to tend to equalise the numbers of whites and of blacks over this round and the preceding round, i.e. the colour should be the reverse of the colour in the preceding round.

    (b) If rule D4(a) fails, then, for each player, the colour should be such as to tend to equalise the numbers of whites and of blacks over this round and the preceding two rounds.

    (c, d, etc.) As rule D4(b), with (b), (c), etc., respectively, substituted for (a), and three, four, etc., respectively, substituted for two; until the coverage has extended back to the second round (Rule D3 has already covered back to the first round.)

5. If rule 4. fails, then:

    (a) If the players are floaters: the player with the lower score takes white.

    (b) If the players are not floaters: the player with the higher balance of upward minus downward floats takes white (e.g. if one player has had one upward and no downward floats, and the second has had two upward and four downward floats, the first player takes white).

6. If rule 5. fails, then decide by lot.

The Italo-Swiss System

In this variation the pairing is automatic, so that nothing is left to the subjective decision of the arbiter and the influence of the lottery is eliminated (except for the first round).

The number of rounds should not, if possible, be less than one third of the number of contestants and not be more than one-half plus 1 of the total number of contestants.

Lots are drawn at the beginning of the tournament to establish the order of the players. This is the only lottery and this order in the tournament table remains unchanged until the end of the competition. The players should be seen as lined up in a circle, following the order of the numbers they drew by lot, clock-wise. The pairs are fixed working clock-wise, *never* going back, and this rotation is continued from the first to the last round.

What this actually entails is working from the top of the tournament table (the player who has drawn the number 1 to the bottom, without ever reverting back. When we arrive at the bottom of the table (the player who has drawn the last number) we then go back to the top and once again work our way down to the bottom, etc.

In the first round the 'rotation' begins with number 1 who plays number 2, and then we get the following pairings: 3-4, 5-6, etc.

To get the pairings for the second and subsequent rounds we first seek out the player with the highest number of points. The 'rotation' begins after the player who had the *white* pieces in the *last pair* of the previous round ('ultimo bianco' - last white). This player may, but need not, also be the player with the highest number of points. In the first case he will be the 'first' player who 'seeks an opponent'. In the second case, one starts from that player and works one's way down to the bottom of the table, looking for the player with the highest number of points, who will be the 'first' player and who has to have a partner (the first pair). When the player with the highest number of points is found, working always in a circle, one works one's way to a partner with the same number of points, and if there is no-one, then to the player with the closest number of points.

One must bear in mind, however, that two players must play against each other only once. If the two players have already played against each other in some earlier round of that tournament, then the rotation is continued to find another opponent with the same (or, if that cannot be found, the closest) number of points.

Hence, we have the first pair. The same system is applied for all the other pairings.

If a player cannot be paired with a player with the same number of points, then one looks for a partner from the group of players with half-a-point less, etc., once again always making sure to apply the principle of rotation.

Adjourned games which have not been completed by the beginning of the round are, when doing the pairing, considered as wins for *both* players.

Towards the end of the tournament it may prove impossible to form the last pair, since these two contestants may have already played against each other. In this case, the next-to-the-last pair is annulled and all combinations are tried with the last four players to compose two pairs of players who have not played against each other. If this, too, proves impossible, then the next-to-the-penultimate pair is also annulled, etc. The aforementioned principles are applied in these operations too, when possible.

In this variation, then, what is important is that the pairings are done automatically, always working in a circle, from the top towards the bottom of the table and back again to the top, and so forth. In the first round or rotation begins with the number 1, and in the next with the player who had the white pieces in the last pair of the previous round. One works one's way from that player looking for the player with the highest number of points. The important principle is that one *never* reverts back, so that the rotation always proceeds forward.

AFTER
ROUND 8

1	T.	2	
2	A.	5	
3	X.	$4\frac{1}{2}$	
4	B.	5	
5	Y.	$4\frac{1}{2}$	
6	C.	5	
7	Z.	$4\frac{1}{2}$	
8	W.	$4\frac{1}{2}$	
9	P.	2	→ 'LAST WHITE'
10	S.	3	

etc.

Let us take the example given above, where the players are lined up along the circumference of the circle, although they could have been lined up in an ordinary tournament table. This represents only part of the contestants: one group which, let us say, has 5 points each (A, B, C) and one other which has half-a-point less (X, Y, Z, W). Working one's way clockwise, one has to find a partner for player A. This will be player B, while player C will have Z for a partner.

If it is impossible to compose a pair among A, B, C, (because they have already played), then again one starts out from A, having determined that he cannot be paired with either B or C, and works one's way *forward* (never back), taking the first player after C from the group with half-a-point less. And so we get pair A-Z. Now we have to find a partner for player B. Since the first group ends with C, we continue the rotation. Z is already taken, and the next player is W, so our second pair is B-W. Finally, we look for a partner for C and the first one we come across in our rotation is X. The pairings, then, are: A-Z, B-W and C-X. Player Y is still free and he will get a partner from the next group.

The white pieces in the first round go to the first player in each pair. In the next rounds, the white pieces go to the player (a) who has had white a fewer number of times than his opponent; (b) if they have both had white the same number of times, to the player who was last to play with the black pieces; (c) if they both meet the conditions of (a) and (b), to the player with the fewer number of points; and (d) if there is no difference between them in any of the three above points, to the player who drew the lower number in the lottery at the beginning of the competition.

If at the beginning the number of contestants is uneven, then an odd number of rounds is played. The contestants who play in the first round are those who have the first numbers on the table, ending with the number which corresponds to the number of rounds minus 1. For example, if nine rounds are being played, only the players with the first eight numbers play in the first round. All other contestants are free in this round. The players to be free in turn in the next rounds are those who played in the first round. For instance, there are 21 contestants and 9 rounds are being played. Playing in the first round are: 1-2, 3-4, 5-6, 7-8, and all the others are free. Number 1 will be free in the second round, number 2 in the third, and so on.

If a player withdraws from the tournament, then the player with the lowest number of points will be 'paired' with the said player, and he will be given one point. Here it is irrelevant if that player has already played with the one who has withdrawn from the competition. The player with the lowest number of points can receive a forfeit point for the second time from the same player who withdrew, provided the former trails by at least one point behind all the others, otherwise the point will go to the next-to-the-last, etc.

The Italian version of the Swiss System has been improved several times. There is also the *Yugoslav Circular Variation*, which is also based on automatic pairings and which differs from the Italian only in certain nuances. These variations of the Swiss System are popular in Italy and in Yugoslavia.

10 Swiss Systems: Team Events

Team Form

Up to this point a player vs. player format has been assumed. However, the Swiss System applies equally well to a team vs. team format. The only basic difference arises in the scoring, since in a team tournament two scores exist: the scores of the individual games and the scores of the team as a whole. The team, or match, score is derived directly from the game score: if a team scores more game points than its opponent, the team wins; if fewer game points, the team loses; if the same number of game points, the team draws.

Some directors argue that pairings and scoring should be by game points, as more differentiated pairings are possible (since the number of game points possible greatly exceeds the number of match points possible). Other diectors argue that match points are preferable for pairing and scoring to avoid the possibility that a team might win more matches, but lose to a team which has won fewer matches yet accumulated more game points. These diectors also point to the use of game points as contrary to the spirit of a team tournament.

As an example of the minor adjustments that might be made to the Swiss rules to provide specifically for a team tournament, the rules of the US Chess Federation are given. As the USCF conducts its two national team tournaments according to match points, these rules provide for pairing and scoring by match points rather than game points.

USCF Form

Pairing Rules of the US Chess Federation Ratings-Controlled Team Swiss Tournaments.

Basic Rules
1. Most of the rules for Ratings-Controlled Individual Swiss Tournaments apply to teams in Swiss tournaments. Some rules are modified as indicated below.

Pairing Cards
2. A card similar to that used for Individual Swiss Tournaments is used, but provision is made for match scores and game points.

Order of Boards
3. Team members should be placed in board order according to ratings, and they must play in that order throughout the tournament. The highest-rated player is Board No. 1, etc. Unrated players may play on any board as long as their position reflects their actual strength in relation to the rated players.

The director may authorize in advance of the tournament that players may be placed out of rating order within a specific point limit, such as 25 or 50 points.

Alternate team members are used according to whatever system is announced in advance.

Team Ratings and Identification Numbers

4. The rating entered on a team's card is the average of the ratings of the regular team members. In the case of unrated players:

    (a) If a top or bottom board is unrated, the rating assigned is 50 points (or some other announced number of points) from that of the player on the next board.

    (b) If a middle board is unrated, the rating assigned is averaged from the ratings of the next higher- and lower-rated players.

Pairing Rules

5. Teams are paired and ranked first by their match scores, then by their ratings.

Color Allocation

6. In each team the colors given to the individual players alternate from Board No. 1 down. If the player at Board No. 1 has white, then No. 2 has black, No. 3 has white, etc. Rule Nos. 17-22 for Individual Swiss Tournaments are applicable to team tournaments, but in each rule the colors referred to are those of the player at Board No. 1.

Scoring

7. Each member of a team scores game points as described in Rule No. 6 for Individual Swiss Tournaments. A team scores one match point for a win against another team, one-half match point for a draw, zero for a loss, on the basis of its game points. A team's match score for a bye is one point. Any round defaulted because of a team's failure to appear within one hour after the starting time is scored as one point for the winning team and zero for the losing team, and the defaulting team is not paired for the succeeding rounds without an excuse acceptable to the director. Defaulted rounds (as those of a late-entering team or of a team which is excused from being paired in a round after the director has been notified in advance that it will be unable to play) are scored as zero. The remaining games of a team which is excused, withdrawn because of a default without notice, or expelled from the tournament are scored as zero. The scores of unplayed games (rounds) are circled on the pairing cards and wall chart. Each team's final position is determined by the total of the match points scored by the team.

11 All-Play-All (Round Robin)

The All-Play-All (Round Robin)

The All-Play-All or Round-Robin System of pairing is accepted as offering the most accurate final standings. This is especially true if it is a double-round event in which players have both white and black against each other.

In the all-play-all, each participant plays each of the other competitors. The order in which a player will play his opponents and the colour of the pieces depends on the numbers the contestants draw by lot at the beginning of the tournament and on the variation of the all-play-all used to play the competition. The Berger pairing system is the most popular.

If an all-play-all is played, in which contestants meet each other more than once, it is best for all players to play one game with each other, as in a single round-robin tournament, and then for the cycle to be repeated with colours reversed, etc.

The Berger System

Before the competition begins, each player draws a number. This automatically determines the pairings and colours for each round, using the Berger tables, which can be found in the Appendix, p. 208.

Berger tables are based on certain principles which we should know so as to be able to use various methods and arrange pairings even without such tables.

First we must remember the following three rules:

Rule 1. If both partners have homogeneous numbers (i.e. both are even or both are odd), then the player with the higher number plays white. If the players have heterogeneous numbers (one even and the other odd), then the player with the lower number plays white.

The last number on the table is the exception if the number of players is even. Then, the upper half of the players and the player with the last number on the table play white and the lower half plays black.

Rule 2. In each round the player who has drawn the number 1 plays the player whose number is the same as the number of the round. The exception is the first round, when he is either given the bye in the case of an odd number of participants, or plays with the last on the table in the case of an even number of participants. In the fifth round, for instance, the player with the number 1 plays with the player with the number 5. This pair is called the basic pair of the round.

Rule 3. Berger tables for an odd number of contestants are identical to tables for an even number with one contestant extra. The only difference is that with an odd number of contestants, the player who, in an even number of contestants, should play with the last number, is given the bye.

Several methods exist for drawing up Berger tables for any number of players. We shall present those which we believe are the simplest and the most suitable in practice.

All-Play-All Procedures

Allot each player a number starting with 1, 2, etc.; if there is an odd number of players issue an extra number to represent the bye.

In round one the lowest number is paired against the highest, the second lowest against the second highest, etc.

In later rounds, the highest number (or bye) is paired in succession (round 2) against one above the middle number, (round 3) against second lowest number, (round 4) against second number above middle, (round 5) against third lowest number . . . For 20 players No. 20's pairings would go round 1: 1 v 20; 2: 20 v 11; 3: 2 v 20; 4: 20 v 12; 5: 3 v 20, and so on in the same pattern. The colours of the highest number always alternate.

Each player (other than the highest) is paired in consecutive rounds with a next higher number except:

a) after pairing v highest odd number the next round is against No. 1.

b) when next number is its own; then it is paired with the highest (or bye) number, and then in following rounds with the number immediately higher than its own.

To determine colours use the following formula:

1. The highest no. (always an even number) has black against all players in the lower half of the numbers and white against the higher half of the numbers.

2. Odd numbered players have white against greater evens, and lesser odds.

3. Even numbered players have white against lesser evens and greater odds.

The highest number alternates colours each round.

To determine which round any two players meet, other than pairings involving highest no. (or bye), add their numbers together; and:

a) if answer exceeds highest no., subtract highest number.

b) if answer is less than highest no., subtract 1.

To determine the pairings for any particular round:

a) first make pairing for highest no. (or bye).

b) calculate figure x by subtracting 1 from round no.; make all possible adding combinations to total this figure x.

c) figure y by adding round no. to highest no.; make all possible adding combinations to total this figure y, except for highest no player.

Example: 18 players, round 6   18 v 12   x = 7   1 v 6   2 v 5   3 v 4; y = 24   17 v 7   16 v 8   15 v 9   14 v 10   13 v 11.

The following table shows how this procedure works:

round I	1–8	2–7	3–6	4–5
round II	8–5	6–4	7–3	1–2
round III	2–8	3–1	4–7	5–6
round IV	8–6	7–5	1–4	2–3
round V	3–8	4–2	5–1	6–7
round VI	8–7	1–6	2–5	3–4
round VII	4–8	5–3	6–2	7–1

Bold indicates that the player has white.

For complete pairing tables based on these procedures see the Berger International Tables, Appendix, p. 208.

A quick method of preparing a pairing table, showing the rounds in which players meet, for any number of players playing each other once is as follows:
1) Construct a chart as follows, e.g. for 8 players:

CHART FOR ALL-PLAY-ALL TOURNAMENT

	1	2	3	4	5	6	7	8	Total
1	X								
2		X							
3			X						
4				X					
5					X				
6						X			
7							X		
8								X	

2) Working across the top row fill in the blank squares the numbers 1 to 7 and do the same down the first column.
3) For the second row, work across from 1 to 7, but leave out the number 2 which falls on the square marked X, the number 2 is then placed at the end. Thus the second row will read 1, −, 3, 4, 5, 6, 7, 2.
4) For the third row, starting with 2, work across, leaving out the number 4, which falls on an 'X'. The third row will thus read 2, 3, −, 5, 6, 7, 1, 4.
5) Complete the sequence for the remaining rows.
6) For the last row, where there are an even number of players, copy the last column. In our example the final table should read:

	1	2	3	4	5	6	7	8
1	X	1	2	3	4	5	6	7
2	1	X	3	4	5	6	7	2
3	2	3	X	5	6	7	1	4
4	3	4	5	X	7	1	2	6
5	4	5	6	7	X	2	3	1
6	5	6	7	1	2	X	4	3
7	6	7	1	2	3	4	X	5
8	7	2	4	6	1	3	5	X

7) Colours are decided as follows:
1. Odd numbered players have white against 'higher odds' and 'lower evens', e.g. 3 has white against 5, 7, 2; black against 1, 4, 6, 8.
2. Even numbered players have white against 'lower odds' and 'higher evens', e.g. 6 has white against 1, 3, 5, 8; black against 2, 4, 7.

'Shifting' All-Play-All

A simple pairing system for informal all-play-all events like lightning tournaments is a 'shifting' one.

Seat all the players at a row of tables with white along one side and black along the other. Play the first round.

At the end of each round all the players but one – who plays in the same fixed place throughout the tournament – move clock-wise to the next free chair. The colours are reversed along the whole row after each round. Continue changing places until all players have met.

If there is an odd number of players, the bye takes the place of the fixed place.

Example

ROUND 1

Ivan	Jules	Pedro	Pablo
(Black)	(Black)	(Black)	(Black)

(White)	(White)	(White)	(White)
Fred	Jan	Albert	Hyrom (or Bye)

ROUND 2

Fred	Ivan	Jules	Pedro
(White)	(White)	(White)	(White)

(Black)	(Black)	(Black)	(Black)
Jan	Albert	Pablo	Hyrom (or Bye)

Master Popović's Variation

Since each contestant in a single-round tournament according to both the Berger System and the shifting variation draws his number by lottery, the order of the opponents and the colours of the pieces in the games may often be more favourable to one player than to players of his strength who are his direct rivals. The colour of the pieces in certain games influences the ultimate standing of the players and this influence is all the greater if the players differ in strength. Consequently, the scores of the first and second leg in double-round tournaments often differ considerably. The order of the opponents also plays a certain psychological role in the final standings. Master Voja Popović's system largely eliminates these shortcomings and therefore merits attention.

We divide the players into two groups, if there is a minor difference between the players, and into three or four groups, if that difference is greater.

System of two groups

We classify the contestants into two groups according to strength: S, for stronger players and W for weaker players who are equal in number.

The first half of the tournament: each player in each group *S* plays against each player in group *W*.

Second half of the tournament: the players in each group play against each other, i.e. each group plays a tournament according to the Berger System, so that *S* play against each other and *W* does the same.

System of three groups

We classify the players according to strength into three groups of equal number: *S* - stronger players, *A* - average, *W* - weaker. Naturally, the total number of the contestants must be divisible by three.

First third of the tournament: *S* - *W*; *A* against each other,
Second third of the tournament: *S* - *A* ; *W* against each other,
Last third of the tournament: *A* - *W*; *S* against each other.

System of four groups

We divide the players into four groups according to strength: *F* - favourites of the tournament, *S* - stronger players, *A* - average players and *W* - weaker players.

First quarter of the tournament: *F* - *W*; *S* - *A*,
Second quarter of the tournament: *F* - *A*; *S* - *W*,
Third quarter of the tournament: *F* - *S*; *A* - *W*,
Last quarter of the tournament: players play against each other in each of their groups.

The group always plays against the other group according to the classical variation of the Scheveningen System. Each player draws his number by lot in his group prior to the beginning of the tournament. When groups play against each other, the colour of the pieces is determined by the following rule: players in the weaker group play white in all odd rounds, and black in even rounds. When players from the same group play each other in the last part of the tournament, the colour of the pieces is determined by the Berger tables.

Let us put forward some of the advantages of this system in, for instance, the variation with four groups:

1. Players in one group have virtually the same order, and after each quarter of the tournament they will have come across exactly the same players. They have the same colour of pieces in each round until they reach the mutual tournament.

2. In the last quarter of the tournament they play amongst themselves, and this, from the viewpoint of sport, provides the greatest interest of the tournament.

3. The round by round placement of the players, when observed separately by groups, is more realistic and more interesting.

Master Voja Popović's variation can also easily be applied to tournaments with groups of players from the same club or country, where their mutual encounters are to be held in the first part of the tournament.

The Holland System

In order to ensure that competition using the round robin system is not too lengthy, the number of contestants should be limited. But this system can be used with a larger number of entrants and still not be too long, provided the players are divided into preliminary groups, then finals are played. By choosing a suitable number of players in the groups and of players who will qualify for the finals, a round robin tournament can be played with a substantially smaller number of rounds than if all the contestants were to play one tournament. One can shorten the procedure still further by not having the players (or teams) who played in the same group in the preliminaries meet again in the finals, and instead have their scores automatically transferred to the tournament table of the finals. The final tournament, then, can be shortened by one or more rounds, depending on whether 2, 3 or more players from each group qualify.

The ideal distribution of players by groups is for them to be as numerically equal as possible and approximately of the same strength. It is better to have one undersized group than an oversized group. If, for instance, we have 49 contestants, the best would be to have four groups with 10 contestants each and one with 9. It would not be good to have three groups with 12 players and one with 13, for the group with 13 contestants would play two rounds more than the other groups.

Shortening the finals by a round can be easily achieved in tournaments made up of two contestants from each of the preliminary groups, by using the method proposed by Soviet international arbiter L. Abramov. In order to write down their mutual score as the result of the first round of the finals, the lots for the final tournament should be drawn in pairs for players from the same group, by drawing out both numbers with one lottery – one of the pairs of the first round – and giving the lower number to the player who had white in the semi-finals in his game with the other.

12 Tie-Breaking Systems

It is an accepted principle in Swiss, as well as round robin tournaments, that tied winners of prizes should be awarded all the cash prizes involved, summed and divided equally. Tie-breaking becomes necessary, therefore only when a prize cannot be divided, as when a championship title or trophy must be awarded to only one person or when only a limited number of players may qualify into a succeeding event. In such cases, tie-breaking serves a necessary function.

Tie-breaking is at best a necessary evil, however. In a round-robin tournament, at least all the players have met the same field, but in a Swiss tournament each player plays a different field. No system for breaking ties in a Swiss System has earned anything approaching general acceptance. The assumptions underlying each system are accepted by some directors and questioned by other directors. Opinions vary even about what tie-breaking systems should measure.

Although tie-breaking is problematical at best when used on the top scorers, it verges on the fruitless when applied to middle and low scorers, as the Swiss System itself is not intended to make accurate differentiations aside from the top few places. After ties have been broken among the top scorers if necessary, the most reasonable thing to do is list the other players in score order and alphabetical order within equal scores. Small differences in tie-breaking points are meaningless.

Some tie-breaking systems are used more widely than others. They are described here in no particular order, but as sometimes the use of one system is not sufficient to break a tie, it is necessary for a director to have an ordered list of systems to use in case more than one is needed. The regulations for the World Junior Championship, for example, provides for the following order: Median, Total Score, Weighted Score, the result of the game played by the players concerned, Partial Score, lowest number of games with white, drawing of lots.

Adjusting Scores for Tie-Breaking

In the Partial Score, Total Score, and Median Systems, reference is made to 'adjusted scores'. It is customary in those systems to make adjustments in the final scores used for tie-breaking to compensate for opponents who won or lost points as a result of unplayed games (byes and games won or lost by default).

Every player who won or lost a point for a game that was not played for any reason receives one-half point as the adjusted score for that game. This adjusted score is used only for the purpose of breaking ties among the players' opponents. A player receives one-half of the final adjusted score of his opponent in any paired, but unplayed (defaulted), won game when his own tie-breaking sum is calculated.

The Partial-Score System (Sonneborn–Berger, Buchholz II)

For each player in the tie is found the sum of the final adjusted scores of all the opponents he has defeated, together with half the final adjusted scores of all the opponents with whom he has drawn (nothing is added for games he has lost).

(Intended to score round-robin tournaments, this system, as applied to Swiss tournaments fails to evaluate losses sustained by tied players.)

The Total-Score System (Solkoff, Buchholz I)

For each player in the tie is found the sum of the final adjusted scores of all his opponents.

(Though the total scores of a player's opponents are used, undue weight may be given to losses to the players with the highest final scores and, as in the Partial-Score System, the scores of the weakest opponents are included.)

The Median System (Harkness)

For each player in the tie is found the sum of the final adjusted scores of all his opponents except the following:
(a) in a tournament of eight rounds or less, the highest and the lowest;
(b) in a tournament of nine to twelve rounds, the two highest and the two lowest; or
(c) in a tournament of thirteen rounds or more, the three highest and the three lowest.

(As with the Partial- and Total-Score Systems, the Median System attempts to evaluate the relative strength of each player's opposition. The extremes at the upper and lower ends of the scale are removed in an attempt to get a more representative measurement of the strength of the opponents.)

The Weighted-Score System (Kashdan)

For each player in the tie, four points are given for a win, two points for a draw, one point for a loss. Wins and losses by default are counted as two points.

(This system is based on a proposal to modify the usual 1-$\frac{1}{2}$-0 scoring to give greater weight to a win and a loss than two draws.)

The Cumulative System

For each player in the tie is found the sum of his cumulative tournament scores after each round.

(This system provides a rapid method for breaking ties without the necessity of waiting for virtually all games to be completed, as required by the Partial Score, Total Score, and Median Systems. However, the results of this system, though they correlate to a substantial extent with those produced by the other systems, do not fully take account of the opponents' strength.)

Tie-Breaking in an All-Play-All Tournament

The standing of players, and teams, at a tournament is determined by the number of points they have compiled. If the awards are in a form which cannot be divided, or if the first two players, or teams, are entitled to qualify for further competition, to win categories, etc., then some sort of differentiation must obviously be made.

There are several ways of doing this, depending on the system of the competition and on whether it is an individual or team event. In order to apply any of these methods, it is essential that it be determined *beforehand* and included in the tournament regulations as a provision which defines procedure in the case of a tie for critical places.

One of the general provisions which can always be applied, in both individual and team competitions, regardless of the system being used for the competition, is a play-off match. If two players tie for a place, their order is determined by a play-off match whose number of games, duration and other conditions are laid down in advance in the tournament regulations of the competition. In the case of a tie among three or more players, a three-way, four-way, etc. match is played. The regulations must provide for what to do in the case of an unresvoled score in such a match – to play on until the first win or to provide some other clause. In team competitions, what usually decides is the best score on the first half of the boards or some other provision: match points in the competition, etc.

This is a realistic and fair way to resolve the matter, but it is also tied in with new financial expenditures, the possible absence of players in team competitions, etc. We therefore list other methods which are used in individual and in team competitions played according to the round-robin system.

Tie-Breaking in individual competitions

The following may be used to break ties in a round robin tournament:
    1. Tie-breaking according to results against the top half.

Players who have tied for a place are ranked in order of the number of points they have acquired against those players who have scored over 50% of the total number of possible points.

This is a practical and good method: it gives priority to those players who scored more points in encounters with stronger players.
    2. Tie-breaking according to the Sonneborn–Berger System.

a) Here, the tie-breaking procedure is as follows: For each player in the tie, one adds up the scores of the opponents he has defeated and half the scores of the players with whom he drew. By comparing these numbers (co-efficients), calculated for each player separately, one gets their order of finish.

The essence of this system, which is officially recognized in the world, is that the points carry more weight when scored against higher-placed contestants. The weak side of this system is that less important games, especially towards the end of the tournament, can often play a decisive role in the order of finish for ties towards the top of the scoreboard.

b) Some ten years ago, Soviet chessplayers and mathematicians T. Shmulyan and V. Dvorkovich found a simpler way to calculate the co-efficients, based on won and lost games. They showed that the players' order of finish in a tie, calculated this way, and their order calculated under a) is always the same.

According to the Shmulyan–Dvorkovich method, co-efficients are worked out in the following way: one adds up the points of the opponents defeated by the given player as well as the points of those to whom he lost. The difference between the first and second total gives us that player's co-efficient. This is a quicker method when the players in question have had few lost games and a large number of draws, which is practically always the case with highly-placed players, who are usually those to be involved in a tie.

3. Tie-breaking according to the larger number of wins. Priority is given to players with a larger number of wins at the tournament.

This method has no scientific justification, since the player who has a larger number of wins than the opponent with whom he shares the same number of points, must also have a larger number of losses. On the other hand, this is of practical importance in that it can work to activate the players' fighting spirit and cut back the number of 'placid' draws.

The aforementioned tie-breaking methods are usually used in tournaments. Two or more players may, even after the application of these methods, still remain tied. Hence, the tournament regulations must provide for more than one way to break ties, using secondary and perhaps even tertiary criteria. One can, for instance, let the score of their mutual encounter decide, and as an ultimate resort, when the two players' scores are the same in all methods, one can draw lots. The organizer decides before the competition which method will be primary, which secondary, etc.

Tie-Breaking in team competitions

There are two possibilities for working out the final placements in team competitions: according to match points and according to game points. The FIDE General Assembly in Paris in 1924 settled this dilemma when it was generally adopted that in all official team competitions placement is to be determined according to game points. This is fair, since each game in team matches is a whole unit itself, so that the team match is actually a compilation of a given number of individual games. By using this method, each individual game increases in importance.

As in individual competitions, there may be a situation in which two or more teams have the same number of points at the end of the competition and the need arises to break the tie. And here, again, there are several ways to establish the order of finish. The primary tie-breaking criterion in team competitions, however, is usually match points. The choice is broader for secondary and other criteria and depends on the organizer. Naturally, the order of all these criteria must be laid down by the tournament regulations in advance.

In Chess Olympiads the classification of teams is decided in the following manner:

1) by the results of the games (total number of points for won and drawn games);

2) in case of equality in the results of the games, by the results of the matches (number of points for won and drawn matches, counting one point for a win and half a point for a drawn match);

3) in case of equality in the results of the games and of the matches, by the result of the matches between the teams in question;

4) if rules 1 to 3 do not produce a decision, by the Sonneborn–Berger system. (For the method of calculating this system for team competitions see Art. 21 of Laws of Chess – FIDE Interpretation 1967.)

This method of tie-breaking could be an example for other round-robin team competitions too.

13 Arbiters and their Responsibilities

The required number of certified arbiters is established before a competition, from which one is appointed as the chief arbiter, and the others are his assistants or deputies. It is the duty of the chief arbiter to make rulings and settle all disputes as the first resort of appeal, and only in his absence can his deputy assume these rights. The number of arbiters required depends primarily on the kind of competition in question, its importance, the system it will be played by and the number of participants. In tournaments played according to the Berger system with up to twenty participants, it is usually sufficient to designate one arbiter and one deputy. In team competitions it is advisable to have, in addition to the chief arbiter, enough assistant arbiters so that one of them can run each match, or, if the matches are played on a small number of tables, for one arbiter to run every 2–3 matches.

The duties of the arbiter during the competition are laid down on general lines by the Laws of Chess of FIDE. The organization and correct running of the competition, however, demands the involvement of the arbiter not only in the progress of the competition itself, but also before it commences: must take part in preparing tournaments (he is usually a member of the organizing committee), work on elaborating the rules of the tournament, take part in establishing the necessary conditions for play etc.

This may be clearer if we divide the duties of the arbiter into three parts: before the competition, during the competition and after the competition.

Duties of the Arbiter before the Competition

One of the first duties of the arbiter is, on the basis of the instructions and conditions of competition prescribed by the organizer, to draw up the regulations of the tournament.

The regulations must be read out prior to the beginning of the competition or submitted to all the contestants beforehand, and they should be signed by the arbiter, a representative of the organizer and all the contestants to denote agreement. If a player fails to do this, but still takes part in the competition, he is considered to have agreed with the regulations. Once the competition has commenced, the tournament regulations can no longer be changed.

Securing and Checking the Necessary Conditions for Play

The arbiter, prior to the commencement of the competition, must check all the conditions for play, secure through the organizer all the necessary equipment, and engage a sufficient number of deputies and auxiliary staff (demonstrators, monitors, controllers, etc.).

1. First, the arbiter must prepare the playing room, check the lighting, heating, ventilation, etc., as well as the other rooms needed for the equipment and documentation, rooms in which the players may rest, rooms for analysis of the games, for newsmen, a snack-bar, etc. If the playing room has a stage, it usually serves as the area of play, provided it is large enough, has good lighting and good ventilation. If the room has no stage, or has a stage which does not meet the necessary conditions, then a part of the room (in front of the stage, for example) is used as the playing area, and it is cordoned off from the spectators area. Only the players, arbiter and demonstrators may be in the playing area; others may enter this area only by permission of the arbiter.

2. The arbiter must also check with the organizer whether all the necessary equipment has been assembled: chess tables, chairs, chess sets, clocks, demonstration boards (if the games are demonstrated in the playing room), and check whether these are in working order and whether they meet the customary norms. Spare sets and clocks should be available. He must also check whether all other accessories have been secured: ashtrays, scoresheets, envelopes for sealed moves, etc.

3. Prior to the commencement of each round, the arbiter must check whether the boards and pieces are properly arranged, the pairs properly distributed, the clocks properly set, whether all the players have scoresheets, whether all the necessary signs have been posted, the pieces on the demonstration boards arranged, etc.

In all games, the white pieces should be arranged facing the same direction, usually on the left facing the stage from the spectators' area.

It is recommended that all clocks be set so that the first-time control is when the hands reach 6:00. The clocks are always positioned so as to face the arbiter's desk or the aisle, so that the arbiter may always be able to observe their functioning, especially during 'time-pressure'.

4. If the games are shown on demonstration boards, then the arbiter should check whether these have been properly set up and whether they are clearly visible from all parts of the playing room, as well as whether the demonstration is progressing properly, for order in the tournament room often depends on the proper demonstration of the games.

Commencement of the Tournament and the Drawing of Lots

The tournament is opened by a representative of the organization running the competition, followed by speeches by the hosts. Then the arbiter reads out the regulations (provided he has not already submitted them to all the contestants) and invites the contestants to draw numbers for registering them in the tournament table. The numbers may be written out on folded slips of paper and placed in envelopes. The players are called by alphabetical order, by titles or in order of how their names are listed in the tournament regulations, to draw the lots. The procedure for the lottery can also be done in some other, more interesting way. The slips of paper with the numbers can be placed in a bouquet of flowers, for instance. This can be left to the imagination of the organizer. The only important thing is that the objects be identical. In big tournaments, the regulations are read and the lottery held one day before the first round.

If a player withdraws from competition after the lots have been drawn but before the beginning of the first round, then the lottery is reheld, except in the following two cases:

a) if, with an even number of contestants, the player to withdraw had the last number on the table (since his withdrawal does not affect either the pairings or the colour of the pieces in the encounters of the other players),

b) If a substitute replaces the player who has withdrawn.

A new lottery need not be held if another two players are to be included in the tournament after the numbers have been drawn, but before the commencement of the first round. Then they are given two neighbouring numbers in the middle of the tournament table, and the tournament numbers of the players who have drawn numbers in the lower part of the table are raised by two. This, again, does not affect the colour of the pieces or the distribution of the pairs who have already drawn their tournament numbers.

A new lottery is not required in tournaments with an uneven number of contestants, if only one player is subsequently included in the tournament. Then he is automatically given the last number.

Duties of the Arbiter During the Tournament

The duties of the arbiter during the tournament are to keep a tidy record of each round, to control the working of the chess clocks, to oversee the proper course of the competition, to ensure order in the playing room and the players' comforts during play, to fix the schedule for the resumption of adjourned games, to supervise the work of the technical staff of the competition, to settle any disputes which may arise and to undertake all preventive measures to check any disputes or conflicts, to penalize any lack of discipline on the part of the players, etc. The arbiter must initiate play (by starting the clocks) and indicate the end of the session. **For an example of an arbiter's record see p. 220.**

If the tournament regulations do not stipulate the order in which adjourned games will be played, then this is decided by the tournament arbiter. Here, the arbiter does not have to go by chronological order. He draws up the schedule for the adjourned games as he thinks best, guided by the principle that he should find the most economical way to use the time reserved for continuations. If players A, B, C and D have adjourned their games: A–D, A–B, C–D, the arbiter will decide to start with continuations A–B and C–D, because they can be played at the same time, regardless of whether game A–D is from an earlier round.

All contestants who have adjourned games, regardless of whether their games are up for play first or not, must come at the hour designated for the commencement of the adjournment sessions. A player with an adjourned game who cannot play it yet because his opponent is engaged in another adjourned game, must nonetheless be in the playing room, because as soon as his opponent's adjourned game is completed, the arbiter has the right to commence his adjournment. The regulations do, however, allow for several minutes of rest (15 to 30 minutes) to be granted to the players in between two adjourned games.

The continuation of the game is usually played until the end of the session, i.e. 2, 4 or 6 hours, depending on how much time is allotted. It is not generally customary to adjourn a game prior to the end of the session so that the same players may play other adjourned games, although in some countries (e.g. the USSR), such provisions do exist. If a player has several adjourned games, then at the end of the first, and after a rest, if granted by the arbiter, he must play the continuation of the second game, at the end of which the continuation of the third game, and so on, as time allows, provided that at least 2 hours remain until the end of the session. If the adjournment session lasts from 16:00 to 22:00, for example, and the player ended his first adjourned game at 20:15, the continuation of the second game cannot be called because only 1 hour and 45 minutes remain until the end of the session.

During the competition, the arbiter must carefully observe the conduct of the players and take timely action when needed. Similarly, the arbiter must keep an eye on relations between the players and see to it that they are correct and sportsmanlike. Moreover, a good arbiter must also undertake all necessary preventive measures to check the outbreak of disputes and conflicts at the tournament and thereby enable the competition to follow its normal course. Any irregularity should be properly and objectively judged by the arbiter who must take a corresponding decision which is unbiased and which is the result of a detailed consideration of all the facts and circumstances, and based on the Laws of Chess of FIDE and on other applicable regulations.

So as to facilitate the work of the arbiter in this matter, we shall enumerate some of the things which may occur in the course of competition and provide some guidelines (which need not always be mandatory) for dealing with them. We can divide these questions of conduct into three groups: first, acts which are contrary to the FIDE Laws of Chess; second, acts which are contrary to the ethics of sport but not to the FIDE Laws of Chess; and third, acts which are part of playing tactics, but which are not based on purely chess elements.

I. Acts which are contrary to the FIDE Laws of Chess

These acts directly clash with the FIDE Laws of Chess and other regulations and they engender corresponding sanctions and penalties. Let us mention those which are most frequent at competitions, although they far from exhaust the list:

1. withdrawing from the tournament,
2. failing to show up for a game;
3. analysing the game in the tournament room;
4. leaving the tournament room or playing area;
5. leaving the table when the said player has the move;
6. talking with other contestants;
7. seeking advice from others or using books, notes, etc.;
8. disturbing the opponent in any way whatsoever;
9. agreeing beforehand on the outcome of the game ('fixing the game').

Leaving the competition, unless there is a quite justified reason, is a serious offence meriting stringent sanctions, for the withdrawal of only one player from the competition is unfair to other contestants. With respect to determining the scores in a tournament played according to the Berger system when such a withdrawal occurs, the arbiter should act in accordance with the Interpretation of FIDE (1970) given with Art. 21. of the FIDE Laws of Chess.

Failure to arrive for the game, as in the case of players who arrive at the chess board over one hour late, incurs loss of the game for that player. There is no need to say that, not only leaving the tournament, but also every individual game which is lost without play, is a gesture of poor sportsmanship.

In view of the effect which games lost without playing may have on the proper course of the competition, it is customary to tolerate no more than two games lost by a player in this way. A third game lost without play (it need not be the third consecutive game), would mean the said player's expulsion from the tournament, the initiating of disciplinary procedure, and, with respect to verification of the said player's results, action in accordance with FIDE Laws of Chess (Art. 21).

No contestant may leave the area designated for the players during the session without the permission of the arbiter. This is understandable, for otherwise, the player could contact other people and receive advice, not to mention the fact that he would be beyond the control of the arbiter and could have recourse to notes, books or analyses. Consequently, failure to respect this rule may result in the imposition of a default by the arbiter on the said player.

The arbiter should not, save in exceptional cases, permit a player who has the move to get up and move away from his table. This can raise suspicions in the opponent's mind that the player is taking advantage of advice from third parties. Even if such suspicions are not always justified, such acts can have a psychologically adverse effect on the opponent and so arbiters are advised to abide by this procedure.

In principle, the arbiter should not permit any discussion between the contestants, for this, too, can be the cause of a great many conflicts. A player who has the move and whose opponent is not at the table may always suspect that the latter, although he may be speaking about something entirely different with some other contestant, is actually discussing their game, and this may psychologically upset him and lead to a dispute. One should be especially rigorous in prohibiting any and all discussion among contestants in team competitions.

Unfortunately, all the things we have mentioned here are taking on growing proportions in modern-day chess, and the battle against them is arduous, for one can seldom find reliable and obvious proof to establish such offences. For example, a dishonest chessplayer has many ways to 'fix' the game: he can 'overlook' a piece, 'overstep' the time limit, not show up for the continuation, seal an illegal move, etc. An experienced arbiter, in assessing all the circumstances, will often be firmly convinced that a game has or has not been fixed, but he may only act with irrefutable proof.

A draw which is agreed upon in advance is a much milder infraction, and the motivations entailed here are of a different nature. Since 'fixing' a game for a draw is a milder infraction than giving away an entire point, the arbiter's sanctions are also less rigid.

II. Acts which are contrary to the ethics of chess

These acts do not directly clash with the Laws of Chess of FIDE, but they do clash with chess ethics, i.e. with 'fair play'. They are all rooted in the player's desire to win not only on the basis of the moves he executes or the taking advantage of human frailties directly tied in with the game of chess, but also on the basis of tricks and cunning. All these acts, although they escape chess sanctions, merit moral condemnation.

Let us mention those which most often arise:

1. refusal to shake hands before the commencement and at the end of a game;
2. arriving deliberately late for games;
3. disdaining the opponent who won the game;
4. setting a trap and then simulating regret as if it had been a crude oversight;
5. pretending to contemplate a move on the queen-side only to quickly execute a well-thought-out move on the king-side;
6. deliberately writing in one move and playing another;
7. playing long or even adjourning hopeless or obviously drawn positions;
8. failure to show up for the continuation of a game;
9. deliberately omitting or adding moves in one's scoresheet in the aim of deceiving the opponent as to the number of moves played;
10. offering a draw in a lost position;
11. agreeing to 'gentlemen's' draws and playing disinterestedly when one has lost one's chance of success;
12. sealing a resignation.

There are players who, in the desire to deceive an opponent who is extremely pressed for time and is not writing down the moves, deliberately omit writing in moves. The opponent, relying on the number of moves he sees on the former's scoresheet, quickly plays more moves than needed until the time-control, and thus makes a crucial mistake.

A player may plan another trick using the same circumstances: he may deliberately write one move down twice and the opponent, if he relies on this number of moves, quietly contemplates his 41st move while his flag drops.

In such situations, the arbiter is powerless: he must declare the default, even if he may be convinced that the victory is a dishonourable one. The blame, however, is partly the loser's, for according to the Laws of Chess of FIDE, no-one has the right to give the players information on the number of executed moves, and if he should see this from his opponent's scoresheet (or, which is forbidden, have even asked him), he must be prepared to suffer the consequences.

There are players who do not resign a game even if the position is completely hopeless, because they want to 'take revenge' for the defeat awaiting them. This can go so far that such a player may adjourn the game in such a position and not show up for the continuation. Such situations can also arise with positions which are an obvious draw. Naturally, here again, the arbiter cannot apply any sanctions, but merely make it clear to the given player that this is an act which is unfair to the opponent, to the organizer and to the public.

Regarding draws 'without play', in exceptional circumstances, such a draw could be tolerated if a player at that moment is obviously unfit to play, or is overtired from previous games which were long and exhausting, etc. All these specific circumstances are hard to define and should be judged by the arbiter. But if a player has the habit of reaching an entire series of such agreements on a draw, then this is obviously not a question of any such exceptional circumstance.

III. Acts which are part of playing tactics

So far, we have considered acts which are contrary to the Laws of Chess of FIDE and acts which clash with the principles of chess ethics, which the arbiter should fight against and check. Now we shall consider acts which, while not based on purely chess elements, are not to be condemned, for they take advantage of weaknesses in the opponent's character, such as carelessness, forgetfulness, inability to portion out his time, etc. There are many examples here but we shall mention only those which are most frequently come across in practise.

Ways and possibilities of taking advantage of an opponent's time-pressure are extremely important for practical chess. Some players do this by playing quickly, although they are not pressed for time, to deprive the opponent of any opportunity to collect himself during the time they would use to think out their moves. There is nothing here which clashes with chess ethics, because time is an element in the game of chess. This can be a good tactic in a weak position and if we know that our opponent is not very capable of handling time-pressure. If a player has a superior or even winning position, however, then playing on the opponent's time-pressure may work like a boomerang.

Such methods are permitted because chess is a complete battle between two people and all means are permitted in this battle for the purpose of taking advantage of the opponent's weakpoints, not only his moves, but also his psychological shortcomings and all objective circumstances. All that is important is that the means used are honest and ethical.

Forgetfulness may seriously harm a player. A contestant's forgetfulness in starting his clock may be used by another dishonestly: even if he has thought of a move, he may not execute it but rather 'think it over' so as to have the time factor work against his opponent as much as possible. Unless the opponent remembers that he has forgotten to stop his clock, he may overstep the time limit.

Duties of the Arbiter at the End of the Tournament

At the end of a competition, the arbiter announces the results and turns the tournament documentation (usually within five days) over to the organizer of the competition.

The documentation of the competition includes the following:
1. The tournament regulations;
2. The tournament tables;
3. The progress tables according to rounds;
4. The programme of the competition;
5. Records of the individual rounds or matches;
6. Records of the playing of adjourned games;
7. The scoresheets of the games;
8. Other documentation (appeals by the contestants, announcements and rulings by the arbiter, rulings by the tournament committee, etc.);
9. The arbiter's final report.

The arbiter's final report should include: the general provisions on the competition, the importance of the competition organizational criticism, publicity effect, characteristics of the competition with special reference to the play of the winner, youth, etc., creative achievements, theoretical innovations, the question of discipline at the tournament, fulfilment of the norms for acquiring or confirming categories.

The arbiter must be thoroughly versed in the rules of the game and chess competitions. He must conscientiously and objectively discharge his duty, maintain a high level of discipline at the competition and quietly and reliably settle any disputes which may arise. The arbiter must try from the beginning to maintain good discipline at the competition. Consequently, he should check the players from being late at the beginning of the game, try not to postpone games unless there is a strong reason for doing so, keep an eye on the proper course of individual games, on the conduct of the contestants and their correct attitude to their opponent, etc.

Experience has shown that the majority of disputes break out in the second half of the competition. This is understandable in view of the fact that mental and physical exhaustion lead to accentuated irritability towards the end of the competition. This means that the arbiter must take steps to prevent any possible disputes or conflicts. He must be sure that he is always near the player who is faced with a critical time-pressure situation.

In settling disputes, the arbiter must take into consideration all the facts leading up to the conflict and must base his objective decision on the rules of play and on the tournament regulations.

The Tournament Committee

The tournament committee consists of three to five members chosen from the players and organizers. Its task is to rule on appeals from contestants concerning the decisions of the arbiter. If a player is dissatisfied with a decision of the arbiter, he has the right to submit (usually within one hour after the session in which the dispute arose) a written appeal to the tournament committee which will review and rule on it within a prescribed period of time.

Until the tournament committee takes its decision, the decisions of the arbiter are executive and appeals do not place an injunction upon them.

The tournament committee reviews appeals from players and after investigating and establishing the facts it makes a ruling to the best of its ability. The tournament committee also settles disputes which arise with respect to interpreting the regulations of the tournament and the Laws of Chess of FIDE.

The decisions of the tournament committee are conclusive.

14 Ratings

Numerical rating of players

Long ago attempts began to find a system for numerically comparing the strength of chess players. The final scoreboard at a tournament offers only the provisional ranking of the participants. The individual results of the majority of players vary from tournament to tournament, so that a rating of players based on the results of only one competition is hardly reliable, nor does it allow for comparison with other players in other tournaments. A general rating system must be able to embrace all active players and to clearly establish the strength of each tournament, which is an essential condition for rating the achievements of chessplayers at various tournaments, including those who have never met each other at the chess table.

The numerical rating system was introduced in 1948 in the Federal German Republic (the Ingo-System), while other systems were developed in other countries - England, the United States, Switzerland, Canada, the Soviet Union, etc. At its Congress in Siegen in 1970, FIDE adopted Professor Arpad Elo's system as the official rating system for international tournaments and for determining norms in winning the titles of international master and grandmaster.

Rating systems do not concern themselves with the quality of the games, but this is not evaluated on the tournament scoreboard either. In other words, rating systems do not uncover any new values, they merely translate the results scored into a universal rating number. However, all systems make use of statistics, probability theory and experience.

Once the players' ratings are in some way determined, one can precisely establish the *strength of each tournament*. This is the number which represents the average of all the participants' ratings. Only then, when brought into context with the strength of the tournament, can the attained number of points by a player be evaluated.

Just as a player's real standing in individual tournaments is more reliable if he has played a large number of games, so the rating of a player is more reliable if it embraces a large number of competitions. The numerical rating of a player based on a small number of competitions will oscillate at first, only gradually to develop and finally offer a reliable indication of the player's practical strength.

Rating systems can be divided into three groups, according to the basic postulates on which they are based:

a) systems based on statistics and probability theory (Elo System);

b) linear systems - where numerical rating is calculated along linear functions (Ingo, British Grading and Swiss systems);

c) empirical systems - in which the proportions are established empirically (the rating system of the Soviet Union).

The need often arises for a player's numerical rating in one system to be translated into its equivalent in another. This may occur when a player has a numerical rating in the system of his national federation, and enters an international tournament using, say, the Elo-system. It took a long time before the closest formulae were found for such translations.

Today the following formulae are in effect and officially accepted:

$$\text{B.C.F. Grading} = 280 - \text{Ingo}$$
$$\text{Elo} = 2840 - (8 \times \text{Ingo})$$
$$\text{B.C.F. Grading} = (\text{Elo} - 600) \div 8$$

The first formula enables us to transform Ingo numbers into Grading numbers and vice-versa, the second to transform Elo numbers into Ingo and vice-versa and the third, which stems from the former two, to transform Elo numbers into Grading and vice-versa.

Rating systems offer a number of advantages for practical chess. Let us mention just a few:

– Each player, if he knows his numerical rating and the strength of the tournament, can work out how many points he needs to retain or improve his rating, which stimulates each player to play his best.

– Each player is given the possibility of assessing his performance objectively from tournament to tournament, and of assessing his prospects at a tournament in which he intends to take part.

– Team captains are facilitated in their task of selecting and arranging their team.

– Organizers have an easier time of composing groups of equal strength in a competition which is to be held in several groups.

– Ratings can be used to determine pairings in some tournament systems, for example the accelerated forms of the Swiss system.

We include a special article on the Elo-system by its inventor, Professor Arpad Elo, but space precludes a discussion of national rating systems. Let us just note that some countries use entirely different systems for rating players. Yugoslavia, for example, uses the titles of master and candidate master, then first, second, third and fourth category players and players without category. In order for a player to earn the fourth category, for instance, he must take one of the first four places in a tournament of players without category of at least 10 participants. At a tournament of first category players, the winner earns the title of master candidate. At tournaments with players of various categories, higher titles are earned by winning a certain percentage of points. A similar system is in use in the Soviet Union and in certain other countries.

A Statistical System for the Rating of Chess Players
By: Arpad E. Elo

I Introduction

The concept of rating chess performances dates back to the 19th century. (Brumfitt, 1891: Landau, 1895). The purpose of these early attempts at evaluating performances was, even as now, to obtain a ranking of the chess masters of the period.

Rating systems which went a step beyond mere ranking and attempted to evaluate relative strengths of chess players evolved in the 1930s and 1940s. The foremost of these was the Ingo System developed by A. Hoesslinger and disclosed in 1948. Variations of the Ingo System were later introduced by K. Harkness (1956) for use by the U.S. Chess Federation and by R. B. Clarke (1957/8) for the British Chess Federation. These systems share a common principle in that they combine the percentage score achieved by a player with the rating of his competition. They received acceptance because they produced ranking lists which generally agreed with the subjective estimates of rankings made by knowledgeable chess players.

During 1959/60 the writer developed a system variously known as the Elo-USCF System, the Elo-FIDE System or just the Elo System. This system is based wholly on statistical probability theory. It is a system which is universal in the sense that it can be applied to any type of competitive activity in which opponents (or even teams) are paired against each other. The system has been described in various publications (Elo 1961; Elo 1967; Elo 1973; Kühnle-Woods 1971), and its basic theory was presented in a privately printed monograph and in the *Journal of Gerontology*. (Elo 1965.) Since 1960 the system has been used by the U.S. Chess Federation for the rating of its entire tournament-playing chess population, and since 1970 by FIDE, both for rating of chess players in international competition and for the basis of international title awards.

II Basic Principles of the Elo System:
Stated simply, the Elo System is a numerical system making use of an interval scale in which differences in rating may be converted into scoring or winning probabilities. And conversely, scoring percentages can be converted into differences in ratings. It is a scientific approach to the evaluation of chess performances.

From even cursory examination of chess cross-tables it can be seen that what is called 'form' of a player varies. The stronger player does not invariably out-perform the weaker; a player has good days and bad, good tournaments and bad. By and large at any point in his career, a player will perform around some average level. Deviations from this level occur, large deviations less frequently than small ones, etc. These facts suggest the first assumption of the Elo System. It is stated in the formal terms of statistics:
A rating scale may be so constructed that many performances of an individual when evaluated on the scale will be normally distributed.

The second assumption concerns the definition of the rating scale intervals. The term *class interval* or *category interval* is well recognized in the chess world although it has been rather loosely used. We distinguish between various levels of proficiency, such as grandmaster, master, candidate master, etc., though even within any one category there exists a spread of proficiencies. But within one category we might expect good all around competition with no one being badly outclassed or outclassing the field. In the Elo System the class interval is given a quantitative definition, namely, the statistical concept of standard deviation in single games.

The concepts of normal distribution and standard deviation are illustrated in the accompanying Figure 1. Here the horizontal axis represents the rating scale with R the average performance of a player. The vertical axis represents the relative frequency with which any deviation δ from R occurs. It is seen that most performances are clustered around R, and other performances with large deviations appear less frequency, though they do occur. The standard deviation is the *measure* of the spread of individual performances, though it must not be construed as the spread itself. About two-thirds of the performances will be found within a range of plus or minus one standard deviation of the average, with the remaining one third outside of the range equally distributed at the two ends of the distribution. The graph shown is known as the normal distribution curve and is the basis of much of probability theory as well as measurement theory. The symbol used for the standard deviation is the Greek letter sigma or σ. Thus in the Elo System the class interval $C = \sigma$.

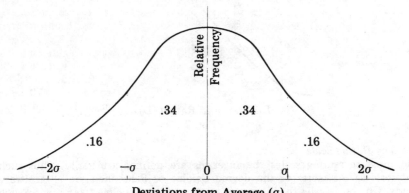

Deviations from Average (σ)
Figure 1

In some sports, such as golf or bowling, where there is an absolute method of scoring, the score achieved by a player is itself the measure of the *performance*. (Of course, even in these cases the difficulty of the course or the condition of the bowling surface may be factors influencing the score.) Chess performances, on the other hand, permit of no absolute method of evaluation. In a single game only three possible scores exist: $1, \frac{1}{2}$ and 0. Even in a tournament the total score of a player reflects only his performance against the particular competition he encounters. Thus another method of evaluating performance, which takes into account the strength of the competition, must be sought.

The mathematical form by which the evaluation of performance may be expressed is not information of an *a priori* nature, but can be deduced from the basic assumptions stated earlier, using the calculus of statistical probability theory. Thus we derive the relation between the probability of a player out-performing (or out-scoring) an opponent in a match (or opponents in a tournament) and the difference in their ratings. This relation is central to the rating system and provides its structural corner stone. (Note: the probability of out-performing an opponent in a single game is the same as the percentage expectancy in an extended series of games.)

The derivation of the basic relation, as well as of the other working formulae of the Elo System, is given in two of the technical references (Elo, 1965). The relation is a form of the *normal probability function* with a standard deviation of $\sigma\sqrt{2}$. This is shown graphically in Figure 2. The horizontal axis represents *differences* in ratings in units of σ, while the vertical axis represents percentage expectancies or probabilities. The graph is also known as the Gauss Error Curve and as the Standard Sigmoid. In tabular form it appears in most works on statistical methods.

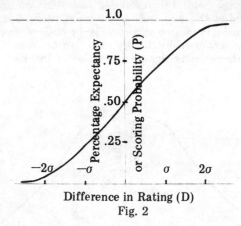

Difference in Rating (D)

Fig. 2

III *The Rating Scale*

On most measuring scales the intervals are defined arbitrarily. Thus such intervals as the meter or the degree Celcius or Fahrenheit are all arbitrary units. On some scales the interval is related to reproducible fixed points, such as the ice point and steam points on temperature scales; on others it is measured by a standard unit, such as the meter, deposited in the International Bureau of Standards. But many scientific scales contain neither reproducible fixed points nor depositable standard units. Examples of the latter type are the Richter Scale for earthquakes and, of course, rating scales for chess players.

The major interval on the FIDE rating scale is the class interval C which we have defined as the standard deviation of performances in a single game, and this has been arbitrarily divided into 200 rating points. The rating scale itself, its range of numbers, is also arbitrary. Like any scale without reproducible fixed points, it is necessarily an open-ended floating scale. Application of the rating system to the entire membership of a national federation requires a range of numbers wide enough to cover all proficiencies, perhaps as many as ten categories, from novice to grandmaster, and enough ballast numbers so no rating ever goes negative. The present range originally took 2000 as the upper level for the strong amateur, or club player, and arranged the other categories above and below, as follows:

Over 2600   – Contenders for the World Championship
2400-2599   – Most International Masters & Grandmasters
2200-2399   – National Masters & Some Candidate Masters
2000-2199   – Some Candidate Masters and Experts
Below 2000   – Various Numerical Categories, etc.

Category designations and proficiencies among federations have become more generally comparable with the adoption of the system by FIDE and by many member federations. However, different federations still have different standards for awarding national titles of 'master', candidate master, etc.

Using the FIDE scale intervals we can re-draw the percentage expectancy curve, this time on what is called normal probability paper, on which the curve turns out to be two segments of a straight line (Fig. 3).

THE PERCENTAGE EXPECTANCY CURVE (Fig. 3)

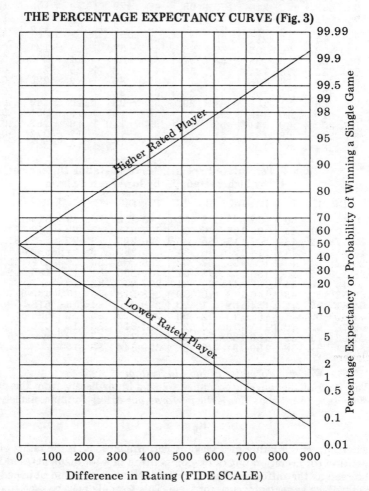

Difference in Rating (FIDE SCALE)

With the aid of this curve rating differences may be converted to percent expectancies, or percent scores may be converted into rating differences. The information contained in the graph may also be expressed in tabular form as follows:

Table 1. Rating Differences from Percent Scores

P	D(P)	P	D(P)	P	D(P)	P	D(P)	P	D(P)	P	D(P)
1.0	*	.83	273	.66	117	.49	−7	.32	−133	.15	−296
.99	677	.82	262	.65	110	.48	−14	.31	−141	.14	−309
.98	589	.81	251	.64	102	.47	−21	.30	−149	.13	−322
.97	538	.80	240	.63	95	.46	−29	.29	−158	.12	−336
.96	501	.79	230	.62	87	.45	−36	.28	−166	.11	−351
.95	470	.78	220	.61	80	.44	−43	.27	−175	.10	−366
.94	444	.77	211	.60	72	.43	−50	.26	−184	.09	−383
.93	422	.76	202	.59	65	.42	−57	.25	−193	.08	−401
.92	401	.75	193	.58	57	.41	−65	.24	−202	.07	−422
.91	383	.74	184	.57	50	.40	−72	.23	−211	.06	−444
.90	366	.73	175	.56	43	.39	−80	.22	−220	.05	−470
.89	351	.72	166	.55	36	.38	−87	.21	−230	.04	−501
.88	336	.71	158	.54	29	.37	−95	.20	−240	.03	−538
.87	322	.70	149	.53	21	.36	−102	.19	−251	.02	−589
.86	309	.69	141	.52	14	.35	−110	.18	−262	.01	−677
.85	296	.68	133	.51	7	.34	−117	.17	−273	.00	*
.84	284	.67	125	.50	0	.33	−125	.16	−284		

Table 2. Percentage Expectancies from Rating Differences.
H: by higher rated; L: by lower rated player.

Rtg Dif	H	L	Rtg Dif	H	LL	Rtg Dif	H	L	Rtg Dif	H	L
0-3	.50	.50	92-98	.63	.37	198-206	.76	.24	345-357	.89	.11
4-10	.51	.49	99-106	.64	.36	207-215	.77	.23	358-374	.90	.10
11-17	.52	.48	107-113	.65	.35	216-225	.78	.22	375-391	.91	.09
18-25	.53	.47	114-121	.66	.34	226-235	.79	.21	392-411	.92	.08
26-32	.54	.46	122-129	.67	.33	236-245	.80	.20	412-432	.93	.07
33-39	.55	.45	130-137	.68	.32	246-256	.81	.19	433-456	.94	.06
40-46	.56	.44	138-145	.69	.31	257-267	.82	.18	457-484	.95	.05
47-53	.57	.43	146-153	.70	.30	268-278	.83	.17	485-517	.96	.04
54-61	.58	.42	154-162	.71	.29	279-290	.84	.16	518-559	.97	.03
62-68	.59	.41	163-170	.72	.28	291-302	.85	.15	560-619	.98	.02
69-76	.60	.40	171-179	.73	.27	303-315	.86	.14	620-735	.99	.01
77-83	.61	.39	180-188	.74	.26	316-328	.87	.13	over 735	1.00	.00
84-91	.62	.38	189-197	.75	.25	329-344	.88	.12			

IV The Working Formulae of the Elo System:

The first of the working formulae follows immediately from the percentage expectancy function. This is the *performance rating* formula, namely:

$$R_p = R_c + D(P) \tag{1}$$

where R_p is the rating of a player's performance, R_c is the rating of his competition (or average rating of his competition in a tournament), and D(P) is to be read as the difference based on the percent score P and obtained from the percentage expectancy curve or table. This formula may be used to determine the initial rating of a player who for the first time competes against rated opposition. It may also be used to determine the average rating of a group of players who compete for the first time against a rated player or the rating of an unrated player who plays a match against a rated player.

A useful modification of equation (1) applicable to tournaments in which all play all, or round-robin tournaments is:

$$R_p = R_a + D(P)\left(\frac{N}{M}\right) \tag{1a}$$

where now R_a is the average rating of all the participants in the tournament, including the player, N is the number of games played, and M is the total number of players.

Another modification of (1) applies to matches in which both participants already have ratings. This is really a special case of a round robin tournament in which M = 2N. Therefore the formula becomes:

$$R_p = R_a + \tfrac{1}{2}D(P) \qquad (1b)$$

where R_a now is the average rating of the two participants.

A performance rating even in a long series may not accurately reflect the strength of a player relative to his competition. A well designed rating system then further combines performance ratings so as to provide the best possible estimate of the current relative strength of the player. This combination is termed the *player rating*, or just *rating*. The player rating will also exhibit some random variability, but not to the degree shown by performance ratings. Player ratings may be computed after each event by what is known as the *current rating* formula:

$$R_n = R_o + K(W - W_e) \qquad (2)$$

where R_o is the pre-event rating, R_n is the new or post-event rating, W is the actual game score (each win counting 1, each draw $\tfrac{1}{2}$). W_e is the expected game score based on R_o, and K is the rating point value of a single game score.

This equation performs the arithmetical operation of averaging the latest performance into the prior rating so as to diminish smoothly the effects of earlier performances, while retaining the full contribution of the latest performance. The logic of the equation is evident without algebraic proof: a player performing above his expectancy gains points, and a player performing below his expectancy loses points.

The coefficient K reflects the relative weights selected for the pre-event rating and the event performance rating. A high K gives high weight to the most recent performance. A low K gives more weight to the earlier performances. Thus K may be used to recognize the varying rates at which change occurs in a player's performance; a player development coefficient in a way. In actual practice K may range between 10 and 32. The lower value 10 is used in FIDE, where rated events are longer and player proficiencies are more stable. USCF uses the higher value 32, since over 80% of the tournaments rated are weekend events of six rounds or less, the player proficiencies vary widely.

The expected score W_e can be determined in either of two ways: a) by summing up the percentage expectancies of the player against the individual opponents, that is:

$$W_e = \Sigma P_i \qquad (3a)$$

or b) by taking the percentage expectancy corresponding to the average difference in rating between the opponents and the player and multiplying this by the number of opponents, that is:

$$W_e = N \times P_a \qquad (3b)$$

Equation (3a) gives the precise value of W_e, however, for most application (3b) yields tolerable results.

V Examples of Calculations:

Example 1. Use of tables and averaging:
Assume that a player participates in a 12 man tournament. His rating is 2350 and the ratings of his 11 opponents are as listed, with the differences and individual percentage expectancies:

Opponent	Rating	Difference	P_i
1	2500	−150	.30
2	2480	−130	.32
3	2430	− 80	.39
4	2400	− 50	.43
5	2375	− 25	.47
6	2365	− 15	.48
7	2335	+ 15	.52
8	2320	+ 30	.54
9	2300	+ 50	.57
10	2280	+ 70	.60
11	2260	+ 90	.62
Totals:	26045	−195	5.24

The average rating of the opponents is 26045 divided by 11 or 2368. This is now R_c. The average rating of all the participants is: (26045 + 2350) divided by 12 or 2366. This is R_a.

Example 2. Use of equation (1) for calculating R_p:
Assume that the player scores 5-6 against the 11 opponents. His percentage score is 5/11 or .455. From Table 1 the D(P) corresponding to this percentage is −33 points. Therefore the performance rating is: 2368 − 33 = 2335.

Example 3. Use of equation (1a) for calculating R_p:

$$R_p = R_a + D(P) N/M = 2366 - 33(11/12) = 2336$$

Example 4. Use of equation (1b)
In the 1972 World Championship match Fischer-Spassky, in the 20 games actually played, Fischer scored $12\frac{1}{2}$-$7\frac{1}{2}$. The pre-match ratings for the participants were 2785 and 2660 for Fischer and Spassky respectively. What were their respective performance ratings for this match?

The average rating of the two participants were 2722.5 and their respective percentage scores .625 and .375 which correspond to a D(P) of +90 points for Fischer and −90 points for Spassky. By equation (1b) we obtain for Fischer:

$$R_p = R_a + \tfrac{1}{2}D(P) = 2722.5 + 45 = 2767.5$$

and for Spassky: 2722 − 45 = 2677.5.

Example 5. Calculation of the expected score W_e.
Returning to example 1 we see the individual percentage expectancies in column four. The summation of these expectancies is 5.24, which is the expected score. Also the difference between the average rating of the competition and the player's rating is -18 points. This difference corresponds to a percentage expectancy against the field of .427. The expected score then is .474 $\times$ 11 = 5.21 game points, in good agreement with 5.24. (It should be noted that while actual scores can vary only in discreet amounts, that is $\frac{1}{2}$ points, expected scores can vary continuously. Small fractions then are hardly significant.)

Example 6. Calculation of a change in rating by equation (2).
Continuing with example 5, we see that the change in rating is given by the term $K(W - W_e)$ in equation (2). Now $W = 5$ game points, W_e may be rounded to 5.2, and using 10 for K we obtain:

$$\text{Change in rating} = 10(5.0 - 5.2) = -2 \text{ rating points.}$$

VI Administration of the Rating System
The administration of a rating system may be conducted on a periodic basis, a continuous basis, or on a combined periodic-continuous basis.

In the periodic method ratings are calculated at definite intervals, say six months or a year using equation (1). R_c is used to express the previous ratings of the opponents. Theoretically the time period may be any interval, but good statistical practice requires it to include at least 30 games to determine a player's rating with 'reasonable confidence'. Formula (1), of course, produces an indeterminate rating for a 100% score or a zero score. Hence it is applicable only when the number of games is sufficient to include a variety of results, that is, some wins and draws and some losses. B.C.F. uses the periodic method.

In the continuous method the ratings of players are readjusted after each event by equation (2). Through this continual readjustment rating differences will eventually be generated which conform to the percentage expectancy curve on which the system is based. In a sense this is a self-correcting method. The method is particularly appropriate to the rating of a large mixed population of chess players within which a substantial fraction of the population may consist of developing players whose ratings are changing rapidly. USCF uses this method.

In the combination method ratings remain in effect for a definite period, say one year. Changes in ratings are, however, computed by equation (2) for each event. At the end of the rating period the changes are totalled and new ratings are issued. The method is most suitable to a chess population wherein proficiencies are relatively stable and the range of ratings is limited to two or three class intervals. This is the method used by FIDE.

The administrator of the rating system may be called upon the solve a variety of calculation problems. The examples already given show how most problems may be solved when all the participants in a tournament already have ratings. Other situations may be encountered, however, especially in the early stages of institution of the rating system. These are:

A. Rating of new players who enter a rated tournament for the first time.

B. Rating a group of players of whom only very few are rated.

C. Rating a group of players, all without ratings.

Actually the basic methods described can be used to solve any of these problems, but they must be applied in steps.

Case A: If there are only a few unrated players participating in a round-robin tournament, then as step one their performances against only the rated players is computed by equation (1). Second, this performance rating is tentatively entered for each of the unrated and R_a is computed for the entire group of participants. Third, after R_a is determined, R_p for each player may be determined by equation (1a). The R_p thus obtained for the unrated will be their initial rating. Finally for the remaining rated players the changes in rating are determined as in examples 5 and 6. This method automatically takes care of the games between the unrated players.

Case B: With only a few rated players among the participants the problem is solved in a similar fashion, only in this case R_a is determined from the performances and ratings of the rated players who now serve as comparison standards. Rewriting equation (1b):

$$R_a = R_p - D(P) (N/M)$$

First $D(P)$ is determined for each of the rated players from their percent score, and this is multiplied by (N/M). Then substituting the actual ratings of these players for R_p, R_a is determined. In general, a rated player may not perform exactly according to form. Therefore to determine R_a with any degree of confidence it is best to have at least three rated players as participants in a tournament. The different values of R_a obtained from the various performances may then be averaged. And once R_a is found, the performance ratings of all the participants can be determined by equation (1a).

Example 7: Assume three rated players, A, B, C, with ratings of 2400, 2320 and 2270, participate in a 15 man tournament, and they achieve scores of $8\frac{1}{2}$-$5\frac{1}{2}$; $7\frac{1}{2}$-$6\frac{1}{2}$ and 5-9 respectively. We tabulate these:

Player:	A	B	C
Rating:	2400	2320	2270
Score:	$8\frac{1}{2}$-$5\frac{1}{2}$	$7\frac{1}{2}$-$6\frac{1}{2}$	5-9
% Score	.607	.536	.357
D(P)	+78	+26	−104
D(P) (N/M)	+73	+24	−97
R_a	2327	2296	2367
Average R_a			2330

It might seem that the values of R_a from the three performances vary widely; however, the standard deviation of performances in 14 round tournaments is $200 \sqrt{2}/\sqrt{14}$ or 75 rating points. The values obtained above are well within this range of the average.

Case C: If a group of players is to be rated, none of them having any rating, the best that can be done is to determine *differences* in ratings. An arbitrary average rating may be assigned to the group and ratings may be determined with respect to this value. Then if subsequently any members of the group interplay with FIDE rated players, the ratings may be brought into conformity with the FIDE ratings. It is not even necessary that all the members of the group have encountered each other as long as sufficient data on the performances of the players exist and provided no sub-group is isolated from the main group. The initial International Rating List was obtained by this method. For this purpose the complete interplay of 210 International Masters and Grandmasters was compiled for the period 1966–68 inclusive. In the first step, from the percent score, the differences of the individual players, with respect to the group average, were calculated. Several cycles of calculations were made, the competition average for each player being re-evaluated after each cycle. The cycles were continued until successive values of the differences showed little or no change. These calculations for so many players were made possible only through modern programmed computers. Actually 8 iterations of the computer were required to provide an acceptable set of differences. Such a set is called a self-consistent set.

Among the 210 players were about a dozen U.S. masters whose participation in U.S.C.F. rated tournaments for a number of years provided well established ratings for them. This made it possible to bring FIDE ratings and USCF ratings into conformity.

In general, round-robin type tournaments are preferable for rating purposes when there are many unrated players among the group to be rated. Swiss type tournaments may be used, but the results, in general, are less reliable. The reliability of results, of course, improves with greater volume of data.

VII Maintenance of Scale Integrity

As stated earlier, the rating scale is an arbitrary and open ended scale on which only differences have a significance. Yet for such purposes as title awards, etc., it is desirable to maintain some sort of scale integrity so that a given rating may represent the same proficiency at one time as at another. The control of scale integrity is the key to the successful operation and acceptance of any rating system.

For successful control of scale integrity, the rating administrator must have some statistical expertise. He should understand the general composition of the ensemble of player's which comprises what we shall call the *rating pool*, as well as the rate and direction of its change. In particular he should be aware of the effect that new and improving players can have on the pool. In general chess players who enter competition early in their lives improve rapidly and at various rates during their youthful years, may remain stable in their middle years and will slowly decline in later years. However, the proficiency in later years will seldom sink to the level at which the player may hae entered the rating pool. We may put this into quantitative form as follows: let R_i = initial rating assigned to a player upon entry into the pool; let R_m = maximum rating achieved by the player during his stay in the pool; and let R_f = final rating upon leaving the pool, whether through retirement or death. During the phase R_i to R_m the player would ordinarily be taking points from the pool and during the phase R_m to R_f he would be returning points to the pool. The net result would be that he took $(R_f - R_i)$ points from the pool. Thus to maintain the integrity of the rating pool, and in turn the rating scale, mechanisms must be built into the rating system which will feed into the pool $(R_f - R_i)$ points for each and every player who enters the pool. If this is not done, the result will be a systematic deflation, a gradual downward trend of all ratings, including those whose proficiency remains stable.

Obviously, whereas R_i is always known, R_f cannot be anticipated. Therefore, the mechanisms which will feed the necessary points into the pool will have to be of a statistical nature and based on probabilistic considerations. In this way the points fed into the pool are more likely to be channelled to those who are entitled to them.

There are two immediate manifestations of deflation. One concerns the improving player whose indicated rating at any time might be less than his actual proficiency. The other concerns his opponents, in a sense, his victims. An under-rated player truly victimizes his opponents, regardless of the outcome of the game, as may be seen from the percentage expectancy table. For example, a 50 point difference between actual and indicated rating can make as much as 7% difference in percentage expectancy, and each opponent of the under-rated player could lose .07K rating points undeservedly. The loss may not be great at any one time, but small losses could accumulate into significant amounts. Accordingly the control of deflation requires mechanisms to accelerate adjustment of the ratings of rapidly improving players, and to protect their opponents from undue loss.

There are various methods, some crude, some sophisticated, for identification of improving players. In general these will be found among low rated players who entered the rating pool relatively recently or among junior players. Players who have newly entered the rating pool and have played less than 25 or 30 games, may be designated as *provisionally rated*. Similarly juniors, say under 18 years of age, may be identified for special treatment.

The most reliable method for identification of an under-rated player is by the player's own performance in an event. A player may be said to be under-rated if his performance, as indicated by statistical tests of significance, is significantly above his expected performance. (This may be the so-called 't-test'.) The test is a common-sense criterion expressed in probablistic terms. In general a performance may be regarded as exceptional if the probability of its occurrence is less than .10 or better yet, less than .05. Each administrator may set the percentage on his judgment of the requirements in his own case. In an application, similar to that in FIDE, and limited to high level and stabilized players, the requirements would have to be most stringent. On the other hand, in an application to a mixed pool containing a large percentage of juniors and players of mixed proficiencies, the requirements could be more relaxed.

In this connection it should be remarked that the standard deviation of the game score of a player in a tournament is at most $\frac{1}{2}\sqrt{N}$, where N is the number of games played. The probability of the actual score exceeding the expected score by this amount is .16. At 1.28 $\times$ this standard deviation the probability becomes .10 and at 1.65 $\times$ the s.d. the probability becomes .05. These figures may be used as partial guide lines to the formulation of regulations intended to control rating deflation. Control of deflation is a complex problem and really cannot be effected by a single mechanism. Some measures are suggested:

1. Whichever method is used in rating administration, whether periodic or continuous, observe an order of rating calculations. New players, of course, must be rated first, then provisional players and then established junior players. Then their post tournament ratings should be entered into the calculation of other established ratings.

2. In the continuous method, different K coefficients may be used for juniors and for others. Alternatively a schedule of K values could be tied to the rating level of a player, a high value of K for low rated and a low value of K for the stabilized high rated.

3. Recognize exceptional performances as indicated by the significance test. This could take the form of award of bonus points for such performances or, which is equivalent, a temporary use of a higher K value.

4. Award of *feedback* points, or compensation points to the opponents of bonus winners. This can take the form of a return of a fraction of the normal gain of the bonus winner to each of the opponents. Alternatively a second cycle of calculation may be used for the opponents with the post tournament rating of the bonus winner being entered into the calculation of the opponents' ratings.

Regardless of what method or combination of methods is used to control deflation, it is still recommended that the ratings of a selected control group of players be monitored periodically to detect any systematic drift in the rating scale.

VIII FIDE Application of the Rating System

There are two phases to the FIDE application of the rating system: maintenance of an official international rating list (IRL) and the specificiation of norms for the awards of international titles.

Tournaments accepted for rating purposes may be either national or international tournaments in which there are at least 10 participants, and at least one-half plus one of the participants have an FIDE rating. Players are included on the IRL only if their ratings exceed 2200 for men, and 1800 for women. Performances of individuals in Swiss type tournaments may also be rated under some circumstances. Regulations covering the rating of Swiss type tournaments are currently under review by FIDE.

Tournaments recognized for title awards must be international tournaments with a minimum of 10 participants. In addition at least 75% of the participants must have FIDE ratings, at least one-third of them must be FIDE title holders and at least one-third must come from other than one and the same member federation.

Titles awarded by FIDE are International Grandmaster, International Master, Woman International Grandmaster, Woman International Master and FIDE Master. Titles of World Master and National Master of FIDE are also under consideration. The awards of these titles are based on the achievement of certain norms of performance and ratings. The performance norms must be achieved in 24 games or more within a three year period and the rating norm must be achieved at the time of the title application. The norms are as follows:

For the title of:	Performance Norm	Rating Norm
World Master (Proposed)	2651 +	2600 +
Grandmaster	2551 +	2500 +
International Master	2451 +	2400 +
FIDE National Master (Proposed)	2351 +	2300 +
Woman Grandmaster	2351 +	2300 +
Woman International Master	2251 +	2200 +

The performance norms as well as other technical aspects of the rating system as used by FIDE are given in greater detail in the FIDE Title Regulations (section C of this chapter).

References

Brumfitt, G. *Statistical Study of Chess Masters 1881–1890; British Chess Magazine*, 1891, p. 388.

Clarke, R. *British Chess Federation Grading System; B.C.F. Yearbook* 1957/58.

Elo, A. E. *Theory of Rating System*. Privately printed monograph, 1965.

Elo, A. E. *Age Changes in Master Chess Performance, Journal of Gerontology*, July 1965, p. 289.

Elo, A. E. *The International Chess Federation Rating System, CHESS*, July, August and October 1973.

Elo, A. E. *U.S.C.F. Rating System, Chess Life*, June 1961. Also *Chess Life*, August 1967.

Englehardt, S. *Schachtaschen Jahrbuch*, Vol. 1, 1951. S. Englehardt Publisher, Berlin-Frohnau.

Harness, K. *Official Chess Handbook*, First Edition 1956, p. 331–360. David McKay Co., Philadelphia, Pa.

Hoesslinger, A. *Ingo System, Bayrischen Schachnachrichten*, April 1948.

Kühnle-Woods, W. *The FIDE Grading System, Chess Express* 1971, Nos. 4/5.

Landau, E. *Zur relativen Werthemessung der Turnierresulte. Deutsche Wochenschach*, Oct. 20, 1895, p. 366.

15 The FIDE Rating System

THE FIDE RATING SYSTEM AND ITS ADMINISTRATIVE RULES
Approved by the 1978 General Assembly

0.0 Introduction

0.1 Section 3.2 of the International Titles Regulations specifies the FIDE Rating System, but the principles and processes of the system are scientific in nature and are not elaborated in the regulations. The basic principles and working formulae are presented here, in sections 1 and 2 of these administrative rules.

0.2 Much of the reporting and records required for titles is also required for ratings, and administration of the two functions is combined in the regulations. The reports, calculations, and records leading to the official rating list are described in sections 3 and 4 of these rules. Portions of this material are also described in the regulations, and at each such point in these rules the section number of the regulations is given.

0.3 Reporting and records may be followed more easily by use of special forms, of which samples are attached

> Form 1 – Tournament Report
> Form 2 – International Title Tournament (ITT) Form
> Form 3 – Player Record

0.4 It is a function of the Congress to establish the policies under which FIDE titles are awarded. It is the function of the rating system to produce scientific measurement information of the best statistical quality, to enable the Congress to award equal titles for equal proficiencies of players, or to make in that policy any adjustment that may be desired. For this purpose the rating system requires proper scientific maintenance and adjustment, both on the short- and long-term bases, and sections 5 and 6 of these rules set forth important considerations in this regard.

1.0 General Principles

1.1 The FIDE Rating System is a numerical system in which percentage scores are convertible to rating differences and conversely, rating differences are convertible to scoring probabilities.

1.2 The rating scale is an arbitrary scale with a class interval set at 200 points.*

1.3 The basis of the system is the normal probability function of statistical probability theory. This is put into tabular form for the conversions indicated in 1.1.

1.4 Table of conversion from percentage score, P, into rating difference, D_p.

P	D_p	P	D_p	P	D_p	P	D_p	P	D_p	P	D_p
1.0	677	.83	273	.66	117	.49	−7	.32	−133	.15	−296
.99	677	.82	262	.65	110	.48	−14	.31	−141	.14	−309
.98	589	.81	251	.64	102	.47	−21	.30	−149	.13	−322
.97	538	.80	240	.63	95	.46	−29	.29	−158	.12	−336
.96	501	.79	230	.62	87	.45	−36	.28	−166	.11	−351
.95	470	.78	220	.61	80	.44	−43	.27	−175	.10	−366
.94	444	.77	211	.60	72	.43	−50	.26	−184	.09	−393
.93	422	.76	202	.59	65	.42	−57	.25	−193	.08	−401
.92	401	.75	193	.58	57	.41	−65	.24	−202	.07	−422
.91	383	.74	184	.57	50	.40	−72	.23	−211	.06	−444
.90	366	.73	175	.56	43	.39	−80	.22	−220	.05	−470
.89	351	.72	166	.55	36	.38	−87	.21	−230	.04	−501
.88	336	.71	158	.54	29	.37	−95	.20	−240	.03	−538
.87	322	.70	149	.53	21	.36	−102	.19	−251	.02	−589
.86	309	.69	141	.52	14	.35	−110	.18	−262	.01	−677
.85	296	.68	133	.51	7	.34	−117	.17	−273	.00	
.84	284	.67	125	.50	0	.33	−125	.16	−281		

1.5 Table of conversion of difference in rating, D, into scoring probability P, for the higher, H, and the lower, L, rated player respectively. For a zero or 100% score D_p is necessarily indeterminate.

D	P		D	P		D	P		D	P	
Rtg Dif	H	L	Rtg Dif	H	L	Rtg Dif	H	L	Rtg Dif	H	L
0 3	.50	.50	92 98	.63	.37	198 206	.76	.24	345 357	.89	.11
4 10	.51	.49	99 106	.64	.36	207 215	.77	.23	358 374	.90	.10
11 17	.52	.48	107 113	.65	.35	216 225	.78	.22	375 391	.91	.09
18 25	.53	.47	114 121	.66	.34	226 235	.79	.21	392 411	.92	.08
26 32	.54	.46	122 129	.67	.33	236 245	.80	.20	412 432	.93	.07
33 39	.55	.45	130 137	.68	.32	246 256	.81	.19	433 456	.94	.06
40 46	.56	.44	138 145	.69	.31	257 267	.82	.18	457 481	.95	.05
47 53	.57	.43	146 153	.70	.30	268 278	.83	.17	485 517	.96	.04
54 61	.58	.42	154 162	.71	.29	279 290	.84	.16	518 559	.97	.03
62 68	.59	.41	163 170	.72	.28	291 302	.85	.15	560 619	.98	.02
69 76	.60	.40	171 179	.73	.27	303 315	.86	.14	620 735	.99	.01
77 83	.61	.39	180 188	.74	.26	316 329	.87	.13	over 735	1.00	.00
84 91	.62	.38	189 197	.75	.25	329 341	.88	.12			

2.0 The Working Formulae of the FIDE System

2.1 For the measurement of a performance:

$$R_p = R_c + D_p$$

---

* This refers to the traditional idea of a class difference which previously had no connection with numbers, such as Grandmasters, International Masters, National Masters, Candidate Masters, etc.

where R_p is the performance rating,
R_c is the average rating of the opponents,
D_p is the difference in rating based on the percent score P and which is obtained from 1.4.

2.2 In an all-play-all or roundrobin type tournament the performance rating may also be expressed in terms of the average rating R_a of the participants instead of R_c:

$$R_p = R_a + D_p \ (N/M)$$

where D_p is the same as in 2.1,
N is the number of opponents,
M is the number of participants or $(N + 1)$.

2.3 In a match, if one player is unrated, the rated player serves as a standard of comparison for the unrated, and equation 2.1 can be used to express the performance rating of the unrated player.

If both players are rated the match becomes a special case of a roundrobin tournament and the performance of either player is expressed by:

$$R_p = R_a + \tfrac{1}{2} D_p$$

where R_a is the average rating of the two participants prior to the match.

2.4 Calculation of a *change* in rating after an event is made by:

$$\Delta R = K(W - W_e)$$

where ΔR is the change of rating,
W is the actual game score, wins counting as 1, draws as $\tfrac{1}{2}$,
W_e is the expected game score,
K is the rating point value of a game point, or development coefficient.

2.5 The expected game score is calculated by:

$$W_e = N \, P_c$$

where N is the number of opponents,
P_c is the percent expectancy based on the difference between the average rating of the opponents and the rating of the player, obtained from 1.5.

2.6 In a round-robin type tournament considerable calculation time may be saved by using the formula:

$$W_e = M.P_a - \tfrac{1}{2}$$

where M is the number of participants,
P_a is the percentage expectancy based on the difference between the average rating of all the participants and the player.

2.7 The development coefficient, K, is used as a stabilizing factor in the system. The coefficient K for a player new to the rating list is set at 25 for the first three events, or 30 games, whichever comes first. After that K is set at 15 as long as the player's rating remains under 2400, and thereafter at 10 permanently.

2.8 The new rating, after one or more performances, may be calculated by:

$$R_n = R_o + \Sigma\Delta R$$

where R_o is the old rating, and
$\Sigma\Delta R$ is the summation of the subsequent rating changes.
Where there is no previous R_o then $R_o = R_u$ (see **4.0**).

3.0 Reporting Procedures

3.1 The principal information, including that required (Title Regs. 3.14) to be reported for a tournament, is conveniently grouped on form 1, attached. It consists of:
  a. Identification of the event, including exact dates of beginning and ending;
  b. Specification of the time limit;
  c. The complete cross-table; and
  d. Proper authentication.

3.2 A proper cross-table should list the players in final-rank order, together with full first names, titles, federation affiliations, and ratings. This information will normally correspond with that appearing in the current official rating list, and any differences, such as a change in name following marriage, should be explained in detail in remarks.

Players without a published rating will be entered under rating at 2200 (1800 for a woman).

For each player, his results against each opponent should be given, as $1, \frac{1}{2}$, or 0, and any result arising from an unplayed game should be marked with an asterisk (*) and explained if necessary. Any unusual circumstances should also be described, if they might affect the validity of the result.

3.3 The effective period for a rating list is the calendar year. The list is applicable to all events begun between January 1 and December 31 (Title Regs. 3.22).

3.4 The rating period begins November 1 and ends October 31. All events ending between those dates are rateable for the next list (Title Regs. 3.21).

3.5 Reports of tournaments must be sent within four weeks after the event ends, to the FIDE-Secretariate (Title Regs. 3.14).

3.6 Each national federation should designate an official to coordinate and expedite qualification matters, and his name should be given to the FIDE Secretariate. Reports, however, are accepted from the arbiter, organizer, or any other reliable source.

3.7 Federations shall be fined Swiss Francs 25 per event for incomplete reports, late reports or no reports at all.

3.8 At the end of a rating period the rating fees mentioned in the financial regulations shall be invoiced to the federations.

4.0 Calculation Procedures

ITT   – International Title Tournament.

IRL   – The Official FIDE Rating List.

R_u – A nominal figure (2200 for a man, 1800 for a woman) for a player never on an IRL, or for a player previously on an IRL but who currently has a rating lower than 2200 for a man, 1800 for a woman.

R_a – The tournament average rating for rating or title purposes.

(Title Regs) – Refer to Title Regulations.

4.1 Upon receipt, form 1 is checked for rateability (Title Regs 3.1) and for qualification as an ITT (Title Regs 4.1; 4.2). For each ITT, form 2 is prepared by the system administrator.

4.2 R_a is calculated for each event. Each rated player is entered at his current IRL rating. Each unrated player is entered at R_u. Each player who is not a member of a FIDE federation is excluded (Title Regs 4.42). R_a is then used to determine the category number and the title norms for the events (Title Regs 4.3).

4.3 After each event, data from form 1 is entered by the system administrator on the form 3 for each participant, and his *rating change* ΔR for the event is calculated by formula 2.4 and entered, with the appropriate coefficient K used.

4.4 The new rating for the next IRL (see 2.8 above) is computed following the closing date, after all permissable events (Title Regs 3.1) have been posted in form 3.

    4.41 The new rating for the next IRL is rounded down to the five which is surpassed.

4.5 Swiss tournaments and team tournaments other than official events are not rated as a matter of course, but only upon request from a player, organizer or a member federation. The report must include a complete cross-table of the event and for each player to be rated a list of his opponents and their ratings, and the results against these opponents.

4.6 Conditions for rating players in Swiss tournaments (Title Regs. 3.12):

    4.61 A player new to the FIDE list can only be rated if he plays a minimum of 9 games against rated opponents.

    4.62 A player already rated can be rated only on his games against rated opponents.

    4.63 If a player new to the FIDE list has played less than 9 games against rated opponents, but participates in another rateable event during the same or the next rating period, his results may be pooled to make up the necessary requirement of 9 or more games.

4.7 Unplayed games, whether because of forfeiture or other reasons are not counted for either rating or titling purposes.

4.8 In the event that an unrated player has a zero score in a tournament the scores of his opponents against him are disregarded for rating and titling purposes.

5.0 Monitoring the Operation of the Rating System

5.1 The rating scale is not only arbitrary, but is also open ended with no fixed or reproducible points on it. Only *differences* in ratings have a significance in terms of probabilities.

5.2 If the composition of the FIDE rating pool changes, or if the pool expands or contracts, the rating scale could drift with respect to the true proficiency of the players.

5.3 The integrity of the system is preserved if ratings of the same value from year to year represent the same proficiency of play.

5.4 Detection of any drift in the rating scale and the preservation of the integrity of the system are important functions of the rating system administrator.

5.5 Detection of drift in the rating scale may be made by suitable surveys, such as:
  a. Monitoring the ratings of a selected group of established players, between ages 25–40, for any change in the average rating of the group.
  b. Monitoring the rating of the top group of players, such as the top 50, for change in the average rating.
  c. Monitoring the distribution of ratings within the rating pool.

5.6 The provisions described under 2.7 and 4.2 are designed for the preservation of system integrity and operation automatically.

6.0 Qualifications for the FIDE Rating System Administrator

6.1 The rating system administrator should have a sufficient knowledge of statistical probability theory as it applies to measurements in the physical and behavioural sciences.

6.2 The rating system administrator should be able to design the surveys described under 5.5; to interpret the results of the surveys; to apply the significance tests as needed; and to recommend to the Qualification Commission whatever controlling measures are needed to preserve the integrity of the rating system.

6.3 The rating system administrator should be able to determine the general composition of the rating pool as well as the direction of its change. In particular he should understand the effect that new and improving players have on the pool; and he should also be aware of the pattern of development of chess proficiency with age.

6.4 The rating system administrator should be ready and able to advice and assist any FIDE member federation in the establishment of a national rating system compatible with the FIDE system.

6.5 In all his activities, as they apply to the administration of the rating system, the rating system administrator should display an objectivity on the same high level as might be expected of a FIDE arbiter.

FORM 1 (for organizers or federations)

TOURNAMENT REPORT

Event Name _____ Place _____ Country _____ Began _____ Ended _____

| Fin. No. | PLAYERS | | | | | Scores (1, ½, 0) vs Opponent No. | | | | | Totals | | Pct W/W+L |
	Name	First name	Title	Fed.	Rating	1	2	3	4	5	W	L	
1						X							
2							X						
3								X					
4									X				
5													

count, or total

Specification of time limit: _____ moves in _____ hours.

REMARKS:

CERTIFIED as a correct report: by _____

Date _____   and by _____

Remarks should include any changes in name, title, or federation from that shown on current rating list; and a description of any special circumstances which might affect the validity of the results.

FORM 2 (for system administrator)

ITT CHECK SHEET

Event _____   Date ended _____

	No. of Players	No. of Title-Holders	No. of Visitors	No. of Rated Players	Total Ratings
All players (from report)					
Less Non-Counteds*					
Net to count					
FIDE minimums (from table)					
Do nets exceed minimums?					

Tournament Average* _____	Tournament Category No. _____	GM Norm _____	WGM Norm _____	IM Norm _____	IWM Norm _____	FIDE Norm _____

REMARKS:

RECOMMENDATION: Subject to remarks (if any), this event is recommended as conformant with the regulations for an ITT of the category indicated.

Date _____   _____ Rating System Administrator

* Non-Counteds include players not from FIDE federations and players who complete less than half the schedule.

* Tournament Average is the average rating of the net counted players, allowing 2200 for each player without a published rating (1800 for a woman).

Table of minimum numbers required:

For net counted total players of	10	11	12	13	14	15	16	17	18	19	20	21	22
Titleds minimums are	5	6	6	7	7	8	8	9	9	10	10	11	11
Visitors minimums are	4	4	4	5	5	6	6	7	7	7	7	8	
and rated players minimum is	8	9	10	11	12	13	14	15	16	17	18	19	20

FORM 3 (for system administrator)   PLAYER RECORD

PLAYER INFORMATION

Date entered	NAME	First name	Fed.	K	Title

RATING RECORD

Event and Results							Publ. Rating			computation of W_e (table 1.5)			
Data from tournament report													
Date	Place	R_a	W	L	$W - W_e$	ΔR	R_o	R_n	$R_o - R_a$	P_a	M	$P_a \times M - 2$ W_e	

Post R_n only after entering all ΔR for the rating period. $R_n = R_o + \Sigma \, \Delta R$.
Post all other rating information after each tournament report.
Post player information as received.

16 International Titles

INTERNATIONAL TITLE REGULATIONS OF FIDE
Approved by the 1976 General Assembly; amended by the 1978 General Assembly

0.0 Introduction

0.1 The FIDE acknowledges solely such chess titles as have been acquired in accordance with its established conditions.

0.2 The international FIDE titles are:

    0.21 Titles automatically acquired through results obtained in certain competitions (tournaments and matches). Such titles are registered by the President of FIDE. (Sections 2.11, 2.22, 2.24, 2.32, 2.33, 2.42, 2.52.)

    0.22 Titles awarded to players on account of results in competitions other than listed under **0.21** above. Such titles are awarded by the General Assembly. (Sections 2.12, 2.21, 2.31, 2.41, 2.51.)

    0.23 Titles awarded for merits in chess activities other than practiced play. Such titles are bestowed or acknowledged, respectively, by the General Assembly.

0.3 Titles listed under subparagraphs **0.22** and **0.23** can be awarded only by recommendation of the Qualification Commission established by the FIDE.

0.4 Members of the Qualification Commission:

    0.41 Elected by the General Assembly for the same period of office as valid for the FIDE President:
A president or chairman
a vice-chairman
a secretary
five experts.

    0.42 Members due to their office:
The President of FIDE, if he is not chairman of the Commission
the Deputy-Presidents of FIDE
the Zonal Presidents of FIDE.

    0.43 As a rule, the Commission makes its decisions during sessions preceding immediately the opening of the General Assembly. When absent a Zonal President may give proxy to a representative.

0.5 If not expressly stipulated otherwise in these regulations, voting is effected as perceived by Art. 4.5, 4.7, 4.8 and 4.9 of the FIDE Statutes.

0.6 Exception: In exceptional cases, the Commission may bestow a title by correspondence voting.

1.0 International Titles

1.1 The Titles of FIDE are:
    1.11 Titles for over-the-board chess:
        Grandmaster
        International Master
        FIDE Master
        Woman Grandmaster
        International Woman Master
        International Arbiter
    1.12 Titles for chess composition:
        Grandmaster of Chess Composition
        International Master of Chess Composition
        International Judge of Chess Composition
    1.13 Titles for Correspondence Chess:
        Grandmaster of Correspondence Chess
        International Master of Correspondence Chess
        International Arbiter for Correspondence Chess

1.2 Titles date from date awarded or registered, and are valid for life.
    1.21 Use of a FIDE title or rating to subvert the ethical principles of the title and rating systems may subject a person to revocation of his title upon recommendation of the Qualification Commission and final action by the General Assembly.

1.3 Titles are awarded by the Congress upon report by the judging unit that the candidate meets the requirements. The judging units are:
    1.31 For over-the-board chess, the FIDE Qualification Commission.
    1.32 For chess composition, the FIDE Permanent Commission for Chess Composition; and
    1.33 For correspondence chess, the International Correspondence Chess Federation. ICCF both judges and awards the titles; upon report of the award, the Congress awards the titles in confirmation.

2.0 Requirements

2.1 *Grandmaster:* Any one of the following:
    2.11 For any player: Qualification for the Candidate Matches for the World Championship.
    2.12 For an International Master or FIDE Master: Two or more Grandmaster results in events covering at least 24 games, and a rating of at least 2450 in the current FIDE Rating List.

2.2 *International Master:* Any one of the following:
    2.21 Two or more International Master results in events covering at least 24 games, and a rating of at least 2350 in the current FIDE Rating List.

2.22 First place in one of the following events:
Women's World Championship
Zonal tournament
World Junior Championship
European Junior Championship
American Junior Championship
Asian Junior Championship
African Junior Championship

2.23 If there is a tie for the first place in a Zonal Tournament and if the players concerned do not qualify by virtue of 2.24, the title will be awarded only after a play-off.

2.24 One International Master result in a FIDE tournament in the cycle of the Individual World Championship, of not less than 13 games.

2.3 *FIDE Master:* Any one of the following:

2.31 Two or more FIDE Master results in events covering at least 24 games, and a rating of at least 2250 in the current FIDE Rating List.

2.32 First place in the World Championship for Under 17.

2.33 One FIDE Master result in a FIDE tournament in the cycle of the Individual World Championship, of not less than 13 games.

2.4 *Woman Grandmaster:* Any one of the following:

2.41 Two or more Woman Grandmaster results in events covering at least 24 games, and a rating of at least 2250 in the current FIDE Rating List.

2.42 One Woman Grandmaster result in a FIDE tournament in the cycle of the Women's Individual World Championship, of not less than 13 games.

2.5 *International Woman Master:* Any one of the following:

2.51 Two or more International Woman Master results in events covering at least 24 games, and a rating of at least 2150 in the current FIDE Rating List.

2.52 One International Woman Master result in a FIDE tournament in the cycle of the Women's Individual World Championship, of not less than 13 games.

2.6 *International Arbiter:* All of the following:

2.61 Thorough knowledge of the Laws of Chess and the FIDE regulations for chess competitions.

2.62 Absolute objectivity, demonstrated at all times during his activity as an arbiter.

2.63 Sufficient knowledge of at least two languages of which at least one is an official FIDE language.

2.64 Experience as chief or deputy arbiter in at least four important chess competitions as defined in 2.65.

2.65 Chess competitions recognized for arbiter application: National individual and team championships
All official FIDE competitions
International Title Tournaments

Matches between federations
International Chess Festivals of not less than 100 participants.

2.71 *Grandmaster of Chess Composition:* The requirements established by the regulations of the FIDE PCCC.

2.72 *International Master of Chess Composition:* The requirements established by the regulations of the FIDE PCCC.

2.73 *International Judge of Chess Composition:* Frequent experience as a judge of important international competitions for chess composition (problems, studies, etc.), with demonstrated absolute objectivity.

2.8 *Correspondence Chess Titles:* The requirements established by the ICCF.

3.0 Measurement of Over-the-Board Play

3.1 *Internationally Rated Play:* The basic data for measurement of chess performances must be broad and ample. Play shall be rated by FIDE when it meets all the following requirements:

3.11 In a roundrobin type tournament at least one third of the players must be rated. If the event has less than ten players, all must be rated.

3.12 In Swiss or team events only games against rated opponents are counted.

3.13 Play must conform to the Laws of Chess. Speed of play may not exceed 45 moves in two hours. Not more than two rounds per day, excepting sessions for adjourned games, are played.

3.14 A proper report, including an authenticated cross table, is sent by airmail to the FIDE Secretariat within four weeks after the end of the event.

3.15 The event and report, as recommended by the rating system administrator and accepted by the Qualification Commission, must be found bona fide and suitable for rating or titling purposes.

3.2 *Official FIDE Rating List:* Each year the Qualification Commission shall prepare a list incorporating the rated play during the year into the previous list, using the unique rating system formula based on the percentage expectancy curve and derived from the normal distribution function of statistical and probability theory. The list shall carry the following information:

3.21 The closing date, normally October 31. Rated play completed after the closing date will enter the computations only in exceptional cases.

3.22 The effective date, normally January 1. The list is applicable to all events beginning on or after that date.

3.23 A list of the rated events entering the computations.

3.24 The name and federation of each player whose rating exceeds 2200 (1800 for women) as of the current closing date or as of any of the two preceding closing dates. The women shall be listed separately.

3.25 The FIDE title held by each player listed.

3.26 The current rating of each player listed.

3.27 A supplementary list consisting of new names only is issued as of July 1 of each year (closing date: April 30).

3.3 *Players new to the List:* A rating for a player new to the list shall be published only if it is based on a minimum of 9 games against rated opponents. If this condition is not fulfilled in one event, then results from other events, played within the same or the next rating period, may be pooled to obtain the initial rating.

3.4 *Rated Players not on the List:* Players who appeared on previous lists but who through inactivity do not qualify under 3.24 are nonetheless considered currently rated at their most recent published rating, and shall be shown on the FIDE Rating List for the next five years.

3.5 *Rated players who through inadequate results* drop below 2200 (1800 for a woman), are carried on the next two lists at 2200 (or 1800 respectively). Such players, however, are not counted as rated players for rating and titling purposes.

3.6 *Unrated Players:* A nominal figure – 2200 for a man, 1800 for a woman – is used to determine a tournament category for title purposes.

4.0 International Title Tournaments

4.1 An International Title Tournament shall have at least 9 rounds. At least one-half of the players shall be titleholders, at least one third shall not come from one and the same federation, and not more than 20% shall be unrated. Generally no more than one round per day shall be played. However, on one or two days, two rounds per day are allowed. Two rounds per day shall not be allowed for the last three rounds of the tournament.

    4.11 For tournaments beginning before the end of 1980 the requirement is: one half titleholders or players with a rating of at least 2300.

4.2 The tournament should, if possible, be conducted by an International Arbiter. The requirements of 3.13, 3.14 and 3.15 must be met.

4.3 Tournaments are classified according to the strength of the participants, as indicated by the average rating. The categories of International Title Tournaments and the minimum percentage scores for title results are as follows:

Average Rating	Tournament Category	GM Result	IM Result	FIDE M Result	WGM Result	IWM Result
2051–2075	1W					76
2076–2100	2W					73
2101–2125	3W					70
2126–2150	4W					67
2151–2175	5W				76	64
2176–2200	6W				73	60
2201–2225	7W				70	57
2226–2250	8W				67	53
2251–2275	1		76	64	64	50
2276–2300	2		73	60	60	47
2301–2325	3		70	57	57	43
2326–2350	4		67	53	53	40
2351–2375	5		64	50	50	36
2376–2400	6		60	47	47	33
2401–2425	7	76	57	43	43	30
2426–2450	8	73	53	40	40	
2451–2475	9	70	50	36	36	
2476–2500	10	67	47	33	33	
2501–2525	11	64	43	30	30	
2526–2550	12	60	40			
2551–2575	13	57	36			
2576–2600	14	53	33			
2601–2625	15	50	30			
2626–2650	16	47				

The average rating consists of a rating figure (from 3.2, 3.4 or 3.6) for each player, which have been totalled and then divided by the number of players.

4.31 Roundings of the average ratings are made to the nearest whole number. The fraction .5 is rounded off upward.

4.32 If the minimum percentage score for any tournament results in a norm having a fractional game point, the norm must be rounded up to the nearest half a point.

4.4 The following additional provisions apply to the computation of title results:

4.41 A candidate may consider himself and all his opponents in a Swiss or team event as a tournament under 4.1.

4.42 Players who do not belong to FIDE federations and the results of play against them may not be counted.

4.43 Grandmaster results in events having less than three Grandmasters are not valid. Scores against previously unrated players are not included in the calculations for a Grandmaster norm. Woman Grandmaster results in events having less than three players with a rating of over 2200 are not valid.

4.44 International Master results in events having less than three International Masters or Grandmasters are not valid.

4.45 At least one title norm must be obtained in a tournament having not more than one round per day.

4.46 Woman Grandmaster results and International Woman Master results in mixed events are recognized.

4.47 If a title norm is sufficient for more than one title then it may be counted toward each.

4.48 Results in events more than five years old cannot be counted in title applications.

4.49 For titling purposes the category and norms are determined at the beginning of a tournament. However, forfeited or other unplayed games are not counted in the score for the norm for the title.

4.50 Title norms shall be regarded as valid if they were valid in accord with the International Title Regulations prevailing at the time of the tournament in which the norm was attained.

5.0 Application Procedure

5.1 An application for title may be submitted to the appropriate judging unit by the candidate, by his federation, or by a member of the judging unit.

5.2 Contents of application:

5.21 Each application must contain the candidate's full name, address, date of birth, and federation affiliation, and sufficient information to establish the candidate's qualifications.

5.22 Standard application forms have been designed for the titles mentioned in point 1.11 and are annexed hereto. Applications for these titles must be presented on these forms, which may be obtained from FIDE headquarters or copied herefrom.

5.23 Applications for titles based on performances in chess events must include a complete, authenticated cross table for each event listed. Applications for the title of International Arbiter must include documentation for each event, listed sufficient to enable the Qualification Commission to determine that each of the requirements of 2.64 and 2.65 have been met.

5.24 Applications for the title International Arbiter should be supported by certificates from individuals whom the Qualification Commission can recognize as competent to certify. For example, qualification under 2.61 or 2.62 could be certified by FIDE officials, by International Arbiters, or by officials of the candidate's federation; qualification under 2.63 could be certified by university language professors.

5.3 Applications will be considered by the Congress if received by the judging unit at least 60 days before the Congress begins.

5.31 A late application will be considered for a title earned within 60 days of the Congress, provided the application is forwarded without delay and in sufficient time for proper processing and review.

To the FIDE Secretariate

I (We), _____

propose that the title

> INTERNATIONAL GRANDMASTER
> INTERNATIONAL WOMAN GRANDMASTER
> INTERNATIONAL MASTER
> INTERNATIONAL WOMAN MASTER
> FIDE MASTER

be awarded to _____

_____

(first name, surname, profession)

born _____ at _____

residing _____

_____

(exact address)

I (We) refer to the enclosed list of results.

_____
(signature)

Application for the award of International Titles

Application for the award of
the title International Arbiter of FIDE

The undersigned, _____
_____ herewith
requests that the title International Arbiter of FIDE be awarded to:

_____
born on _____
residing _____
_____

The candidate possesses an exact knowledge of the playing rules of
FIDE and all other reglementations of FIDE to be observed in chess
competitions.
He(She) speaks the following languages (†): _____
_____

The candidate has worked as chief arbiter during the following
competitions(††): _____
_____
_____
_____

Moreover he(she) has been deputy arbiter in the following competitions:
_____
_____
_____
_____

In his(her) activity as an arbiter he(she) has proved at all times an
absolute objectivity.

Date: _____ Signature: _____

(†)   The candidate should possess a sufficient knowledge of at least two languages
       of which at least one is an official FIDE language.
(††)   It is necessary that the candidate has worked as chief or deputy arbiter in
       at least four important chess competitions.

To be sent to the FIDE Secretariate.

17 Organizing Events

Organizing A Chess Club

Chess clubs are the mainstay of organized chess. They are usually founded by chess enthusiasts and fans. One can found a chess club practically anywhere: in towns, villages, business enterprises, factories, schools, private homes, apartment house communities, sports clubs, colleges – wherever there are even just a few chess fans. Clubs are important for creating a regular chess life.

A group of chessplayers usually meets and forms a *preliminary committee* for founding a chess club. This committee will hold one or more meetings at which it will draw up a plan for founding the club. The task of the committee is to carry out the necessary preparations: to investigate possibilities for the club to obtain the support of some firm, enterprise, or organization; to find suitable premises; to draw up a plan for financing the club; and to prepare the club's inauguration. Often, of course, the club will have to live off of its own income, derived from membership fees or some other form of activity.

When the preliminary committee decides to found a club, then it should find the best way to inform chessplayers of the club's inauguration. In many countries it is customary to invite guests, such as prominent people from the world of culture and sport, local officials, etc.

The agenda of inauguration is quite straightforward: the president of the preliminary committee delivers a speech in which he explains why the club is being founded, the draft rules of the club are proposed, and after they are approved the club's officers are elected, and a programme and financial plan are adopted. In many countries it is legally required to inform the competent authorities when any association is being founded.

The rules of the club usually include the following: the name of the club, its purposes and tasks, membership rights and duties, organs and structure of the club (assembly, executive board, supervisory board), property and financial assets of the club (sources of income, inventory, library, etc.).

The *executive committee* usually consists of a president, 1 or 2 vice-presidents and several members, the majority of whom are charged with special duties (chess among young people, ladies' chess, finance, professional work, competition, organizing lectures in the club, etc.). The executive board also often has a secretary who handles administrative matters.

A representative of a higher chess forum from the given territory may be invited to the founding assembly, and once it is actually constituted the club and its members should register with that forum.

Once the club is founded, active work begins on ensuring that the members take regular part in the work of the club. One of the first steps is to organize competitions in the club itself. One can start with tournaments, out of which the best qualify for the final club championship. A ladder may be instituted whereby members are given the chance of challenging those above them to a match, and this can be a standing competition in the club. Matches with other teams, be they friendly or league matches, are extremely important for the club. The club should offer variety and attractions for all its members. Junior and ladies' competitions, etc., should be organized. Lightning games are extremely popular in all clubs. Virtually every chess club holds regular lightning tournaments to which it admits guests. Lectures on chess and simultaneous and other exhibitions should be included in the programme so as to get all the members involved in club life.

It is extremely important to engage capable and agile organizers who, true enough, will have fewer opportunities of playing chess, but who, in return, will get great pleasure out of seeing the fruits of their labour. Energetic organizers are a guarantee of the club's success.

Preparing and Organizing Chess Competitions

It is widely held that it is relatively simple to organize a chess competition: the equipment required is not expensive, and no special stadiums are required to hold the competition. And yet, chess has its own specific qualities which make it stand apart from other branches of sport. Chess competitions last much longer than competitions in other sports. A tournament demands a lot from the organizers and participants in terms of time and effort, and this also means in terms of money. And finally, since chess is not as spectacular a sport as some, it cannot count on covering the costs of competition from ticket returns.

Chess competitions vary in both purpose and form. International Master V. Vuković said that one can, albeit imprecisely, speak of three levels of chess competitions and of treating chess as a game. At the first and extremely large-scale level, chess is above all a socially useful recreation. At the second level, chess is a kind of intellectual sport, and at the third, at the master and grand-master level, it is an art. 'Chess organizers are primarily concerned with this second, medium level of club and tournament players, and it is here that the problem of running a competition is at its most complex, for, as a rule, players have different attitudes towards chess. Some merely love chess as a game, others love their club and others still, 'personal success'.

Organizing chess competitions, then, is more complex than it may appear. The important thing is what kind of a competition is in question and what its purpose is. It is not all the same whether you organize a mass competition with a large number of chess fans taking part, or a first-rate competition of international standing, with renowned grandmasters taking part. The conditions under which the competition is organized are also important; sometimes these are pioneer attempts, the first steps taken in the life of an organization, and sometimes they are part of a programme of a strong chess organization which has considerable experience and perhaps a long tradition in organizing chess competitions. Consequently, one cannot provide organizers with a single pattern which they can use to plan everything down to the last item.

First steps

So, where should one begin in organizing a chess competition? The entire project usually begins with an idea born in the minds of organizers of a club, federation or enterprise, and sometimes this is simply an effort to implement the already established programme of a club or organization. As in other fields, the driving force here is provided by chess enthusiasts. Regardless of the intended level of the competition, an organizational committee is usually set up at the very start to handle everything. This body encompasses capable organizers for technically carrying through the competition, as well as prominent public and cultural figures who will help the competition to be a success. When large competitions are being organized, an honorary committee is also usually set up with prominent personages for its members.

Chess does not enjoy the same status in all countries, nor is its financing the same everywhere. In some countries, competitions are part of an established annual plan, and chess falls within the scope of the ministry for sport or some other state or social organ. In some western countries, chess enjoys only partial subsidy, while in others it is left to private initiative. There are also other variations. In Yugoslavia, for instance, the chess organization gets a subsidy from the state for financing international competitions according to an established programme (Olympiads, FIDE competitions, etc.), but players receive no salaries for playing chess. Chess obtains most of its funds, however, from local sources - individual towns and enterprises - which are used to finance virtually all competitions. Yugoslavia organizes a record number of 20 and more international tournaments a year, thanks to cooperation with tourist and local organizations. In Spain too, chess maintains good cooperation with tourist organizations.

Chess affords great publicity for the venue of the competition. Many small places have become famous through traditional chess tournaments. Many firms, banks, etc. are interested in financing such competitions. When mass competitions are in question, funds should be sought from corresponding institutions - schools, trade unions, etc. A great deal depends on the imagination of the organizers. Thanks to their inventiveness, their ability to make use of existing conditions, and to awaken an interest in others, including private benefactors, many important competitions have been held. There is no question that collecting the funds is the greatest obstacle in carrying out any idea, including the field of chess!

Timely Preparation

Timely preparations should be made for each competition if the technical organization is to be satisfactory and if the invited players are to come. International tournaments have mushroomed over the past few years, so that preparations for a large tournament must be made a year in advance if one wants famous grandmasters to take part. In organizing such tournaments, one usually starts out by ensuring the participation of a few 'key players'. Hence, establishing the list of participants, planning the tournament and sending the invitations is one of the first tasks of the organizational committee. It is much simpler, of course, when organizing local competitions, or competitions planned by a club or chess federation.

Planning Chess Competitions

For each competition the organizer should determine its purpose, date and venue, the system which will be used for play, the number of contestants and how they will be determined, as well as the financial conditions of the competition.

One should distinguish between two groups of competition: one embraces official competitions, and the other, all other competitions and events, including special purpose and publicity competitions.

If the competition is not along official lines, then the organizer can be not only chess federations but also any other chess organization. Today, many tournaments are organized by various firms and benefactors.

When drawing up the plan, one must not forget to ensure that the dates of the competition do not clash with some important competition of general importance, whose date was fixed earlier.

Organizational Committee

An organizational committee is usually elected to prepare and carry through a chess competition, and it is charged with the following:

a) to draw up a preliminary financial estimate, and to announce and draw up regulations for the competition which will later be adopted and confirmed by the organizer;

b) to secure the tournament rooms, necessary equipment, accommodation for the contestants and execute all other technical preparations

c) to settle all organizational problems which may crop up during preparations for and in the actual course of the competition;

d) to submit a report and documentation at the end of the competition to the competent chess forum.

The number of members in the organizational committee depends on the importance, character, and scope of the given competition. If it is a high-ranking competition, then the number of members will be larger, and often it is necessary and advisable to form special sections within the organizational committee for certain fields.

For a major competition, one can provide for the following sections:

1. section for the press and publicity, with the task of preparing material for the press and other media, setting up a press bureau, organizing simultaneous displays and chess lectures, etc.;

2. welcoming and accommodation section which helps to settle all questions concerning the room and board of the contestants;

3. section for technically preparing the competition, with the task of arranging the player room, heating and ventilation, securing the equipment, organizing the ticket office, monitors, demonstrators and executing technical preparations for each round;

4. bulletin section, which publishes the bulletin;

5. financial section, which ensures that the funds for the tournament are used and spent according to the previously prepared financial plan, and that the necessary revenues are realized;

6. controlling and executive section composed of the arbiter, his deputy and members of the tournament committee and their deputies. The arbiter of

the competition directly manages over the competition and his duties are defined by the Laws of Chess of FIDE.

Announcement of the Tournament and Tournament Regulations

Once the date is set, the material funds secured and the list of contestants compiled, an announcement of the tournament is drawn up. The announcement should be sent to all contestants no less than 30 days before the beginning of the competition, and in the case of tournaments of major importance, several months in advance. The announcement should contain the following: the aim and purpose of the competition; venue and date; the number of contestants and names of those invited; the financial and other conditions of the competition (travel expenses, accommodation, etc.); prizes, time of arrival of the contestants and whom they should report to on arrival; and the dead-line for submitting applications.

The tournament regulations are more detailed and are drawn up by the arbiter of the tournament according to the instructions and conditions of the organizer. Each set of regulations should contain the following basic particulars:

1. name and purpose of the competition;
2. name of the organizer, date and hour of the opening of the tournament and the drawing of numbers, the tournament venue and the duration of the tournament;
3. list of the contestants;
4. time of play for each individual round and adjournment sessions, and schedule of free days;
5. regulations according to which the competition is being played, rate of play and time-control;
6. any supplementary provisions and interpretations of FIDE Laws of Chess;
7. the names of the arbiters of the tournament, their deputies and the members of the tournament committee;
8. the appeals procedure;
9. the possibility of postponing games;
10. the category and title norms, or other qualifications – here, special provisions should exist which can be applied in the case of a tie;
11. prizes;
12. any other provisions.

Technical and Other Preparations

In preparing for a competition, the organizational committee handles all technical and financial matters. The tournament arbiter takes on the responsibility for the competition from the moment it actually begins. However, he and the organizational committee must also cooperate during preparations for the competition. The organizers take care of accommodation for the contestants and welcoming them, acquiring the necessary equipment for the competition, engaging a playing room, preparing the playing room, etc. The arbiter must be engaged in all this as well: he must give advice as to the playing conditions, the lighting, the standard of the equipment, etc.

The technical organization of chess tournaments has not really advanced greatly since the London and other tournaments one hundred and more years ago. To be precise, the organization of chess competitions has not taken advantage of some of the achievements of science, so that demonstration of the games, for instance, is often still at the level it was during the Steinitz-Zukertort match. It is only of late that efforts have been made to show games on electronic or automatic boards or on closed circuit television. The ideal would be to have the move played by the contestant automatically transmitted onto the demonstration board as he makes it. Such boards already exist, but the problem is that players would have to use special chess pieces in order to be able to transmit the moves. Chess clocks have not really advanced all that much either since the 1883 London tournament. Designers are only now beginning to devise electronic and digital clocks, and ways of automatically demonstrating the time shown on the player's clock.

There is no school for chess organizers, but they learn their trade well, primarily from each other. In many ways, the Fischer–Spassky match in Reykjavik in 1972 later served as a model for the technical organization of matches. This especially applies to showing the games via closed circuit television. There have also been other FIDE competitions, especially Olympiads and Candidates' Matches, which have been at a similarly high level, and others have tried to emulate these. Only recently, as interest in chess has spread, has greater attention been devoted to the technical organization of competitions and efforts been made to provide spectators with better facilities for following the games. In the Candidates' Matches in 1977 in Lucerne, Evian, and Belgrade, certain novelties were introduced in demonstrating the games such as semi-automatic transmission of the moves and presentation of the time on the chess clocks.

The tournament playing room
No prescribed standards exist for the playing room in a chess competition. In its regulations for competition FIDE provides for the following general conditions: the room should be comfortable for the contestants and amenable to the normal course of chess competition, and it should, first and foremost, offer the greatest comfort to the players. The area for the players should be separate from the spectators' section: the actual distance between the two depends on the importance of the competition. The regulations for the world title match, for instance, prescribe that the distance between the players and the spectators should be at least 12 meters. Of course, there are competitions, especially mass and team competitions, where this is not easy to achieve, but the arbiter should try to ensure as favourable conditions as possible.

The playing tables should be arranged so as to give the players ample room. The stage should be well-lit, and the temperature and ventilation in the playing room itself should be well regulated. It is extremely important to ensure silence during a chess competition and, consequently, playing rooms which do not allow this should be avoided.

There should also be several other rooms apart from the actual playing room itself, such as a room for the arbiter where he can keep the equipment, etc., a room for the players who have finished a game to analyse it, and rooms for the press at larger competitions.

Equipment

For a chess competition we need tables, chess sets, chess clocks and other equipment. For a long time there was no regulation as to standards for chess equipment. A FIDE Bureau Commission (E. Edmondson, L. Schmid and B. Kažić) drew up the first such regulation, which was approved by FIDE in 1975 (see the interpretation to Art. 21 of the Laws of Chess of FIDE). There is no single type of clock or of pieces valid for all official competitions. The regulations of FIDE matches stipulate that the players may agree as to the pieces they will use in the match, the type of clock they will choose and other equipment. In the absence of such an agreement, the arbiter of the competition shall decide on the equipment.

In principle, the pieces and the chess tables or boards should be of a dull or neutral finish, never shiny, and the colour should be pleasing to the eye. Chess clocks also should not be shiny, and should be of proper size, suitable for allowing the arbiter to control their functioning quiet in operation and easy to read. Attempts have been made recently to devise clocks with a special dial for the last few minutes before time-control. Experiments with digital chess clocks have yet to eliminate some of their drawbacks, but they will probably be perfected soon. Today, there are clocks which show the last minute by seconds.

There are no regulations as to the tolerance to be allowed for chess clocks which run slow or fast. Chess arbiters who have verified the precision of various clocks know that differences can be great. Usually, however, one tolerates up to two minutes ahead or behind time over a period of 24 hours. Naturally, the ideal is to have the clock run with precision and fulfill all the aforementioned conditions.

A few days before the competition, the arbiter should check the functioning of the clocks used in the competition. During actual play, he should also check the functioning of the chess clocks and verify whether they are precise. This can be done every hour.

The arbiter must be careful and regularly check the clocks. We may recall a comic case recorded in Soviet chess literature. In the 1930s, F. Duz-Khotimirsky and G. Levenfish played against each other in a match between Moscow and Leningrad. At the time there were not enough chess clocks to go around and an arbiter came to the rescue with his 'antique' clock. What made this clock special was that one side worked faster than the other. Whether by accident or out of a feeling of kinship for his compatriot Levenfish, he placed the 'faster side' towards Duz-Khotimirsky. The latter, however, arrived somewhat early and, since he did not like having the clock on his left-hand side, he moved it to the right, knowing nothing, of course, about the working of that particular clock. Later on, Levenfish, whose clock seemed to run 'at the speed of light', appealed to the arbiters. A scandal ensued, and the culprit was declared to be the person who had lent the clock.

FIDE regulations do not specify anything about the chairs, which should be taken to mean that this is left to the discretion of the contestants, should someone have any reason to ask for chairs other than those provided by the organizers.

The Demonstration Board

The demonstration board is primarily to enable the spectators to follow the course of play. Many organizers make the mistake of omitting demonstration boards and in doing so they deprive the audience of following the course of play. When there are no demonstration boards, the spectators tend to crowd around the players' boards, thereby hampering the work of the arbiter. Competitions lose a great deal in terms of their publicity effect when they do not show the games: it is no wonder that the spectators lose interest when they cannot follow the course of play.

Today, magnetic demonstration boards are widely in use; for larger competitions their dimensions are usually 1.30 × 1.30 metres, up to 2m × 2m. Boards which are too small are unsuitable for competition and can serve their purpose properly only for lectures in a club or school.

The pieces for the demonstration board should be as simple and clear as possible. The best arrangement is to have the board itself painted in some pastel colour, and the pieces in colours which stand out against the squares which they occupy so that, for example, the black pieces are not invisible on black squares. Instead of black pieces, it is better to have a dark colour, and the white pieces can be light yellow so as to distinguish them from the white squares. In any case, one should make sure that the colours are not shiny. It is important to be able to distinguish between the pieces - bishop and pawn, king and queen, for instance.

Along with the demonstration board one should have a model of the clocks to show both players' time. Next to the clock there should be an indicator showing how many moves have been played.

The arbiter decides how the demonstration boards will be arranged in the room, clearly visible to the audience. They are usually positioned on the stage where the players are, but they can be placed in another arrangement as well.

The regulations do not prohibit a player from looking at the position on the demonstration board. Some players often cast a glance at the demonstration board, especially when their opponent has the move and is thinking at the table. In the final Candidates' Match in Belgrade in 1977, an unusual dispute broke out. Grandmaster Spassky, when he had the move, went from the chess table to an armchair behind the curtains where he sat and looked at the position on the demonstration board. He came out onto the stage only to execute his move and thus sat at the chess board only for brief intervals. This method of play 'via the demonstration board', is highly unusual! FIDE will probably give a more detailed interpretation on this method.

Lighting in the Playing Room
This is an extremely important question which should be carefully studied before the competition begins. One should bear in mind that lighting on the stage is ideal when it is as close to daylight as possible. As a rule, the stage where the competition is played should be better lit than the audience section. The playing room should model itself after theatre and cinema auditoria: a brightly lit elevated stage and brightly lit demonstration boards. The lighting in the room should be checked at the time of day when the games are being played - the lighting may seem good during the day, only for it to prove to be insufficient at night.

The regulations for the world title match provide certain norms which can serve as a model for other competitions. 'Illumination on the chess table shall be variable between 120 and 180 footcandles with dimmer control, from fluorescent lamps in the 300 K range, shielded by milk-white flat acrylic plexiglass (or equivalent) no closer than 5 metres to the floor'. It should also be pointed out that all direct lighting, especially reflectors which disturb the contestants, should be avoided. Such direct lighting is also usually uncomfortably hot.

FIDE introduced the above-mentioned lighting norms chiefly on the basis of a suggestion by Sicher's representatives. Good lighting at tournaments is usually considered to be from 800 to 1,000 lux.

Arranging the Playing Room
The director or arbiter of the competition decides on the arrangement of the playing room and correspondingly instructs the organizers and technical staff. The arrangement will not be the same for an individual tournament and for team competition. The system according to which the competition is played may also be of importance.

The tables should be positioned on the stage so that pairs in the first row (in the case of several rows) do not obstruct the pairs in the second row. The distance between the tables should be wide enough for the player to get up from his chair without touching the neighbouring players. The aisle between two rows of tables should be no less than 1.5 metres wide.

The tables are positioned in order of the Berger tables, and may sometimes be placed so that the most interesting pairs are in the front row. The white pieces are usually placed on the left-hand side (facing the stage from the audience), and the black on the right-hand side. The names of the players should be marked on the tables. The player's names should also be inscribed on the demonstration board, White on the left-hand side and Black on the right, or alternatively above or in the lower part of the demonstration board.

At international competitions, the tables usually have the national flags of the players; the flags may also stand on the stage itself or in front of the building where the competition is being held. Flowers on the stage and in the room create a pleasant atmosphere. Note that the stage should also have a table for the arbiter.

The playing room should also provide other comforts for the spectators and players. The actual arrangement should be such as to separate the spectators from the players.

The playing room should be fully ready at least one day before the competition actually begins, so that the contestants have time to look over the room and the conditions for play. Before each round, the arrangement of the room should be ready at least 20 minutes before play begins. The arbiter should be in the room half-an-hour before the beginning of each round, presuming that the duty organizer has already completed all the technical preparations.

Major competitions, of course, such as Olympiads, require lengthy and thorough preparation. At the Olympiad in Havana, in 1966, some one thousand people helped with the organization, which was preceded by seminars for the demonstrators, for the arbiters, etc. Before each competition, the arbiter should thoroughly study the regulations and rules. Some arbiters like to study the contestants as well so as to know their habits, any earlier disputes they may have been engaged in, etc.!

Miscellaneous Equipment

Players at all serious chess competitions write down the moves, and special scoresheets are usually provided for them. Special scorecards, envelopes for adjourned games, posters and other publicity material, programmes with the biographies of the players, badges, etc. are usually printed for major competitions. The scoresheets should be large enough, and should also indicate the time-control. The best layout is for the first page of the scoresheet to provide enough room for 40 or 56 moves, with the 40th move underlined. This is for cases when time-control is after the 40th and 56th move. The second page should have enough room for up to the 88th move.

The envelopes for sealed moves should be large enough to be able to hold the scoresheet without having to fold it several times. The face of the envelope should have printed symbols for the white and the black pieces, so that all the player has to do is to write in the square occupied by the piece (this is a better system than diagrams). It is impractical to give the player a special paper, apart from the scoresheet, for him to write down his sealed move, for this creates confusion. The sealed move is inscribed on the scoresheet used for recording the game.

The arbiter should have many other articles and office material in stock, including pencils for the players, spare scoresheets, diagrams, etc.

Informing the Spectators, Press Service

All necessary information as to the course of the competition should be made available to the spectators and journalists in the tournament room. A large table should be drawn up with the scores of the players and the names of the contestants in order of the lots they have drawn. The scores are written in after each round, and better still after each completed game. There should also be another table indicating the situation after each round.

It is customary to set up a special bulletin board for the regulations of the competition, the schedule of the rounds, diagrams of adjourned games, etc. It is also advisable to have the pairings put up under signs such as 'Playing Today' and 'Playing Tomorrow'.

Organizers of many competitions quite unjustifiably forget journalists and their need to perform their duties well and quickly. Organizers, thereby, merely detract from themselves, for they kill the publicity effect of the competition. Even at competitions of major importance, there have been recent cases in which the organizer provided only two telephones for several scores of foreign and domestic newsmen. Naturally, at the end of each round there is then a great commotion.

Big competitions must provide a large number of telephone lines and telex machines, so that newsmen may quickly report on each round as it ends. Newsmen should also have their own room, with typewriters, papers, etc. The organizer should secure special facilities for newsmen, provide bulletins of the competition, and he should choose a person to tend to the functioning of the press centre.

All important competitions release a bulletin with all games, and attention should focus on printing the bulletin quickly so that it may reach the contestants, journalists and spectators as speedily as possible.

Health Care for the Contestants

This question has long been regulated in many sports, especially at sports olympiads. In chess, however, this is something new, and in its present regulations for zonal and interzonal tournaments, FIDE notes that organizers should ensure health care (treatment and medicine) for the contestants. Such medical assistance is customary for competitions in any field, including chess, in some countries.

In principle, each competition should have an official doctor. He is usually a chess fan and is well-acquainted with the psychology of the players. The official doctor decides whether a game can be postponed due to illness: the regulations usually settle the question of how many times a game may be so postponed. Often this depends on whether it can be played by the end of the competition, without extending the programme.

A player may not be able to play in the playing room due to illness. It is difficult to force his opponent to play in a hotel or hospital room, for the opponent may not feel psychologically up to it, he may fear for his own health, etc. In these cases, the matter can be settled only by agreement with the opponent of the indisposed player.

The Arbiter's Documentation

Different federations have different levels of chess arbiters – club, regional, federal; FIDE awards the title of International Arbiter. Federations usually organize seminars and even examinations for arbiters. Some countries have not gone very far here, while others have precisely mapped out all the duties of the arbiter.

The documentation should enable the situation in a competition to be clearly seen at each moment. The arbiter should have a table with the recorded scores at the end of each game, a progress table by rounds, and records of all played rounds and of adjourned games. All this should be in a folder together with the scoresheets (the original copies) on which the players have written down the moves of the games. The scoresheets for the games should be prepared before each round, with the names of the players, the round and the date, and the number of the given game (according to the Berger tables) written in.

At tht end of the game the players hand both scoresheets with both their signatures, to the arbiter. The arbiter enters the scoresheets into the record for the given round.

The arbiter should also have a special folder containing all the necessary documents: the tournament regulations, appeals by the contestants, rulings of the tournament appeals commission and everything else connected with the competition. The arbiter should have the addresses and telephone number of all contestants throughout the tournament, as well as of the members of the organizational committee, appeals committee, doctor, etc. In big competitions there will be a secretary who keeps all the arbiter's records and handles his administrative affairs.

At the end of the competition, the arbiter draws up the table of competition according to the standings (and not the drawn numbers). The arbiter submits this and his report to the competent organizer, federation, FIDE, etc.

Various countries have certain procedures for recording the rounds, etc. It is somewhat more complicated to keep a table for team competition, but

Soviet arbiter I. Alexeyev has found a way to record team scores and the scores of the individual members of each team. We include some forms for such scorecards at the end of this book. See **Appendix p. 221.**

Before the Competition
Everything we have said about organizing competitions should be adjusted to the level and importance of the competition, and to local circumstances. The contestants, arbiters and organizers usually hold a meeting on the eve of the competition to pinpoint all the technical details. They may also discuss the regulations and details of the competition. Usually, however, the regulations are submitted to the players beforehand and cannot be changed without the approval of the organizer who prescribed them. Changes may be considered only with the approval of all the contestants and the organizers. It is especially inadvisable for the host to change the programme of competition; this requires the consent of the contestants. FIDE recommends that international tournaments be played according to an established rhythm, i.e. that the rounds always be played at the same time, and that the resumption sessions follow the same pattern. Grandmasters do not like the last round to be played at a different time – in the morning, for instance.

The numbers may be drawn at a 'technical meeting' as the contestants like to know in advance whom they will be playing. This procedure may be carried out formally, the day before the commencement of the competition, as part of an official programme opening the competition.

FIDE has adopted recommendations on the organization of international tournaments which are not mandatory, but advisory, and may be of use to the organizers of competitions. We therefore include them in this book.

Recommendations to Organizers of International Tournaments Accepted at the 1970 FIDE-Congress
The following advice and recommendations are of general nature. They apply to all international tournaments, not only to FIDE-Tournaments, but to all tournaments that are recognised as international in accordance with the stipulations of FIDE.

These recommendations have been prudently and cautiously formulated and are not in the form of imperative demands. All the more reason for every organizer of an international tournament – in particular a FIDE-Tournament – to know the ensuing advice and recommendations and carry them out in practice as far as possible.

They are indeed recommendations, but for the most part urgent recommendations:

A. Hotel accommodation and Transport
1. Every player should have, as far as possible, a single room.
2. When this is absolutely impossible – e.g. when local hotel accommodation is inadequate – then you must exercise especial care in arranging for two players to share a double room. Consider the problem for a long time and consult both the players concerned and the chess federation (or federations) to which they belong. Take into account the question of different languages and also of differences in disposition.

3. Should a player inform you that he will be accompanied by another person (wife, second, representative of a chess federation, etc.), ask him in good time if he wishes to share a double room with this companion.

4. When the walking distance between the hotel of the player and the playing room is more than (say) ten minutes, then consider whether it would be better to book only a room with breakfast for a player in his hotel, giving him a daily sum of money for the remaining meals (lunch and dinner), and thereby allowing him to decide for himself where and when he can take these other meals.

5. When the walking distance between the hotel of the player and the playing room is more than ten minutes, then you are in fact faced with the problem of the transport of the player concerned. Please see if you can give the player free transport between the hotel and playing room. It would be incorrect to saddle the player with charges for this. You can, for example, include a sum for such expenses in the daily pocket-money.

6. Make sure in advance that the rooms reserved for the players are of good quality and are situated in the quietest possible area.

7. Arrange beforehand with the hotel, or hotels, about the manner in which the players are treated.

8. Most foreign chess players are strangers in your town. As such, try to help them by, amongst other things, giving them a good town-map and time-tables of bus, trams etc.

9. Try to arrange that players receive free transport in the public transport services.

10. If it should be necessary to put the players up in more than one hotel, make sure that they live under approximately equal circumstances, and have approximately the same distances to the playing-room.

B. The Tournament – What is comprises and entails

1. The invitation to any international chess tournament should be furnished at least four months before the event takes place. At least two months before the tournament takes place a definite decision from the players invited should be at hand.

2. With important tournaments it should be checked whether it is not possible to bring in a principal arbitrator who does not belong to one of the countries taking part.

3. According to the statutes of the World Chess Federation all chess federations and players are equal.

4. If at an international tournament the tournament organizers arrange a fixed date for arrival and inform the players, it is desired that for this day someone from the tournament organization should be present at a place notified to the players in advance so as to assist the incoming players if necessary.

5. It is normally not sufficient to let the player know in advance in which hotel he will be living. It is desirable that you should furnish him in advance with an address he can contact, where on arrival he can reach someone belonging to the tournament organization, who can help and advise him.

6. When a player lets you know in advance on what day and at what hour he will arrive, make sure that he is met on arrival. He is, after all, your guest!

7. If you wish to communicate something to a player, consider which language the individual players understand.

8. Take care that each player receive a playing-schedule together with clear indications of the address of the playing-room, date, time and address of the opening ceremony and of the drawing of the lots and times of playing.

9. If several adjourned games have to be played in another room than the tournament room, make sure that the players are informed.

10. Before beginning the tournament, make sure that the player, or his federation, understands the language.

11. When you are at liberty to determine the hours of play, take into account in the first place the interest of the players and not the convenience of the spectators.

12. Experience has shown that players prefer to start a fresh round early in the afternoon (e.g. at 13.30 h), and like to continue the adjourned game after a break of $1\frac{1}{2}$ hours on the same day (in this instance at 20.00 hours). In this way you can prevent players from worrying about the adjourned game over night.

13. For all participants of the international chess tournaments medical aid must be guaranteed during their stay. In case of inconveniences of the player the tournament director should decide about the further participation in the tournament after having consulted the doctor.

Before the beginning of each tournament, make sure that an adjournment in the tournament is possible due to health reasons, and how often an adjournment is allowed.

C. The Playing room and its accommodation

Here too, and especially here, it goes without saying that the interests of the player are paramount. We give some examples.

1. The playing tables should not be placed too near each other.

2. See to it that the players can walk up and down the playing arena.

3. Make sure that the spectators cannot enter the playing arena.

4. Appoint someone whose duty it shall be to ensure that the whole playing room is quiet during the play.

5. Make sure that a reasonable distance divides the spectators from the playing arena.

6. Try and prevent the spectators from crowding up against the playing arena by the institution of demonstration boards.

7. Make sure that the chess boards of the players are adequately lit and that they do not shine in the light.

8. Make sure that there is no draught in the playing room.

9. Make sure that neither entrance nor exit doors create a noise.

10. When there is a buffet in the vicinity of the playing arena make sure that it is not a source of any noise that may disturb the players.

11. Take care that the temperature of the playing room is good and that there is plenty of fresh air.

12. Pay great heed to any reasonable request or complaint by the players. Try and solve their problems to the best of your ability.

13. Try out the floor of the playing room beforehand. See if any disturbing noise is created when one walks on it.

14. When the tournament controller has not sufficient knowledge of the various languages make sure that he always has at his disposal one or two qualified interpreters.

15. Make sure that the players' chairs are good and comfortable.
16. In order to provide a representative display at each international tournament the national flags of the participants should be hoisted in the playing room or else in front of the playing room. In any case a table pennant with the national emblem of the player should be placed in the playing room.

D. Propaganda and the Press
Organizers of an international tournament are usually interested in seeing that their tournament receives as full coverage as possible in newspapers and chess magazines. One of the strongest reasons for this lies in the most important objective of creating propaganda for chess, and in this connection we draw your attention to the following hints and suggestions.
1. Send out in good time, that is, some weeks before the commencement of the tournament, a full press report to all relevant newspapers and chess magazines.
2. Shortly before the commencement of the tournament send the exact tournament list to newspapers, radio and television. As far as possible this must be accompanied by interesting details.
3. Arrange to have a conference with the press and the representatives of radio and television some time during the opening ceremony, and with this in mind invite them to the opening ceremony. Afford them with the opportunity of speaking freely with the players after the opening ceremony. Furnish them with full and as good information as possible.
4. Try to ensure that the press representatives publish a daily report (in the widest sense possible) of the tournament. At the very least, make sure that your national press agencies speedily receive the tournament results daily (by telephone).
5. Make sure, as far as possible, that during the tournament there will always be present an active member of the organization committee with the special duty of informing and aiding the press.

E. Help for the journalists
Organizers of very strong international tournaments must realize that very often foreign journalists will come to the tournament to report it in their national newspapers or chess magazines. Hence, it is highly desirable that the tournament organizers should see to it that these journalists have a press room at their own disposal. It should contain separate telephones and also a telex. More journalists do not need though spare typewriters might come in useful. Naturally all costs of transmission will be paid for by the journalists (or their newspapers in the case of reverse charges etc.).

F. Tournament bulletin
When a tournament organization decides to publish a Tournament Bulletin, which happens very often nowadays, it is naturally of much interest in seeing that as many copies of this bulletin are sold as is possible.
1. Announce as early as possible, at least 3 months before the commencement of the tournament, in the chess press, both national and international, that you are publishing such a bulletin. It is imperative to give both the price and the address from which the bulletins are to be ordered. If possible also give something about the probable contents.

2. In the interest of chess, tournament bulletins should be given free to the press, especially the national and international chess press. Mention the price and the address where they may be ordered. If possible write something about the supposed contents.

3. It is very important that the bulletin should appear quickly. This does not only concern the daily circular letter, but also the complete edition after the completion of the tournament. The good impression made by a bulletin is often totally spoilt by a delay in expedition.

18 International Organizations

A. The World Chess Federation (Fédération Internationale des Echecs - FIDE)

This is the international coordinating organization in the domain of chess which was founded on July 20, 1924 in Paris. FIDE unites the national chess federations and directs the chess world. Its motto is *'Gens una sumus'* - 'We are one people'.

FIDE issues the rules of chess and the provisions pertaining to the organization of the World Championships and all other FIDE chess competitions. It awards the international chess titles.

FIDE's ground principles are democracy and equality among its members. For the purpose of facilitating administration, FIDE is divided into zones formed chiefly by geographic location. As of early 1979 FIDE boasted 106 members, divided into the following 11 zones:

Zone 1 (West European): Andorra, Belgium, England, France, Guernsey, Ireland, Luxembourg, Monaco, Netherlands, Scotland, Spain and Wales;

Zone 2 (Central European): Austria, Denmark, Faroe Islands, Finland, German Federal Republic, Iceland, Israel, Norway, Rhodesia and South Africa, Sweden, Switzerland;

Zone 3 (East European): Bulgaria, Czechoslavakia, German Democratic Republic, Hungary, Poland and Romania;

Zone 4: U.S.S.R.

Zone 5: U.S.A.

Zone 6: Canada.

Zone 7 (Central American): Bahamas, Bermuda, British Virgin Islands, Colombia, Costa Rica, Cuba, Dominican Republic, Ecuador, El Salvador, Guatemala, Guyana, Honduras, Jamaica, Mexico, Dutch Antilles, Nicaragua, Panama, Puerto Rico, Trinidad and Tobago, US Virgin Islands, Venezuela;

Zone 8 (South American): Argentina, Bolivia, Brazil, Chile, Paraguay, Peru, Surinam, Uruguary;

Zone 9 (West Asian): India, Iran, Iraq, Jordan, Kuwait, Lebanon, Mongolia, Pakistan, Sri Lanka, Syria, United Arab Emirates and Yemen Arab Republic;

Zone 10 (Far East, New Zealand, Australia): Australia, China, Hong Kong, Indonesia, Japan, Malaysia, New Zealand, Papua New Guinea, Philippines, Singapore and Thailand;

Zone 11 (Mediterranean Zone): Albania, Cyprus, Greece, Italy, Malta, Portugal, Turkey and Yugoslavia.

Zone 12 (African Zone): Algeria, Gambia, Ghana, Libya, Mali, Mauritania, Mauritius, Morocco, Nigeria, Seychelles, Tunisia, Uganda, Zaire and Zambia.

FIDE's Organizational Structure

FIDE's highest organ is the General Assembly, where each member-federation has one vote. Other FIDE organs and officials include: the Central Committee, which is composed of about 25 members; the Bureau, consisting of the FIDE President, four Deputy Presidents, the Secretary-General and four members elected by the General Assembly; the permanent and temporary commissions; the President and three Deputy Presidents; the Zonal Presidents; General Secretary; and the Treasurer and the Auditor.

The Zonal Presidents are automatically members of the Central Committee, as are all Bureau members. The Central Committee includes another nine members elected by the General Assembly.

The most important permanent commissions are the Qualification Committee (which recommends the awarding of international titles) and the Rules Commission (which makes proposals to the General Assembly on interpreting the Laws of Chess).

The FIDE President and other officials are elected for four-year terms of office.

FIDE's Competencies

FIDE does not interfere in the internal affairs of its members, but it is fully authorized in the field of world chess. Its most important competencies include: prescribing rules for organizing the world chess championship, the junior world championship, the world ladies' championship, the world team championship – 'chess olympiads', as well as the championships of individual continents, awarding international chess titles (international masters, grandmasters, international arbiters etc.) and formulating and interpreting the Laws of Chess.

The International Correspondence Chess Federation and the Permanent Commission for Chess Composition work as autonomous organizations within FIDE.

FIDE's System of Competition

After Alekhine's death, FIDE took over all competencies in organizing the world individual championship. FIDE had previously had no substantial influence on the world champion title matches or on the choice of challengers. World champions decided themselves on whom they would play and the conditions of the match. A system of competition was established at FIDE's General Assembly in 1947 which begins with zonal tournaments and goes on to interzonal and candidates' competitions, ending with the match for the world chess title. FIDE runs all these competitions and prescribes the rules. This system has been kept throughout the postwar period, with the exception of minor changes: a candidates' tournament was played up to 1965, but since then candidates' matches have been held. The entire system, from the zonal tournaments to the world title match, takes three years.

According to the schemata adopted by the FIDE General Assembly in 1977, *zonal tournaments* are held in each of the 12 FIDE zones; all federations, depending on their prowess in chess, have the right to delegate a certain number of representatives for the zonal tournament. A certain number of the top-placed players from each zonal tournament qualifies for the *interzonal tournament*, which is played the year after the zonal tournaments. The interzonal stage for men is played in two tournaments of 18 players each. For ladies, however, there is only one interzonal tournament.

To illustrate, let us look at the number of players qualifying from each of the zonal tournaments:

from Zone 1: 2 men, 2 women,   *from Zone 7:* 2 men, 2 women,
from Zone 2: 3 men, 2 women,   *from Zone 8:* 3 men, 2 women,
from Zone 3: 5 men, 5 women,   *from Zone 9:* 1 man, 1 woman,
from Zone 4: 5 men, 5 women,   *from Zone 10:* 2 men, 2 women,
from Zone 5: 3 men, 2 women,   *from Zone 11:* 3 men, 3 women,
from Zone 6: 1 man, 1 woman,   *from Zone 12:* 1 man, 1 woman.

In the interzonal tournaments for men, the six players who took third to eighth place in the previous Candidates' Matches also have the right to take part. The same applies to the interzonal tournament for women.

Both mens' interzonal tournaments should be approximately of the same playing strength. The FIDE Bureau is responsible for dividing the players into the two tournaments.

FIDE tournaments are played according to a programme of six rounds in nine days (three rounds, one day reserved for adjourned games, three rounds, one day reserved for adjourned games, free day, etc.). The rate of play is 2 hours and 30 minutes for the first 40 moves and 16 moves for each subsequent hour of play.

The Candidates' Matches, which are played the year after the interzonal tournaments, have eight players: the three top players from each of the interzonal tournaments and the two players from the previous final Candidates' Match. If, in the interim, the winner of the match has become the world champion, then the former world champion has the right to play in the Candidates' Matches. The matches are played on the knockout system: quarter-finals of 10 games, semi-finals of 12 games for men, and 10 for women, and finals of 16 games for men, 12 for women.

The winner of the final match earns the right to challenge the world champion to a match the succeeding year. According to the present rules, the first player to win six games becomes the world champion. Should he lose the match, however, the world champion has the right to play a return match the next year.

A new cycle of zonal tournaments begins in the same year as the match for the world title.

'Chess Olympiads' are the world team championship; from the outset, they have been FIDE-organized (the first Olympiad was played in London in 1927). The teams are of four players, with each team having the right to two reserve players. Since World War II, the number of teams at the Olympiads h has been steadily rising, so that a system of preliminary and final groups was instituted. The XXII Chess Olympiad in Haifa, and the XXIII in Buenos Aires, however, were played according to the Swiss System. This was so as to reduce the length of the competition and thus reduce organizational expenses. The General Assembly will decide whether to make this system permanent.

'The Student Olympiad' has been held since 1954, but as of 1979 it is to be played every other year. Students up to the age of 27 play in teams of four with two reserves.

The World Youth Team Championship was only introduced in 1978. It is open to national teams composed of four players and two reserves under the age of 26 on September 1 of the year in which the tournament is held. This competition is to be held every even year.

The Women's Olympiad has been held, albeit irregularly, ever since 1956. It is now usually held together with the Men's Olympiad. Each team consists of three players and one reserve.

The World Junior Championship was instituted in 1951. It is open to chess players under the age of 20 on September 1st of the year in which the tournament is held. This competition has been held annually since 1974 (formerly every other year). It is now played according to the Swiss System (13 rounds).

The World 'Cadet' Championship (Under 17) is held each year. Each federation has the right to one representative (and the organizing federation to two). It is open to chess players under the age of 17 on September 1st of the year in which the tournament is held. It is played according to the Swiss System (11 rounds).

Continental Competitions. FIDE also sponsors the team championships of Europe, America and Asia, as well as the youth championships of individual continents. There is also the European Junior Ladies' Cup, the European Club Cup, etc.

FIDE Titles

While chess titles have long existed, and the title of grandmaster appeared early this century, FIDE officially introduced titles only at its 1950 General Assembly, when the first grandmasters and international masters were officially proclaimed. Initially, titles were awarded on the basis of votes in the Qualifications Committee, but after 1958 rules were established with qualifications which had to be fulfilled by the candidate. Since FIDE's General Assembly in 1970 adopted the Elo-system for rating tournaments and the strength of players, this was accepted in ensuing years as the basis for the Rules on awarding chess titles. We present these Rules separately. The 1976 General Assembly also adopted the title of FIDE ladies' grandmaster.

B. International Correspondence Chess Federation (ICCF)

This is an independent federation which cooperates with and recognizes FIDE as the supreme world chess organization. ICCF organizes competitions in correspondence chess, and also awards titles (grandmasters of correspondence chess, international masters of correspondence chess and arbiters). These titles are also confirmed by the General Assembly of FIDE.

ICCF has established its own system of competition: world championships (individual and team), qualification tournaments according to categories, and special correspondence tournaments.

The Rules of Competitions determine the right to play in the world championship final: the best players from the previous championship, the best players in the semi-finals, etc. The qualification tournaments, however, of which there are five classes, are open to all players, depending on their strength.

The Correspondence Olympiad is played in a three-year cycle, with preliminary competitions for selecting the teams for the finals.

The customary rate of play for ICCF correspondence competitions is 20 moves in 60 days (not counting the mailing time).

ICCF has approximately 60 members. Its president is Hans Werner von Massow – Ottersbekallee 21, Hamburg 19. ICCF also has its own Statute and rules. Anyone interested in correspondence chess should inquire at ICCF headquarters.

C. Permanent Commission for Chess Composition

This Commission was founded within FIDE and it deals exclusively with chess compositions (problems and studies). The Commission has its president and officers, and it holds annual meetings at which candidates are proposed for the titles of grandmaster, international master and arbiter of composition chess. FIDE's General Assembly verifies these titles. The Commission issues FIDE Albums with selected compositions from given periods. These are actually a kind of anthology of composition chess, and they include only the best achievements; a criterion for awarding titles is the number of compositions a given author has in the Album.

D. Other Organizations

FIDE cooperates with several organizations dealing in particular fields of chess: The International Association of Chess Reporters (AIPE), the International Committee for Silent Chess (ICSC), and the International Braille Chess Association. The latter organizations hold special competitions in their particular fields. Cooperation with FIDE chiefly entails exchanging information on their respective activities.

Addresses

FIDE Bureau, Passeerdersgracht 32, Amsterdam, Holland;
Commission for Chess Compositions, Mr Jan Hannelius, Lukonrinne 32, 36200 Kangasala, Finland;
Association of Chess Journalists, Mr S. Novrup, Forh. holms Alle 33, 3, 1904 Copenhagen V – Denmark;
'Chess Informant' (publication with FIDE information), ul.7 juli 30, Belgrade, Yugoslavia.

19 The Laws, their Interpretations and Author's Comments

The Rules of Chess (A Short History)

Although chess is a centuries-old game, there were no official unified rules of chess until fifty years ago. The founding congress of the World Chess Federation (FIDE), held in Paris in 1924, included, among its priority programme tasks, the codification of rules which would be binding for all members. At its congress in 1929, FIDE adopted the unified rules of the game.

One can find rules regulating the movement of the pieces in the oldest chess manuals – those of Juan Ramirez de Lucerna, Damiano, Ruy Lopez, and later those of Philidor and others; but the technical aspects of organizing competitions remained unknown until the nineteenth century. Although chess, in terms of how the pieces are moved, basically assumed its present-day form by the end of the fifteenth century, various rules existed in different countries concerning castling, stalemate, capturing 'en passant', the promotion of pawns, etc. Italy, for instance, held out against the rules adopted by other countries for a long time, and it was not until 1881, at the tournament in Milan, that it adopted the modern-day rules concerning castling, pawn promotion and capturing 'en passant'. Many rules which seem straightforward enough to us today, in fact went through a complicated evolution before bcoming generally accepted. For instance, at one time dice were used to decide who would play the first move, white or black, while overstepping the time-limit and tardiness in arrival for a game were penalized by invoking fines, etc.

In the nineteenth century, some chess clubs and national federations had their own rules of play, and even published books containing these as well as certain other rules for competitions. Around 1850, for instance, a brochure was published in Paris entitled *Régle de Jeu des Échecs* (Delarue Publishing House), and in 1857 official rules were published in Russia. Many countries adopted the Rules of the German Chess Federation, which were applied in many tournaments played in the nineteenth century, and even later. The first modern international tournament in London in 1851 was also played 'in accordance with the rules of the chief European Chess Clubs'. The 1862 tournament in London was played according to rules based on the proposals put forward by H. Staunton in *Praxis* in 1860. His code was adopted by many organizers and players in England and America.

There was no time-limit for thought at the 1851 tournament in London, and this was a problem in many later tournaments, when sandglasses were mainly used. The double chess clock, invented by Thomas Bright Wilson of Manchester, was used for the first time at the tournament in London in 1883 and it left its mark on the further evolution of the rules of play and tournament regulations, whereby the rate of play became an important factor in the chess game.

The founding of FIDE provided the conditions for introducing some uniformity into the rules used within certain countries. Even after 1929, many national federations retained supplementary rules which were valid for domestic competitions. Even now, for instance, the Soviet Chess Federation uses its own code for domestic competition, but the Laws of Chess of FIDE are used in international competitions in the Soviet Union.

In 1952 FIDE published a new edition of the Laws of Chess (again in French, as those of 1929). The Laws were amended at annual meetings of the General Assembly, and interpretations were provided for individual articles. FIDE published the third official edition, with the official interpretations given to date, in 1966 in French. In 1974, the Permanent Rules Commission of FIDE published a new edition, for the first time in English, of the Laws of Chess of FIDE. New interpretations and minor amendments to the Laws were provided at subsequent FIDE General Assembly meetings, and this practice of improving the Laws on the basis of competition experience will most certainly be fostered and continued.

The text of the Laws of Chess given here is the latest edition issued by FIDE, and includes FIDE interpretations and changes up to and including the FIDE Congress in San Juan in 1979. In addition to the official text of the Laws, it offers the official interpretations of the Permanent Rules Commission of FIDE. The Laws and official interpretations are binding for all FIDE competitions and for international tournaments.

In addition to the Laws (in normal type) and the official interpretations (in italics), this book includes 'Notes' (in small type) in which the authors describe and explain given cases which have arisen in tournaments as well as cases which are not embraced by the FIDE interpretations. The advice given by the authors may help arbiters when faced with certain disputes and when having to make a decision at a competition. Of course, the author's explanations are only advisory and it is up to the arbiter to decide whether or not he will accept them. The authors have endeavoured to keep their interpretations within the spirit of the Laws of FIDE, and not to contradict the official Laws and interpretations, even when, personally, they may not agree with them. For, here again, what is important is which Laws are valid and accepted by FIDE. Arbiters and national federations may, however, ask for amendments to or changes in the Laws, should they believe them to have shortcomings.

Laws of Chess of the World Chess Federation (FIDE)

In the author's notes to these Laws, the duties of an arbiter may be assumed by a Tournament Committee or Match Captains.

FIDE INTERPRETATION (1958). GENERAL OBSERVATIONS. The Laws of Chess cannot, and should not, regulate all possible situations that may arise during a game, nor can they regulate all questions of organization. In most cases not precisely regulated by an Article of the Laws, one should be able to reach a correct judgment by applying analogously stipulations for situations of a similar character. As to the arbiters' tasks, in most cases one must presuppose that arbiters have the competence, sound judgment, and absolute objectivity necessary. A regulation too detailed would deprive the arbiter of his freedom of judgment and might prevent him from finding the solution dictated by fairness and compatible with the circumstances of a particular case, since one cannot foresee every possibility.

The decisions of this Commission are founded on the above general principles.

FIDE INTERPRETATION (1974). During recent years the Commission has been more or less overwhelmed by a steadily growing number of proposals and questions. That, of itself, is a good thing.

However, there is a marked tendency in those many questions and proposals to bring more and more refinements and details into the Laws of Chess. Clearly the intention is to get more and more detailed instruction concerning 'how to act in such and such a case'. This may be profitable for a certain type of arbiter, but at the same time may be a severe handicap for another, generally the best, type of arbiter.

The Commission in its entirety takes the firm position that the Laws of Chess should be as short and as clear as possible. The Commission strongly believes that minor details should be left to the discretion of the arbiter. Each arbiter should have the opportunity, in case of a conflict, to take into account all the factors of the case and should not be bound by too detailed sub-regulations which may not be applicable to the case in question. According to the Commission, the Laws of Chess must be short and clear and leave sufficient scope for the arbiter to deal with exceptional or unusual cases.

The Commission appeals to all chess federations to accept this view, which is in the interest of the hundreds of thousands of chess players, as well as of the arbiters, generally speaking. If any chess federation wants to introduce more detailed rules, it is perfectly free to do so, provided –

(a) they do not in any way conflict with the official FIDE rules of play;

(b) they are limited to the territory of the federation in question; and

(c) they are not valid for any FIDE tournament played in the territory of the federation in question.

PART I. GENERAL LAWS

Article 1. Introduction

The game of chess is played between two opponents by moving pieces on a square board called a 'chessboard'.

Article 2. The Chessboard and its Arrangement

2.1. The chessboard is composed of 64 equal squares alternately light (the 'white' squares) and dark (the 'black' squares).

2.2. The chessboard is placed between the players in such a way that the corner square to the right of each player is white.

2.3. The eight rows of squares running from the edge of the chessboard nearest one player to that nearest the other player are called 'files'.

2.4. The eight rows of squares running from one edge of the chessboard to the other at right angles to the files are called 'ranks'.

2.5. The rows of squares of the same color, touching corner to corner, are called 'diagonals'.

Article 3. The Pieces and their Arrangement

3.1. At the beginning of the game, one player has 16 light-colored pieces (the 'white' pieces), the other has 16 dark-coloured pieces (the 'black' pieces). **3.2.** These pieces are as follows:

A white king	usually indicated by the symbol ♔
A white queen	usually indicated by the symbol ♕
Two white rooks	usually indicated by the symbol ♖
Two white bishops	usually indicated by the symbol ♗
Two white knights	usually indicated by the symbol ♘
Eight white pawns	usually indicated by the symbol ♙
A black king	usually indicated by the symbol ♚
A black queen	usually indicated by the symbol ♛
Two black rooks	usually indicated by the symbol ♜
Two black bishops	usually indicated by the symbol ♝
Two black knights	usually indicated by the symbol ♞
Eight black pawns	usually indicated by the symbol ♟

3.3. The initial position of the pieces on the chessboard is as follows:

Article 4. The Conduct of the Game

4.1. The two players must alternate in making one move at a time. The player with the white pieces commences the game.
4.2. A player is said to 'have the move' when it is his turn to play.

Note to Art. 4.1.:
Players alternate in making one move at a time until the game is ended in one of the ways prescribed in articles 10, 11, 12, 17 and 18.

Article 5. The General Definition of the Move

5.1. With the exception of castling (Article 6.1), a move is the transfer of a piece from one square to another square which is either vacant or occupied by an enemy piece.

5.2. No piece except the rook, when castling, and the knight (Article 6.5) may cross a square occupied by another piece.

5.3. A piece played to a square occupied by an enemy piece captures it as part of the same move. The captured piece must be immediately removed from the chessboard by the player making the capture. See Article 6.6b for capturing 'en passant'.

Note to Art. 5.2.:
Only the knight may 'jump' over a square occupied by another piece. The method of castling is given in the next article. Then the rook which is doing the castling crosses over the square to which the king has been moved. The formulation of this article is imprecise. At a tournament in Moscow in 1962, a player executed a Queen-side castling despite the fact that the knight occupied square b1. He referred to the formulation of this article which says that during the castling the rook may leap over other pieces. The meaning of this article, however, is that when castling, the rook is transferred across the king which is moved two squares over, but except for this particular case, the rook cannot cross over other pieces.

Note to Art. 5.3.:
Only an enemy king cannot be captured. It can, however, be 'attacked', i.e. it can be threatened by capture in the next move. This occurs when an enemy piece threatens the square occupied by the king. When the king is thus attacked by an enemy piece or pawn, then one says that the king is 'in check'. It is not obligatory to announce a check, but the player whose king is in check must parry the check with his next move (Art. 10). If the check cannot be parried (as described in Art. 10), then the king is mated and the player who has mated the enemy king wins the game (Art. 11.1.).

Claiming a check which does not in fact exist or a non-existent mate is of no consequence.

Article 6. The Moves of the Individual Pieces

6.1. *The King.* Except when castling, the king moves to any adjoining square that is not attacked by an enemy piece.

Castling is a move of the king and either rook, counting as a single move (of the king), executed as follows: the king is transferred, from its original square, two squares toward either rook on the same rank; then that rook toward which the king has been moved is transferred over the king to the square immediately adjacent to the king.

Castling is impossible –

(a) if the king has already been moved, or

(b) with a rook that has already been moved.

Castling is prevented for the time being –

(a) if the king's original square or the square which the king must cross or that which it is to occupy is attacked by an enemy piece, or

(b) if there is any piece between the king and the rook toward which the king is to be moved.

6.2. *The Queen.* The queen moves to any square (except as limited by Article 5.2) on the file, rank, or diagonals on which it stands.

6.3. *The Rook.* The rook moves to any square (except as limited by Article 5.2) on the file or rank on which it stands.

6.4. *The Bishop.* The bishop moves to any square (except as limited by Article 5.2) on the diagonals on which it stands.

6.5. *The Knight.* The knight's move is composed of two different steps; first, it makes one step of one single square along the rank or file and then, still moving away from the square of departure, one step of one single square on a diagonal.

6.6. *The Pawn.* The pawn may move only forward.

(a) Except when making a capture, it advances from its original square either one or two vacant squares along the file on which it is placed, and on subsequent moves it advances one vacant square along the file. When capturing, it advances one square along either of the diagonals on which it stands.

(b) A pawn attacking a square crossed by an enemy pawn which has been advanced two squares in one move from its original square may capture this enemy pawn as though the latter had been moved only one square. This capture may be made only on the move immediately following such an advance and is called capturing 'en passant'.

(c) On reaching the last rank, a pawn must be immediately exchanged, as part of the same move, for a queen, a rook, a bishop, or a knight of the same color as the pawn, at the player's choice and without taking into account the other pieces still remaining on the chessboard. This exchanging of a pawn is called 'promotion' and the action of the promoted piece is immediate.

FIDE INTERPRETATION ART. 6.1 (1971). If a player in castling starts by touching the rook, he should receive a warning from the arbiter, but the castling shall be considered valid.

If a player, intending to castle, touches king and rook at the same time and it then appears that castling is illegal, the player has to move his king. If the king has no legal move, the fault has no consequences.

FIDE INTERPRETATION ART. 6.1 (1974). The Commission regards the warning by the arbiter an adequate means of dealing with those who castle in the wrong manner.

The Commission disagrees with the principle that if the king has no legal move, then a move with the rook shall be made, which would apply if the move was initially one with the rook alone.

FIDE INTERPRETATION ART. 6.1 (1975). Question: If a player moves his king two squares, intending to castle with the king's rook, and it then appears that castling is illegal, can the player castle on the other side (provided, of course, that casling on that side is legal)?

Answer: The answer is yes. The player has to make any legal move he chooses with his king, from its original square. There is no reason why that legal move should not be castling on the queen's side.

FIDE INTERPRETATION ART. 6.6c (1971A). In a game between Player A (White) and Player B (Black), B played on the 45th move . . . c2–c1 (P–QB8). However, he neglected to exchange the pawn immediately for a queen. On his scoresheet he had written 45 . . . c2–c1Q (P–QB8/Q) and stopped his clock afterwards. Then he left the board. At the time, his opponent

was not present. When A returned to the board, he protested because B had not immediately exchanged the pawn on c1 (QB8), though B told him the piece on c1 was a queen. The arbiter decided as follows: A's clock was restored to the position it had before the move . . . c2–c1 (P–QB8) was made. B had to make his move 45 . . . c2–c1Q (P–QB8/Q) again, as it was obvious that he intended to promote that pawn to a queen. Then the game was resumed in the normal way.
The Commission confirms the decision of the arbiter.
FIDE INTERPRETATION ART. 6.6c (1971B). In a competition, if a new piece is not immediately available, the player should ask for the assistance of the arbiter before making his move. If this request is made and there is any appreciable delay in obtaining the new piece, the arbiter should stop both clocks until the required piece is given to the player having the move. If no request is made and the player makes his move and stops his clock without exchanging the promoted pawn for a new piece, he is breaking the Laws of Chess and should be given a warning or a disciplinary penalty, such as the advancement of the time on his clock. In any case, the opponent's clock should be set back to the time it registered immediately before the player stopped his clock, the position on the board should be reestablished to what it was before the player moved his pawn, and the clock of the player having the move should be started. The player should then make his move correctly, in the manner specified in Article 6.6c.
FIDE INTERPRETATION ART. 6.6c (1973). The penalty referred to in FIDE Interpretation Art. 6.6c (1971B) is meant to be indefinite. The penalty should depend on the circumstances.

Note to Art. 6.1.: Castling
Diagram 1 allows Black to castle with the rook on h8; castling the other way is impossible because the king will have to cross a square attacked by an enemy piece. in Diagram 2, castling is possible but only with the rook on a8, on the other side the king would have been placed in check; the black rook *can* cross the b8 square even though this is attacked.

Diagram 1   **Diagram 2**

Note to Art. 6.6.: Capturing 'en passant'
In diagram 1, after white plays 1g2–g4, Black has no choice but to capture the pawn 'en passant'. i.e. he must play 1 . . . h4 × g3 since this is the only move open to him.

Article 7. The Completion of the Move

A move is completed –
1. in the case of the transfer of a piece to a vacant square, when the player's hand has released the piece;
2. in the case of a capture, when the captured piece has been removed from the chessboard and the player, having placed on its new square his own piece, has released the latter from his hand;
3. in the case of castling, when the player's hand has released the rook on the square crossed by the king; when the player has released the king from his hand, the move is not yet completed, but the player no longer has the right to make any other move than castling; or
4. in the case of the promotion of a pawn, when the pawn has been removed from the chessboard and the player's hand has released the new piece after placing it on the promotion square; if the player has released from his hand the pawn that has reached the promotion square, the move is not yet completed, but the player no longer has the right to play the pawn to another square.

FIDE INTERPRETATION ART. 7.1. See FIDE Interpretation Art. 11.1 (1958).

Note to Art. 7.:
The ruling on the completion of a move is important, because it is only when the move is completed that the player is entitled to stop his clock. Should he do this before executing his move, he can be penalized in keeping with Art. 20.4.
Note to Art. 7.1.:
The player is not considered to have executed his move as long as he keeps his

hand on the piece, but he must move that piece, if any move with that piece is legal. A piece may be moved if in the process it does not open up a check to its own king and if there is at least one square, free or occupied by an enemy piece, to which that piece can be moved. If a move with the touched piece is impossible, then touching the piece is of no consequence and the player can move any other piece.

Note to Art. 7.: The Completion of the Move.
The player, in moving the piece to a given square and declaring check, may still not have released the piece from his hand. In this case he is still entitled to move that piece to another square, regardless of whether he declared a check (his hand did not release the piece and the move was not completed).
Note to Art. 7.3.:
When a player moves the king the two squares of a castling move and releases it from his hand, then he must complete the castling on that side, if it is legal. (Art. 6). If castling on that side is illegal, then the player must make, if possible, another legal move with the king, including castling on the other side.

However, if, in planning to castle, the player first moves the rook and subsequently discovers that castling is impossible, he must move the rook.
Note to Art. 7.4.:
In the case of promotion, a move is considered completed only when the piece to which the pawn has been promoted is played on the promotion square and then released from the hand. As long as the player keeps his hand on the piece replacing the pawn, he may return the piece in his hand and promote his pawn to any other piece. To all intents and purposes this means that the player's statement as to the piece to which he is promoting his pawn is of no significance, and the same holds true if a player writes down the name of the promoted piece on the scoresheet. Only what is executed on the board is of any validity.

If a player has released from his hand a pawn which has reached the promotion square, then the new piece may be placed only on that square. If the player has not released the pawn from his hand, then it may be promoted on some adjoining square.

If the player releases the pawn on the promotion square, then the move is completed only after the piece into which he wishes to promote that pawn is placed on the square, and he may not stop his clock until this entire procedure of promotion is completed, including the setting down of the new piece.

If the player has not got on hand the piece into which he wishes to promote his pawn, he may request help from the arbiter, who may stop the clock should he feel that some time may be required to supply the piece.

What happens if a player, White for instance, has a pawn on g7, and without touching it, places and releases a new queen on g8, but upon realizing that Black would then be stalemated, replaces it with a rook? White's intention was clear and he must promote the pawn to the queen; not to do so would mean to withdraw the move. It is not permitted to place pieces on the chessboard except in accordance with the Laws. If, however, in placing the queen on g8 the player did not release the piece from his hand, then he may promote the pawn to any piece on g8 (or f8 or h8, providing that he can capture an enemy piece on these squares).

Article 8. The Touched Piece

8.1. Provided that he first warns his opponent, the player whose turn it is to move may adjust one or more pieces on their squares.

8.2. Except for the above case, if the player having the move touches -
(a) one or more pieces of the same color, he must move or capture the first piece touched that can be moved or captured; or
(b) one of his own pieces and one of his opponent's pieces, he must capture his opponent's piece with his own piece; or, if this is not possible, move his own piece; or, if even this is not possible, capture his opponent's piece.
8.3. If the move or capture is not possible, the player is free to make any legal move he chooses.
8.4. If a player wishes to claim a violation of this rule, he must do so before he touches a piece himself.

FIDE INTERPRETATION ART. 8.1 (1974). A player who wishes to adjust one or more pieces when his opponent is absent may make the adjustment after warning the arbiter of his intention.

FIDE INTERPRETATION ART. 8.2 (1972). In a recent game the player with the white pieces claimed that his opponent violated Article 8.2 by touching a piece, then moving a different piece. Black denied the accusation, and an arbiter was called to the board. There was no independent witness of any kind to the alleged violation, so the arbiter rejected the claim for lack of evidence.

The Commission declares that the arbiter was correct. As in the case of all other Laws, unbiased evidence is required to support any claim by a player that his opponent violated a Law. If the accused player denies the allegation and it is impossible to prove otherwise by the testimony of an official or other disinterested witness, it is just a question of one player's word against that of his opponent. An unsubstantiated claim would have to be rejected.

FIDE INTERPRETATION ART. 8.2 (1974A). A player who touches more pieces than those indicated in this Article may be penalized at the discretion of the arbiter.

FIDE INTERPRETATION ART. 8.2 (1974B). Question: If a player reaching for a piece to make a move (but not having touched it yet) touches another piece with his arm in passing, is this grounds for the opponent to claim that the player must move that piece?

Answer: A piece is considered to be touched under this Article only when a player touches it with the intention of making a move with it. Doubtful cases are left to the discretion of the arbiter.

FIDE INTERPRETATION ART. 8.2b (1975). Question: White has a pawn on c5 and a queen on c4, and Black has a rook on d6. White intends to play cxd6. Many players are used to touching first the piece to be captured and, with the same hand, at (nearly) the same time, the capturing piece. In this example White touches the black rook, and in the following fraction of a second, he reconsiders his intended move and touches the white queen. According to Article 8.2b he can play any move he likes with the queen, and the fact that he touched the black rook does not count anymore. The Article gives priority to a move with the player's own piece over the capture of an opponent's piece. In most cases, would it not better correspond to the original intention of the player to give priority to the capture?

Answer: The Commission declines to give an Interpretation on the basis of hypothetical cases alone. It should be remarked, however, that the seemingly

'obvious' solution (changing the order of possibilities in Article 8.2b) is no good, because in that case another hypothetical case could be constructed, in which the reverse could happen.
FIDE INTERPRETATION ART. 8.4 (1974). The enforcement of this Article by the arbiter does not require a claim to be made.

Note to Art. 8.1.:
Provided he has the move and first warns his opponent, the player may adjust his own and his opponent's pieces on their squares. This is usually done by saying 'j'adoube' (French for 'I adjust') to the opponent. If the player does not first warn his opponent that he wishes to adjust the piece, then he must play the touched piece. If the opponent is absent from the board, the player must inform the arbiter of his intention. One can hardly ask of a player who is under time-pressure to look for the arbiter. It is only logical that it is enough for him clearly to announce his intention to adjust the piece before witnesses.

If the player adjusts pieces when it is not his turn to move, he is disturbing his opponent and may be penalized in accordance with Art. 19.1c.
Note to Art. 8.2.:
This article, more than any other in the Laws of Chess, has been changed several times at FIDE General Assemblies. Even the present formulation has given rise to different views. Provision 8.2, when a player touches one or more pieces of the same colour, appears to be clear. In this case he must move or capture the first piece he has touched. Nor is there any question raised in the case of the player who touches his own and an enemy piece – he must capture his opponent's piece with his own. According to Art. 8.2b, however, if this is not possible then he must move his own piece (if the move is possible). If even this is not possible, then he must capture his opponent's piece with any of his own pieces which are in a position to capture. Hence, the Laws give priority to moving one's own piece, and only then to capturing the opponent's piece (the Soviet Chess Code gives exactly reverse priority to touching and capturing the opponent's piece, which seems more logical).

Suppose in this position (Diagram) Black has (first) taken the Ph2 but with Be6. This is an impossible move. According to Art. 8.2(b) priority is given to moving one's own piece and Black is obliged to play with Bc6 any possible move (he does not have to make a capture). Only if a move with Bc6 is impossible does Black have to take the pawn on h2 (i.e. to play Bd6 x h2).

It is left to the discretion of the arbiter to settle the case of a player who touches several pieces. It would be logical for the arbiter, in this case too, to take into account which piece was touched first and to be guided in his decision by the intention of the player who touched the pieces. The arbiter should differentiate between accidentally and intentionally touched pieces and, as suggested by FIDE's interpretation 1974B, should not be formalistic.

Note to Art. 8.3.:
The 'touch move' rule is applied in all cases. The only exception is when the player cannot make a move with his own touched piece, and cannot capture the touched enemy piece with any of his own pieces. Then the touching of the pieces is of no consequence (there was a time when this resulted in a 'penalty move by the king', but this provision no longer exists).

Article 9. Illegal Positions

9.1. If, during a game, it is found that an illegal move was made, the position shall be reinstated to what it was before the illegal move was made. The game shall then continue by applying the rules of Article 8 to the move replacing the illegal move. If the position cannot be reinstated, the game shall be annulled and a new game played.

9.2. If, during a game, one or more pieces have been accidentally displaced and incorrectly replaced, the position shall be reinstated to what it was before the displacement took place, and the game shall be continued. If the position cannot be reinstated, the game shall be annulled and a new game played.

9.3. If, after an adjournment, the position is incorrectly set up, the position as it was on adjournment must be set up again and the game continued.

9.4. If, during a game, it is found that the initial position of the men was incorrect, the game shall be annulled and a new game played.

9.5. If, during a game, it is found that the board has been wrongly placed, the position reached shall be transferred to a board correctly placed and the game continued.

FIDE INTERPRETATION ART. 9.1 (1963). Question: How are the words 'during a game' to be interpreted if a game has been submitted for adjudication? Specifically, is the game considered to be still in progress for the purposes of Article 9.1 if, before the arbiter has registered the result of the game after adjudication, it is established that an illegal move was made or that one or more pieces were accidentally displaced and incorrectly replaced?

Answer: The Commission declares that in such cases a game submitted for adjudication is considered to be still in progress for the purposes of Article 9.1.

FIDE INTERPRETATION ART. 9.4 (1958). Question: What is the procedure when it is established in the course of a game that the game began with colors reversed?

Answer: The Commission declares that this is a situation of the kind indicated in Article 9.4.

FIDE INTERPRETATION ART. 9.4 (1960). In a Swiss-System tournament, the arbiter made a mistake by giving to Player X the white pieces and to Player Y the black pieces instead of the opposite. After detecting the mistake some days later, Player Y claimed that the game should be annulled and a new game played in its stead, with Player Y having the white pieces.

The Commission declares that in accordance with the fundamental principles of Articles 9.4 and 9.5, the claim, since it was submitted after the end of the game, must be rejected.
FIDE INTERPRETATION ART. 9.4 (1973). The Commission states that in the case of FIDE Interpretation Art. 9.4 (1958) it does not matter who made the mistake (even if it was the arbiter as well as both players). The rules must be obeyed in any case.
FIDE INTERPRETATION ART. 9.4 (1979). Question: The board was placed with a black square at the right. The queens and kings were facing each other, with white queen on white square. The game was played until one player gave checkmate. The arbiter rules that the checkmate stands, since any question of an illegal position had to be claimed during the game.
Answer: The decision of the arbiter was correct.
FIDE INTERPRETATION ART. 9.5 (1973). This Article applies only in the case where the initial position of the piece on the chessboard accorded with that specified in Article 3.3 except that each of the squares on which the pieces rested was of the opposite color. Otherwise, Article 9.4 applies.

Note to Art. 9.1.:
An illegal move may be claimed only *during the game*. An adjourned game is not considered as completed, and consequently, an illegal move·made before the resumption of the game may be claimed upon its continuation. The position is reinstated to what it was before the illegal move was made, and the time is calculated in accordance with Art. 14.7 (as in the case mentioned in 9.2). An illegal move means one which is not in accordance with the Laws (an illegal or impossible move of a piece, an impossible castling, opening up one's own king to check, etc.).
Note to Art. 9.3. and 9.4.:
Another possible illegal position is when the pieces are incorrectly set up at the very beginning of the game or at the continuation of an adjourned game. In the first case, the game is replayed from the beginning, and in the latter, from the correct position as it was on adjournment. In both instances, as well as in those mentioned in 9.1. and 9.2., the correction may be made only if the player claims the illegality prior to the end of the game.
Note to Art. 9.5.:
The position and board are not considered to be wrongly placed if the white pieces are set up on the eighth and seventh ranks (some boards are marked by letters and numbers), and the black on the first and second ranks. The board is considered to be wrongly placed if the square to the right of the players is not white. In this latter case the position is transferred to a board correctly placed and the game is continued.
In all cases enumerated in this article, claims made after the game is finished, as envisaged by Art. 11, 12, 17 and 18, should be rejected and the attained result registered.

Article 10. Check

10.1. The king is in check when the square it occupies is attacked by an enemy piece; in this case the latter is said to be 'checking the king'.
10.2. Check must be parried by the move immediately following. If the check cannot be parried, it is said to be 'mate'. (See Article 11.1.)
10.3. A man blocking a check to the king of its own color can itself give check to the enemy king.

Note to Art. 10.1.:
It is not obligatory to declare check. Declaring a non-existent check is of no consequence, provided that it is not done deliberately to disturb the opponent (which is punishable according to Art. 19).
Note to Art. 10.2.:
Check may be parried:
a) by moving the king to a square which is not threatened by an enemy piece,
b) by capturing the opponent's piece which is checking the king and
c) by placing one of one's own pieces on one of the squares lying between the king and the attacking enemy piece. This last means of defence is evidently not possible when the check comes from the knight or in the case of a double check.

Article 11. The Won Game

11.1. The game is won by the player who has mated his opponent's king.
11.2. The game is won by the player whose opponent declares he resigns.

FIDE INTERPRETATION ART. 11.1 (1976). Question: (1) Player A makes a move that gives stalemate. This move is so menacing (e.g., a threatened mate in one) that his opponent, Player B, resigns. It is subsequently noticed, either by the player or by a spectator or the arbiter, that the last move was a stalemating move. What is the result?
(2) Is the situation affected in any way by the nature of the person who points out the stalemate? For example, if it is a spectator who points it out, is the result of the game any different?
(3) If Player A gives checkmate without realizing it and then Player A resigns, possibly after one move or more has been made, and afterwards it is pointed out or noticed by Player A that mate was given, what is the result of the game?
(4) Is this situation affected by who points out the mate?
   Answer: The Commission reiterates the principle that what happens in consequence of an action or of an omission after the termination of a game is without importance. A checkmating or stalemating move ends the game regardless of subsequent actions or omissions. Spectators are not to speak or otherwise to interfere in the games. However, if a spectator points out an irregularity, the arbiter may initiate action on his own, but should severely warn the spectator against future interference or even expel him from the tournament room.
   FIDE INTERPRETATION ART. 11.2 (1971). If a player shakes hands with his opponent, this is not to be considered as equal to resigning the game as meant in Article 11.2.
   FIDE INTERPRETATION ART. 11.2 (1979). Question: In a Swiss System tournament the result of a game was reported as a win for white. The pairing for the next round was made on that basis. Later it was discovered that black won. The two players agreed that black actually won. Should the result on the scoreboard remain for the later rounds or be corrected?
   Answer: The result should be corrected. Pairing for any rounds already played should remain, but pairings for all later rounds should be based on the true results.

Note to Art. 11.1.:
Mate means the game is over and here there is little ambiguity. The player who moved and released the piece which mated his opponent's king wins the game, even if the flag on his clock falls afterwards, even before he starts his opponent's clock.

Note to Art. 11.2.:
A verbal declaration of resignation is recognized by the Laws as a way of ending the game. Consequently, once such a declaration is made, it cannot be retracted. There have been cases in which a player, thinking that he had no other choice, announced his resignation and then, realizing that he had been mistaken, attempted to retract his statement. The arbiter should not permit this; he must register the result on the basis of the first statement, even if the scoresheet is unsigned and the clock has not been stopped.

There are several ways in which players admit defeat: by stopping the clock, knocking over the king, signing the scoresheet, extending a hand to the winner, etc. What is important is that it is clear to both the arbiter and the opponent that defeat has been acknowledged.

Nonetheless, there is some confusion over this. The Soviet book 'The *Organization and Judging of Chess Competitions* offers the example of master V. who executed a combination entailing the sacrifice of a piece, but this merely led to a draw. His opponent F. contemplated for a while and then, in the belief that there was nothing to be done, stopped the clock and wrote 'resigns' on his scoresheet. His opponent took this to mean tacit acceptance of a draw and wrote 'draw' on his scoresheet. The demonstrator took player V.'s scoresheet and put 'draw' on the demonstration board. At this point player F. crossed out what he had written and wrote 'draw' instead. In this case the arbiter should have proceeded from the fact that it was F.'s turn to play and that he had stopped the clock and resigned the game, so that what followed was irrelevant.

Something similar occurred in a game at a tournament in the Federal Republic of Germany. This is a strange case of mutual surrender. Black moved his pawn g7–g5, but his opponent, who did not see that he could capture the pawn 'en passant', interpreted this as mate and signed his resignation. Meanwhile, Black realized that he would be mated if White captured the pawn 'en passant', and without waiting for a reply, he also signed his resignation. In this case the game should have been won by Black. He made a move and his opponent responded by resigning. White was the first to respond (resign); only then did Black declare himself.

Another example comes from a tournament in Bulgaria during which a player signed his resignation, in the belief that he had overstepped his time-limit. Immediately afterwards it was established that he had made the 41st move. His statement on resigning the game remained in effect, however, because this ended the game.

Consequently, one can conclude that a declaration of resignation is sufficient proof for ending the game. The same could be said of the case in which the player stops the clock, when there is no doubt that this is a gesture denoting the end of the game (for, otherwise, the player is not entitled to stop the clock – this is the job of the arbiter). With regard to stopping a clock the arbiter must not be a pedant; a misunderstanding may have occurred. For instance, a player first stopped the clock and then placed his sealed move in the envelope. His opponent asked that this be considered as resigning the game because he had stopped the clock. The arbiter, however, did not accept this.

There have been cases in tournaments where a player declared a mate to his opponent and the latter instinctively stopped the clock and extended his hand, only to realize that there was no mate. This mistake, however, cannot be corrected and the resigned game remains in effect.

Irrefutable proof of the resigned game is the scoresheet with the outcome and the signature of the player which he turns over to the arbiter. One cannot consider the procedure of resigning as completed, however, if the player writes 'resigns' on his scoresheet, but retains the scoresheet, still pondering whether or not to hand it in.

According to FIDE's interpretations, extending one's hand to the opponent need not be taken as a sign of resigning the game. Obviously, the interpretations here allow for the possibility of a misunderstanding in which one player thinks that the game is drawn, and tacitly agrees to divide a point, while the other thinks that he has a won game and takes the handshake as a sign of resignation. Similar confusion is possible when stopping the clock.

The arbiter should be capable of distinguishing the intentional from the unintentional. Mate and a declaration of resignation remain the clearest evidence of the end of the game. If a stalemate position occurs, however, and the player fails to notice it and resigns the game, then the statement carries no weight because the game had already ended with the stalemate.

This article says nothing about declarations of resignation made when the game is not in progress, e.g. during the adjournment period. Statements of resigning the game made over the telephone, or through another person, etc., are unreliable and may be denied. Consequently the best thing is for the arbiter to obtain written confirmation of the result.

This article speaks about two ways in which the player wins the game. Article 17 is devoted to other cases in which the player may lose the game.

FIDE's Laws of Chess do not at any point stipulate that for a won game the player gets one point, for a draw half a point and for defeat no point. The history of chess competitions has known of other ways for counting draws (as a quarter of a point, etc.) and there are still demands today for a reform. As is known, until 1867, drawn games were replayed, and this posed problems for the organizers. It was then that the British Chess Association adopted the rule of giving half a point to each player in the case of a draw. The first tournament applying this new rule was played in Dundee in 1867, and it was later gradually adopted at other tournaments and in other countries. Nevertheless, there were still some later efforts to bring about some reform in this system (such as at the tournaments in Monte Carlo in 1901 and 1902). Until the end of the nineteenth century, stalemate was also variously counted in different countries (in Spain and Portugal it was considered as a kind of victory, etc.).

In the desire to encourage playing for a win and to stop too many placid draws, FIDE, at its meetings over the past few years, has considered some ideas for tabulating chess scores differently. Draws, for instance, could be scored differently when one side has a material advantage and the other only the king, stalemate would also be given a different score, etc. Even earlier, former world champion Emanuel Lasker had proposed that mate be worth 10 points, stalemate 8, etc.

Nevertheless, chess has so far retained the traditional system of alloting one point for a won game, half a point to each of the two players for a draw, and no points for a loss. This is applied in all FIDE and other competitions, but it is interesting to note that this traditional system is not mentioned anywhere in FIDE documents.

Article 12. The Drawn Game
The game is drawn –
  1. when the king of the player whose turn it is to move is not in check

and the player cannot make any legal move. The king is then said to be 'stalemated'.

2. by agreement between the two players.

3. upon a claim by one of the players when the same position is about to appear (a) or has appeared (b) for the third time, the same player having the move each time. The position is considered the same if pieces of the same kind and color occupy the same squares and if the possible moves of all the pieces are the same.

The right to claim the draw belongs exclusively to the player –

(a) who is in a position to play a move leading to such a repetition of the position, if he first declares his intention of making this move, or

(b) whose turn it is to reply to a move that has produced the repeated position.

If a player makes a move without having claimed a draw in the manner prescribed in (a) and (b), he loses the right to claim a draw; this right is restored to him, however, if the same position appears again, the same player having the move.

4. when a player having the move demonstrates that at least fifty consecutive moves have been made by each side without the capture of any piece or the movement of any pawn.

This number of fifty moves can be increased for certain positions, provided that this increase in number and these positions have been clearly established before the commencement of the game.

FIDE INTERPRETATION ART. 12.4 (1978).
1. In endings king and two knights against king and pawn, the 50-move rule will be extended to 100-moves if the following conditions are met:
a) The pawn is safely blocked by a knight
b) the pawn is not further advanced than for Black: a4, b6, c5, d4, e4, f5, g6, or h4: for white; a5, b3, c4, d5, e5, f4, g3, or h5.
2. Other endings will be considered by the Rules Commission if researched in detail and submitted to the Rules Commission with supporting evidence.

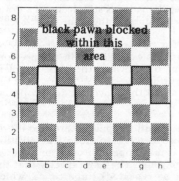 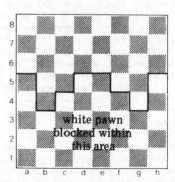

The two diagrams illustrate the area within which the black and white pawns respectively must be blocked for the new (1978) rule to apply.

FIDE INTERPRETATION ART. 12.3a (1974). A requirement to the effect that a player should not only declare his intention of making a move leading to the repetition of the position but also execute the declared move on the board is not necessary. It is clear that the player who claims the draw has to make the intended move in any case, but the Commission is of the opinion that the declared move should not be immediately executed on the board.

FIDE INTERPRETATION ART. 12.3 (1964). Concerning the repetition of a position on the chessboard, a position should not always be considered the same if pieces of the same kind and of the same color occupy the same squares (static identity), but only on the additional condition that the possibilities for moving these pieces are also the same (that is to say, that there is also dynamic identity). If one adds this last stipulation, a player would thus no longer be entitled to demand a draw if, after the repetition of a position, the right to castle or to take a pawn en passant had been lost.

FIDE INTERPRETATION ART. 12.4 (1958A). Question: Can a player lose the game by exceeding the time-limit when the position is such that no mate is possible, whatever continuation the players may employ (this concerns Part II of the Laws)?

Answer: The Commission declares that the Laws must be interpreted in such a way that in this case, as in the case of perpetual check, a draw cannot be decreed against the will of one of the players before the situation foreseen in Article 12.4 is attained.

FIDE INTERPRETATION ART. 12.4 (1958B). The Commission declares that this Article concerns only the possibility of indicating in the regulations for a certain tournament or match certain positions for which the number of fifty moves may be increased.

FIDE should not assume the responsibility for inserting into the Laws details which might be revealed as incorrect as a result of future investigations.

Note to Art. 12.1.:
Stalemate, like mate, means the end of the game. A player at a tournament resigned the game when he was in a stalemate position, but did not see it. In this case, the game is declared a draw, since whatever transpired afterwards is irrelevant. The game ended upon the emergence of the stalemate position. When stalemate results from a sealed move, the game is still declared a draw, even if the player does not come for the resumption of the game (Art. 17.2.).

Note to Art. 12.2.:
As in when resigning a game, it is enough for both players to agree orally on ending the game with a draw. The same principles indicated in the previous article apply as proof of the offer, including offers when the game is not in progress, i.e. clear proposals and irrefutable evidence.

Article 18 of the Laws speaks in detail about the procedure for proposing a draw.

Note to Art. 12.3.:
The right to claim the draw when the same position appears three (or more) times belongs exclusively to the player whose turn it is to move. The position need not appear three times consecutively; it may appear through an undetermined number of moves in the course of the game. The Laws specify that the same position has to appear (rather than be repeated) three times, which means that the first position is also considered as a position to have appeared in the game, if the same player has the move.

An important amendment is that introduced by the FIDE Interpretation (1964), according to which the position is considered the same only if the possibilities for moving the pieces are also the same. A few examples may best illustrate the provisions stipulated in this article.

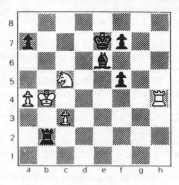

Diagram 1

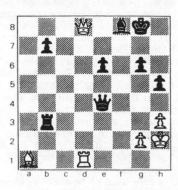

Diagram 2

The case in diagram 1 is very simple: this position (with White to move) will appear three times. This was followed by 45.Ka5, Rc2 46.Kb4, Rb2 (second time the same position) 47.Ka5, Rc2 48.Kb4. Here Black claimed a draw, declaring he would play 48 . . . Rb2; the same position will appear for the third time, with White to move. The Arbiter confirmed the draw (the Spassky-Korchnoi Match, Belgrade, 1977-78, Game no. 16).

An example from the Kushnir-Gaprindashvili match (Game 10, 1972) is shown in diagram 2. The game continued: 40 . . . Qf4+ (this position will appear three times) 41.Kh1, Qe4 42.Kh2, Qf4+ (second time), 43.Kg1, Qe3 44.Kh2, Qf4+ (this was the sealed move! The position is repeated three times.) When the game was to be resumed, Black claimed a draw but this was refused by the arbiter, because the sealed move was considered as already completed. According to Art. 12.3a, the player who is in a position to play a move leading to a treble repetition has first to declare his intention to play this move (before making it). In this case Black had to claim a draw before she sealed the move.

Diagram 3

Diagram 4

One other, more complicated case (from a Bobotsov–Tsvetkov game) is shown in Diagram 3. In this (initial position) White had the move: 41.Be2, Bb7 42.Bf1, Bc8 43.Bd3 (the same position, but with Black to move!) Bb7 44.Qd2, Bc8 45.Kg2, Bb7 46.Qe1, Bc8 47.Kf3, Bb7 48.Kf2, Bc8 (third time the same position, but this time with White to move). A claim for a draw could not be accepted since the same player had not had the move each time.

The position in diagram 4 is a good illustration for the FIDE interpretation (1964) that the position is considered the same only if pieces of the same kind and of the same colour occupy the same squares and also if the possibilities for moving these pieces are the same. The position is a composition (by N. Petrović and Z. Maslar) and White should mate in 6 moves. The solution is not 1.Qg7 because of 1 . . . 0-0-0. If 1.Nf6, ef 2.Qxc7, then 0-0 and again there is no solution. The right solution is: 1.Ne5! Rf8 2.Nd7, Rh8 (the same position, but still a difference: Black no longer has the right to castle on the King-side!) 3.Nf6! Kf8 4.Nd7+ Ke8 (Now the initial position appears for the third time, but still with one important difference: Black has lost the possibility to castle on both sides! Because the possibilities for moving the pieces are not the same, a claim for a draw could not be accepted) 5.Qg7 and mate on the next move.

The rule used to be that the clock of the player who claimed the draw had to be in motion while the claim was being verified. It depended, too, on the player, arbiter and other circumstances as to how much time would be spent on this operation. FIDE's 1976 Interpretation stipulates that five minutes be added on the clock of the player claiming a draw on the basis of a thrice occurring position (as if he had spent those five minutes for thought), regardless of how long the actual verification of the claim takes. This new rule is good in that it equalizes all cases and the player need not suffer the effects of an arbiter who is slow in verifying the claim. The bad side of this provision, however, is that the arbiter, by adding exactly five minutes, may on occasion face a difficult situation when the player has to overstep the time-limit by a second or two. On the other hand, the new interpretation does give the arbiter the chance fully and without haste to establish whether the claim is justified, for a mistake on the part of the arbiter could result in serious consequences.

The new interpretation, however, now raises the practical question of how the arbiter is to execute the operation of adding five minutes. Until now the rule was that the clock of the claimant was left ticking while the claim was being verified. Now, however, the arbiter must stop the clock, record the exact time he reads on it and then, after the verification, add five minutes.

Of course, here again, the principle applies that if the claim was justified, the arbiter declares a draw, even if the claimant overstepped his time limit with the five minutes added. Conversely, in the case of an unjustified claim where the player exceeds his time limit with the additional five minutes, he loses the game.

The player who has called for a draw, claiming that the same position has appeared three times (with the same player having the move each time, the same pieces in the same position and the same possibilities for moving these pieces), cannot retract his claim during the verification. This is what emerges from the present FIDE provisions. The Soviet Chess code allows for the player to withdraw his claim provided that he plays his declared move; meanwhile his opponent has the right to consider the withdrawn claim as an offer of a draw.

The arbiter must verify in the presence of both players whether the same position has arisen three times at a board other than the one on which the game itself is being played. He must leave the position which has arisen in the game intact, and, with the help of another chess set and the scoresheets on which the players write down their moves, determine whether the same position has appeared three times, with the same player having the move and the same possibilities for moving the pieces. Sometimes the arbiter may use two boards to verify the claim, one for setting up the position claimed by the player to have appeared three times, and the other for executing the moves written down on the scoresheet.

It is important to point out the stipulation of Article 13.2.: the player does not have the right to claim a draw unless he has accurately recorded each move. At the chess Olympiad in 1952, Reshevsky, who was extremely pressed for time, stopped writing down the moves, as did his opponent Stahlberg. When his time-trouble had passed, Reshevsky claimed that the same position had been repeated three times. The arbiter, who also used the scoresheets of the demonstrators, turned down Reshevsky's claim. The continuation was rescheduled three times, and three times Reshevsky refused to come. 'The position has now, indeed, repeated itself three times', said some jokingly.

The Laws' new stipulations are now rigorous and do not allow any claim of a draw based on moves which are not written down.

The interpretation of Art. 18.2. describes what happens if an arbiter makes a mistake in verifying a claim. It transpires that both players should be extremely careful and should immediately ask for a new verification if they think they are in the right. A particularly dangerous mistake is to admit that the same position appeared three times, without this being true. The other side should insist on correcting the mistake immediately.

Note to Art. 12.4.:
The first paragraph of this article poses no difficulty for the arbiter. What is important is that fifty consecutive moves by Black and by White have been played. If, for instance, the last capture of a piece or moving of a pawn was on the 40th move by White, then a draw will be declared after the 90th move by White, provided that no piece has been captured or pawn moved in the interim (of either White or Black).

The second paragraph of this article, however, is the greatest mystery in the present FIDE Laws. Fortunately, such cases are rare, so that their consequences are not often felt. This paragraph does not specify which positions can be considered as exceptions, to what number these moves may be increased for these positions, nor what it means that these positions must be clearly established 'before the commencement of the game'. Does this mean that such exceptions should be listed in the Regulations of the tournament, or during the game when such a position appears? All this is unclear. It is no wonder that French master André Chéron writes that this is a rule 'which is not a rule'. Chéron lists four types of exceptional positions which require more than 50 moves for a win, but a win is feasible. They apply to endings: 1. a rook against a bishop (the weaker side has his king in the corner); 2. two knights against a pawn; 3. some positions in which one side has rook and pawn, and the other bishop and pawn (for instance, White has the rook and pawn on a2, and Black has the black square bishop and pawn on a3); and 4. various kinds of studies and problems. In all the cases listed by Chéron a win is possible, but it requires over 50 moves without capturing pieces and moving pawns. Chéron says, however, that it took him several months to study some of the positions, such as a position with rook against bishop, and 'what will the poor arbiter of a competition do when during a game a player asks that a certain position be considered as an exception?'

Some of the Laws' interpretations stipulate that a position may be considered as an exception provided that the given case is already 'known to literature'. This, however, is not enough. Let us say that we have Chéron's example for the ending, with the rook against the bishop and the king of the weaker side in the corner, only instead of the bishop occupying c4, it occupies d3. How can the arbiter, even if he is a grandmaster, establish during a short period of time whether there is a theoretical win here?

Chéron suggests that this incomplete FIDE rule be reformed and proposes that the number of moves be raised for all types of positions where there is even a single exception (so that the number of moves for all endings of rook against bishop, would be raised, regardless). FIDE, however, has yet to adopt this. The Soviet Chess Federation has excluded from its code the provision for the possibility of increasing the number of 50 moves for exceptional positions. Before the commencement of the Final Candidates' Match in Belgrade between Victor Korchnoi and Boris Spassky in 1977, the arbiter called a meeting of both players' seconds, which was attended by the president of FIDE and other officials. The purpose of that meeting was to regulate, through a supplementary protocol, all the technical details and ambiguities in the Regulations and Laws. There was also a discussion on paragraph two of Article 12.4, and the following was unanimously concluded: 'Since neither side has asked for any exceptions for any position, it has been agreed to declare all games a draw in which fifty consecutive moves have been made without capturing pieces or moving any pawns.'

There have been instances when players have asked for the number of moves to be increased to over the figure stipulated in this article. It is not known, however, that arbiters have been willing to accept this. In the game between Kostić and Rabar at the Yugoslav Championship in 1945, for example, the ending that arose was two knights against a pawn, and the same ending reappeared in the Bobotsov–Bogatirchuk game at the 1954 Olympiad, but the arbiters' commission rejected the request to raise the number of moves to 60. Soviet sources mention a drastic case of a game in which 48 moves were made without capturing any pieces or moving any pawn, only for the stronger side to declare mate in three moves. The arbiter was mistaken in allowing a mate on the 51st move.

FIDE will probably have to study this provision of 50 moves more thoroughly, and at present one must agree with Chéron that this is a 'rule which is not a rule'.

In conclusion it should be pointed out that many national federations have adopted the rule that draws be declared for positions where theoretically there is no possible win for either side. According to the FIDE interpretation, however, such positions are not considered a draw, which means that a win is possible even in a position which leaves only one king against the other (because the time limit may be overstepped). It is questionable whether in such a position the time factor is any longer of importance. Nonetheless, we must abide by the official FIDE interpretation as long as it is in effect.

It was suggested to the Rules Commission that under Art. 12.4 a game be declared a draw if it is theoretically impossible to give mate. The Commission has given some reasons against this: 'The Commission saw justification in the suggestion, but refrained from a definitive decision at this time on two grounds.

First, it is not entirely true to say that when such a point in the game is reached, the fact of time is no longer of consequence, as the player who has managed his time better earlier in the game should not be deprived of that advantage later in the game. Second, although a few cases of theoretically impossible mate (e.g. lone king vs. lone king) can be simply defined, there are many positions which would be very complicated to define (e.g., blocked pawn structures). The Commission hesitates to embark upon a new Law which would, almost of necessity, be incomplete'. (FIDE Congress, 1977.)

The Laws rightly do not mention 'perpetual check' as a possible form of a draw. The arbiter does not have the right to declare such cases a draw, because the player may refrain from checking, he may make a mistake, etc. But 'perpetual check' does inevitably lead to a draw, either by repeating the positions or by ultimately boring the players themselves.

A 'grandmaster draw' is a synonym in chess argot for a draw reached after only a few moves when the real fight should be about to begin. Art. 18 of the Laws speaks about these 'premature draws'.

PART II. SUPPLEMENTARY LAWS FOR COMPETITIONS

Article 13. The Recording of Games

13.1. In the course of play each player is required to record the game (his own moves and those of his opponent), move after move, as clearly and legibly as possible, on the scoresheet prescribed for the competition.

13.2. If, extremely pressed for time, a player is obviously unable to meet the requirements of Article 13.1, he should nevertheless endeavour to indicate on his scoresheet the number of moves made. As soon as his time-trouble is over, he must immediately complete his record of the game by filling in the moves omitted from his scoresheet. However, he will not have the right to claim, on the ground of Articles 12.3 or 12.4, a draw based on any moves which were not written down in accordance with the prescriptions of Article 13.1.

FIDE INTERPRETATION ART. 13.1 (1970). Question: A player, referring to the Laws of Chess, asked his opponent to make his move first and only then to write it down on his scoresheet. It is thought not to be correct to write down the move first and only then to make it on the board. The arbiter of the tournament in question judged the case to be insignificant.

Answer: The Commission is of the opinion that every player who has the move has the choice.

FIDE INTERPRETATION ART. 13.1 (1973). In a tournament game, a player who was not short of time (his opponent was, though) recorded his moves two at a time (one move for White, one move for Black), as was his habit. Several players have the same habit. The arbiter told him that he should record his moves one after another. The player considered this to be an unnecessary disturbance and an indirect help for his opponent, who was in time-trouble.

The question is: is it a breach of Article 13.1 of the Laws of Chess if the moves are not recorded separately, but in pairs (White and Black together), if the player concerned is not in time-trouble?

Answer: Technically speaking, this is indeed a breach of Article 13.1. However, the arbiter should intervene only when the arrears in scorekeeping are more than one move for White and one move for Black.

FIDE INTERPRETATION ART. 13.2 (1958). Question: How should the words 'extremely pressed for time' be interpreted?

Answer: the Commission, referring back to what has been stated in the General Observations (FIDE Interpretation Art. 1 [1958]), is of the opinion that in each particular case the interpretation should devolve on the arbiter of the competition.

FIDE INTERPRETATION ART. 13.2 (1959). The words 'extremely pressed for time' figuring in Article 13.2 cannot be precisely defined. It is the arbiter's task to find out, considering time, the number of moves, and the character of the position at the moment, if these words apply to a player's situation. In this case the arbiter's opinion decides.

If the arbiter thinks the above words do not apply, but if the player refuses to record the game according to Article 13.1, then Article 17.4 should be applied.

If the player does not refuse to comply with the arbiter's request, but declares that he cannot complete his scoresheet without consulting his opponent's, the request for this scoresheet must be made to the arbiter, who will determine whether the scoresheet can be completed before the time-control without inconveniencing the other player. The latter cannot refuse his scoresheet for two reasons: the scoresheet belongs to the organizers of the tournament and the reconstitution of the game will be made on his opponent's time. In all other cases the scoresheets can be completed only after the time-control. At this point two situations may prevail –

(a) if one player alone has not completed his scoresheet, he will do so on his own time; or

(b) if the two players have not completed their scoresheets, their clocks will be stopped until the two scoresheets are completed, if necessary with the help of a chessboard under the control of the arbiter, who will beforehand have noted the position.

If in case (a) the arbiter sees that the complete scoresheet cannot help in reconstituting the game, he will act as in case (b).

FIDE INTERPRETATION ART. 13.2 (1967). During the course of a game the two players, under extreme time-pressure, did not write down their moves after move 30. After a series of moves they agreed that they had played at least 40 moves. Being unable to reconstruct the course of the game without the help of a chessboard, they asked permission of the arbiter to reconstruct the game. The arbiter gave permission, and the reconstruction started. The arbiter stopped the clocks, but during the course of the reconstruction the clock of the player with the black pieces was started by the player with the white pieces because the player with the black pieces had started to reflect on the game. At the beginning of the reconstruction the player with the black pieces disposed of one minute and a half for reflection. During the reconstruction this player exceeded the time-limit, and it was discovered that he had made only 39 moves.

The Commission's opinion, as no other details are available, is that the player with the white pieces won the game. (See also FIDE Interpretation Art. 13.2 [1974A]).

FIDE INTERPRETATION ART. 13.2 (1972). Question: Concerning Article 13.2 of the Laws about keeping score, is a player in time-trouble obliged to stop his clock with the same hand with which he keeps score?

Answer: The Laws of Chess make no such requirement, whether or not the player is in time-trouble, nor is there any law that requires a player to stop his clock with the hand he uses to make moves on the board.

FIDE INTERPRETATION ART. 13.2 (1974). If an arbiter stops the clocks for reasons mentioned in FIDE Interpretation Art. 13.2 (1967), then only the arbiter decides when the clocks should be put in motion again.

Note to Art. 13.1.:
This provision requiring the players to record their moves is the cause of frequent dispute, since it does not specify the sanctions to be taken against the player who does not abide by this obligation. The Laws explicitly note one sanction – that the player cannot ask the game to be declared a draw on the grounds of Art. 12.3. or 12.4. Upon completion of the game, the players must turn over to the arbiter their scoresheets with all the moves in the game written down. The defeated player is usually loath to write in the moves he omitted while under time-pressure, because he knows he has already lost the point one way or another, and it is hard to see how the arbiter can penalize him. Nevertheless, the winner can be expected to hand in a properly filled in scoresheet, and the same can be expected of players when a point is divided. Otherwise, the arbiter can refuse to acknowledge the result.

This article says nothing about situations in which the player, because of a physical handicap, is unable to write down the moves or even press the clock. Such cases do exist, and usually, when they arise, the arbiter allows the player to have a representative who will do all this in his stead. So as not to have a situation in which only one side has such assistance, the other player is usually also allowed the same privilege, or it is agreed for one person to write down the moves for them both. Prior to the Final Candidates' Match in Belgrade in 1977, Korchnoi had a car accident in which he injured his right hand. He could not use it either to press the clock or to write down the moves. Spassky agreed to have the clock placed on Korchnoi's left-hand side, and it was also agreed that instead of writing down the moves, Korchnoi could merely mark the number of moves made with his left hand. They further agreed to give Korchnoi the right to claim a draw if the same position repeated itself three times, even though the moves would not be written down on his scoresheet (Art. 13.2). The organizers appointed a person to chalk the moves on a board. This agreement was made, but later things reverted to normal when the match was postponed for five days at the advice of the doctor, by which time Korchnoi was able to write down the moves normally.

Of course, with the exception of such cases in which the player is not able to write down the moves, no help whatsoever is allowed the player and he must write down the moves himself.

According to the Laws, it is irrelevant whether the player first makes his move and then writes it down on the scoresheet or vice-versa. There have been situations, however, such as at a ladies' tournament, where the player wrote down the move on the scoresheet and then waited for the coach's reaction. Naturally, the arbiter must not permit this.

Note to Art. 13.2.:
The term 'extremely pressed for time' is not elaborated, and it is left to the arbiter to decide when he can temporarily allow a player not to write down the moves. This depends on the time the player has left, on the number of remaining moves and the position. In principle, the player may be granted this benefit if only five minutes are left until the time-control. Often, both players are pressed for time and then the arbiter must first take into consideration the clock situation and only then the possibility of himself recording the moves made. This, however, is not his duty. In his book *The Funny and the Serious*, Grandmaster Kotov describes an arbiter who started writing down the moves when the players were greatly pressed for time, and yelled: 'Slow down, I can't keep up with you'. The arbiter does not have to accept such amusing roles, but it is his right to use these notes in order to establish the actual situation.

While FIDE's 1976 interpretation gives the arbiter the discretionary right to intervene should he feel that the players have played the necessary number of moves, it is far better for the arbiter to refrain from getting involved in the time-pressure, and instead to wait for one of the player's flag to fall. When one of the player's flag falls, he must prove that he has played the prescribed number of moves and must write them down on the scoresheet. The opponent's scoresheet and a reconstruction of the game on another board, as well as help from the arbiter, may be used to fill in the missing moves.

If both players have incomplete scoreshsets, then, with the assistance of the arbiter, an attempt is made to determine the actual situation. If it is impossible to establish that the prescribed number of moves has been made, then, as a rule, the game is lost by the player whose flag has fallen, for the burden of proof that he has executed the prescribed number of moves basically rests on him.

Neither the arbiter nor anyone else may warn a player that he has played the prescribed number of moves, nor may they interrupt the game before one of the player's flag falls. The arbiter, then, does not intervene, until one of the player's flag drops. It would be a mistake for the arbiter to stop the clock when there is a case of time-pressure, in order to allow the players to fill in their scoresheets or resolve any differences in the number of moves.

The arbiter should not give any sign confirming that the time-trouble is over. Some arbiters like to stand by the players for the duration of the time-trouble, and immediately leave once the prescribed number of moves has been made. He should try to be inconspicuous (to stand off to the side) and to go inconspicuously to other boards. At the Moscow tournament in 1935, Grandmaster Flohr asked the arbiter during his game with Capablanca how many moves he had made. The arbiter knew that he should not give out such information, but he made a mistake and gestured towards the demonstration board. Such information is not always reliable and the arbiter should not offer even such assistance.

Article 14. The Use of the Chess Clock

14.1. Each player must make a certain number of moves in a given period of time, these two factors being specified in advance.

14.2. Control of each player's time is effected by means of a clock equipped with a special apparatus (flag) for this purpose.

14.3. At the time determined for the start of the game, the clock of the player who has the white pieces is set in motion. In the continuance of the game, each of the players, having made his move, stops his own clock and starts his opponent's clock.

14.4. When determining whether the prescribed number of moves has been made in the given time, the last move is not considered as completed until after the player has stopped his clock.

14.5. Every indication given by a clock or its apparatus is considered as conclusive in the absence of evident defects. The player who wishes to claim any such defect must do so as soon as he himself has become aware of it.

14.6. If the game has to be interrupted for some reason for which neither player is responsible, both clocks shall be stopped until the matter has been adjusted. This should be done, for example, in the case of an illegal position to be corrected, in the case of a defective clock to be exchanged, or if the piece which a player has declared he wishes to exchange for one of his pawns that has reached the last rank is not immediately available.

14.7. In the case of Articles 9.1 and 9.2, when it is not possible to determine the time used by each player up to the moment when the irregularity occurred, each player shall be allotted up to that moment a time proportional to that indicated by the clocks when the irregularity was ascertained. For example, after Black's 30th move it is found that an irregularity took place at the 20th move. For these thirty moves the clocks show 90 minutes for White and 60 minutes for Black, so it is assumed that the times used by the two players for the first twenty moves were as follows:

$$\text{White} \quad \frac{90 \times 20}{30} = 60 \text{ minutes}$$

$$\text{Black} \quad \frac{60 \times 20}{30} = 40 \text{ minutes}$$

FIDE INTERPRETATION ART. 14.3 (1958). Question: How should this Article be interpreted in a case where the player with the black pieces is absent as well as his opponent?

Answer: The Commission considers that Article 14.3 should be applied in all its rigor.

FIDE INTERPRETATION ART. 14.3 (1967). Question: Is an arbiter entitled to call a player's attention to the player's neglect to stop his clock and/or to the fact that the opponent has made a move and put the clock of the player in motion?

Answer: The opinion of the Commission is that an arbiter should refrain from any action of this kind.

FIDE INTERPRETATION ART. 14.3 (1973). FIDE Interpretation Art. 14.3 (1967) is based on the conviction, which the Commission maintains, that the normal handling of the clock should be done solely by the players. If a player forgets to stop his clock when he has made a move, that is his responsibility. The arbiter's function is not to correct the faults or omissions of the players in this respect. Furthermore, a correcting action of the arbiter should not depend on whether he notices these mistakes.

FIDE INTERPRETATION ART. 14.4 (1974). The flag is considered to have fallen when the arbiter observes the fact. In cases where no arbiter is present, the flag is considered to have fallen when a claim has been made to that effect by a player.

FIDE INTERPRETATION ART. 14.4 (1976). In formal competitions, Article 14.4 provides that a move is not considered as completed until after the player has stopped his clock, in accordance with Article 7 (this general principle applies whether there is at the board a witness to these actions or not).

In other words, the player's flag must remain unfallen after the opponent's clock has been started. (Exception: Rarely a player's own flag will fall while his opponent's clock is running. This circumstance, if it can be clearly proven, implies an evident defect of the flag.) Only if it can be clearly proven that a checkmate or stalemate had been completed on the board or that a claim of a draw by repetition had been made under Article 12.3, is it of no importance whether or not the player was able to stop his clock before his flag had fallen.

FIDE INTERPRETATION ART. 14.4 (1979). Question: A player resigned.

Later he noticed that his opponents flag had already fallen. The arbiter decided that the player had actually won by forfeit. The commission is asked to determine whether over-stepping the time limit is equal to checkmate in ending the game.

Answer: The commission ruled that resignation or agreement to draw remains valid even when it is found later that the flag had fallen.

FIDE INTERPRETATION ART. 14.4 (1979). *Question: After sealing his move and stopping his clock, a player noticed that his opponent's flag had fallen. The Arbiter ruled that the claim was too late, and the game should be continued.*

Answer: The Arbiter's decision was correct.

FIDE INTERPRETATION ART. 14.5 (1958). *Having been asked for more exact definitions as to what constitutes evident defects of a clock, the Commission replies by referring back to the general principles clearly outlined in the General Observations (FIDE Interpretation Art. 1 [1958]).*

FIDE INTERPRETATION ART. 14.5 (1971). *With regard to Articles 14.5 and 14.6, the arbiter should endeavour to check all clocks periodically to make sure that they are operating properly.*

A clock with an obvious defect should be replaced, and the time used by each player up to the moment when the game was interrupted should be indicated on the new clock as accurately as possible.

If one unit of the defective clock has stopped, the corresponding unit of the new clock should be advanced so that the total time indicated by the two units is equal to the time the session of the competition had been in progress.

If both units have stopped, the difference between the total of the times registered by the defective clock and the elapsed time of the session should be divided in half and each unit of the new clock advanced by this amount.

If any of the above clock adjustments would result in an indication that a player had exceeded the time limit, or if the time used by each player cannot be accurately determined, the arbiter may set the hands of the new clock in accordance with his best judgment.

FIDE INTERPRETATION ART. 14.5 (1973). *The last paragraph of FIDE Interpretation Art. 14.5 (1971) clearly indicates that the correction of the hands of the clock(s) should not lead to disastrous results for one (or both) of the players. For that very reason, the last paragraph of the Interpretation gives the arbiter the option to use his own judgment.*

FIDE INTERPRETATION ART. 14.5 (1974). *The Commission is of the opinion that with regard to FIDE Interpretation Art. 14.5 (1973) the players involved should never have the right to deal with the situation of a defective clock. This task belongs exclusively to the arbiter.*

FIDE INTERPRETATION ART. 14.6 (1972). *Question: With regard to Article 14.6, is the sudden illness of a player during the course of a game or the sudden decease of a close relative covered by this Article?*

Answer: With regard to Article 14.6, if the sudden illness during the course of a game is deemed to be of a short duration, then the answer is yes, but if it is not regarded as likely to be brief, the answer is no. In this case and also in the case of the sudden decease of a close relative, the matter must be left to the discretion of the arbiter.

FIDE INTERPRETATION ART. 14.7 (1975). *Question: In a game as part of a team match, both players were short of time as the time-control ap-*

proached. Both made their moves in time, and the game was then adjourned to allow both clubs to decide what claim to submit to the adjudicator; the rules of the competition stipulated that after the first full session of play, the game should be sent for adjudication rather than continued.

Before either team had submitted an adjudication claim, but two or three days after the match, one player discovered that his opponent had made an illegal 33rd move, the game having been adjourned at the 40th move. Examination of both players' scoresheets confirmed that the move had been illegal.

The arbiter of the competition ruled that since neither club had submitted a claim to the adjudicator at the stage when the illegality had been discovered, the game could not be regarded as completed. He decided, however, that since the game could not be continued without a major distortion of the time situation, the player who had made the illegal move should lose the game. The club concerned appealed against this decision. The appeals committee overruled the earlier decision and ordered the game continued from the stage where the illegality occurred. They further ruled (a) that the player who had made the illegal move should move the piece which he had touched to make the illegal move and (b) that to offset the distraction produced by the resumption of the game, the player who had made the illegal move should be allocated only 5 minutes on his clock, while his opponent should be allocated 24 minutes, in accordance with Article 14.7.

Would the Commission care to comment on the issue raised by this case?

Answer: The decision of the arbiter of the competition (loss of the game for the player who made the illegal move) was wrong. The decision of the appeals committee (to give the right portion of time to the player who did not make the illegal move and to give considerably less time to the player who made the illegal move) was wrong. The formula of Article 14.7 should have been applied to both players, not to just one of them. There is no indication whatsoever that the formula of Article 14.7 may be ignored; neither is there any indication in the Laws themselves nor is there any Interpretation to this effect in existence. Leaving alone the reasons of the appeals committee for its decision, it should be remarked that the faulty decision made might easily be seen and felt as a kind of punishment, which should be avoided at all cost.

Note to Art. 14.4.:
The number of moves which have to be made during a given period of time is determined in advance by the rules of the competition. If a player has begun a game without being acquainted with the rules, he may not use this as an excuse. It is his responsibility to study the rules of the competition prior to the game.

The amount of time allotted for a given number of moves, or 'rate of play', normally depends on the importance of the given competition. Top-ranking international competitions today usually adopt two-and-a-half hours for the first 40 moves per player, whic means that the entire session lasts five hours. If the game is not completed at the end of the first 40 moves, then it is continued at a rate of 16 moves per hour. The first time-control is after the first five hours of overall play (at the 40th move), after which time and the number of executed moves are controlled at the end of every two hours of overall play (at the 56th, 72nd move, etc.). This rate is applied in virtually all FIDE competitions.

Competitions at various levels, however are played at different rates, with 18, 20 or 24 moves per hour. There are also competitions with a rapid rate of play of 30 moves per hour or even '60 moves in 60 minutes'. According to the Rules for awarding international titles, FIDE takes into consideration only tournaments whose rate is not more than 45 moves in two hours. The usual rate for many local and team competitions is 40 moves in the first two hours and sometimes still more.

Note to Art. 14.2.:

FIDE gives only a general outline of the standard of chess clocks. Unfortunately, there are various kinds of clocks, with different characteristics, different 'flags', mounted in different places, as well as in different sizes, etc. While technology has greatly advanced since that London tournament in 1883, when the double chess clock was used for the first time, chess clocks have not undergone any major improvement. It is only of late that there have been attempts to design electronic clocks and make improvements on classical clocks.

The drawback of many of today's clocks is that the flags are too small and are difficult to see, so that the arbiter must be nearby in order to see them fall. Apart from flags, many clocks also have built-in hands to show that the clock is working. But confusion arises when these devices resemble the flags in colour and shape. Many of today's clocks are miniature in size and are therefore difficult to read, and they are often boxed in shining aluminium or similar casings, which is unpleasant for players and arbiter alike. The flag on some chess clocks starts to rise five minutes before it falls (before the minute hand reaches the number 12), while other flags begin to rise three minutes earlier, and others still one minute before the flag falls. There is no question that the latter version is the worst and that there should be a minimum of three minutes, and that the standard should perhaps be five minutes.

Recently, clocks have been manufactured with a special dial for the last five minutes or even for the last seconds. This mechanism is automatically turned on in the last minutes of play.

The precision of chess clocks is a special concern and the arbiter should check it prior to the beginning of and during the competition itself. The arbiter should run the clocks for several days before the commencement of the competition, and check each clock (on both the left and right sides) against a precise wall clock. During the game the arbiter should check each clock after each hour of play.

Note to Art. 14.3.:

At the time determined for the start of the game the clock of the player who has the white pieces is set in motion. This is usually done by the arbiter or his deputies. At large competitions (olympiads, team competitions, festivals, etc.), at the sound of the gong designating the commencement of competition, the player who has the black pieces sets the clock in motion, and if he is absent, then this is done by one of the organizers. Of course, this may also be done by the player who is white, after making his first move. In some countries (the United States, for instance), the custom is for White, if his opponent is absent, to start his opponent's clock, but to make his move only when the latter arrives. This, however, is not sanctioned by FIDE regulations, nor can it be seen at international competitions.

The Laws do not regulate many of the 'technical' details in handling chess clocks, which is understandable. Nonetheless, arbiters should be acquainted with standard practice. In the United States, for example, the chess clock is placed to the right of the players with the black pieces (probably so as to give him some sort of 'compensation' for the fact that his opponent has the advantage of the first move). This also applies to lightning chess competitions virtually everywhere. Conversely, in the Soviet Union, the clock is placed facing the arbiters, with its back to the audience, hence to the right of the player with the white pieces.

One can easily see from photographs of various matches that practice in placing the clock varies. Both versions have their good and their bad sides. In one case, it is not entirely desirable for White to have the first move and also (if right-handed) to have the clock 'by his hand'. On the other hand, if the clock is placed to the right of the player with the black pieces, then the names of the players on the demonstration board would not necessarily be in keeping with their position at the table. However, the first principle in positioning the clock should be that it must always be easily visible to the arbiter. Everything else should be subordinated to this one consideration. Then the arrangement of names on the demonstration board may be adjusted to the situation at the table. Since the procedure in lightning chess competitions is to have the clock to the right of the player with the black pieces, perhaps this should also be adopted for tournaments and matches.

Finally, let us bring up one more practical question concerning clocks. The clock should be set so that the minute hand crosses the figure 12 at the time-control, so that the fall of the flag shows when the time limit expires. The custom at competitions is to set the hands at 3:30, which means that time-control will be precisely at 6:00. Then one has an extremely good picture of the time, as the hands do not 'interfere' with each other, as would be the case if the clock were set at 9:30. If the time-control occurs at the end of two hours (i.e. after four hours of overall play), then accordingly it is best to set the clock at 4:00., etc.

Article 7 of the Laws stipulates when a move is considered to be completed. It is only then that the player has the right to stop his clock and put his opponent's clock in motion.

Note to Art. 14.4.:

The last move of the time-control is considered to be completed when it has been executed according to Article 7 of the Laws and when the opponent's clock has been put into motion. If the player has made a move before the flag has fallen, but when stopping his own clock (or even forgetting to press it) the flag falls, he is considered to have overstepped the time limit and loses the game, except when he has given a mate with this move (and thus wins the game) or has created a stalemate position (and the game is declared a draw).

Diagram 1 (below) shows a famous position (from the game Levitzky-Marshall, 1912). Black has played 23 . . . Qc3–g3!! (and White resigned). Let us suppose in this position Black is in time trouble and the game continued: 24.h2xg3 and Black has answered with 24 . . . Ne2 and at that moment the flag on his clock fell. Black still wins the game, because 24 . . . Ne2 was a mating move. One other hypothesis: White plays 24.Qxg3, after which Black again played 24 . . . Ne2 and his flag fell. He loses the game, because his 24 . . . Ne2 was in this case not a mating move.

Diagram 2 (below) is an example of stalemate (a composition of Platov).

Diagram 1   **Diagram 2**

After 1.Rg3, fxg3 2. Kg1, Qb8 (or any move) and the game is drawn even if one of the players has now overstepped the time limit.

The fall of the flag incurs no consequence if a draw has been claimed according to Art. 12.3., and it is established that the claim was correct and a draw is declared. If it is established that the claim was incorrect (the same position did not appear three times), then the player whose flag fell loses the game.

The fall of the flag means the end of the game if the player has overstepped the time limit. This, however, should be observed by the arbiter or by the player himself. Mate or stalemate can always be established by reconstructing the game. The fall of the flag, however, can no longer be verified, if the player or arbiter does not notice it on time. Sometimes, the flag falls and no one notices it or does so only after several moves. Consequently, FIDE's interpretation says that the flag is considered to have fallen when the player has made a claim to this effect or the arbiter observes the fact.This is of importance in some cases, and the fall of the flag cannot be equated with situations in which a mate or stalemate position arises, which automatically means the end of the game, for with the fall of the flag there is the additional condition that it be observed.

At an international tournament (Vrsac, 1977), grandmaster M.'s flag fell on the 40th move. The arbiter saw the flag drop and point it out. Player Q., his opponent, suggested that they verify the number of moves they had made – one had 40 moves written down and the other 41. The players agreed that 41 moves had actually been made and decided to continue the game. The arbiter accepted their verification. Player Q. was to seal his move. He pondered for quite some time and finally suggested that the point be divided. M. accepted the proposal.

One hour later, the editor of the bulletin observed that, in actual fact, only 40 moves had been made. Q. lodged a complaint with the tournament committee, noting that exceeding the time limit is equivalent to mate, i.e. it means the end of the game. The complaint was rejected. The reasons? Time-forfeit is not the same as mate and stalemate, but rather is the right to make a claim which must be verified by the players or by the arbiter. Both players had agreed that everything had been as it should be and had agreed to a draw. This was the end of the game.

At a tournament in Lublin, grandmaster T. resigned a game. The spectators drew his attention to the fact that his opponent's flag had dropped, and a dispute ensued. Which was to prevail: the resigning of the game or the fact that the flag had fallen several seconds earlier, but had not been either claimed or observed by the players? The mere fact that the flag had fallen does not automatically mean the end of the game. This should be verified by the arbiter and the loss of the game registered. In this case the game had been resigned regardless of the fall of the flag, and this is what stands as valid, since it was only subsequently that the fall of the flag was noticed. This is the meaning behind FIDE's 1974 interpretation to Art. 14.4 that the flag is considered to have dropped when the arbiter so establishes.

Note to Art. 14.5.:
The principle that the fall of the flag is conclusive evidence of the exceeding of the time-limit is generally accepted. The only difference is in interpreting the term 'evident defects'. It is left up to the arbiters to use their best judgement in interpreting this phrase, but even in such exceptional cases, some logical principles can be followed.

To illustrate an 'evident defect' let us mention the 13th game of the 1966 Spassky–Petrosian match. As Spassky was contemplating his move, Petrosian's clock suddenly started to run. No one noticed this until Petrosian's flag fell, although it was not his turn to make a move nor should his clock have been running. Naturally, the arbiter accepted this as an evident defect and turned Petrosian's clock back to the position it should have been at by calculating how much time remained until the end of the game, how much time Spassky had left, and allowing the rest to Petrosian.

The first case of 'evident defects', then, would be when the player 'oversteps' the time-limit because both clocks are working at the same time. The second case is when the minute-hand bypasses the flag, so that it does not fall, although it is clear that the minute-hand has crossed the figure 12. Here, the player has overstepped the time limit and loses the game. A third instance is when the minute-hand lifts the flag, but the flag does not fall and remains stuck in a horizontal position, although the minute-hand has clearly crossed the figure 12. Here again, it is clear that the player overstepped the time limit. And finally, yet another possible mistake is when the hands on the clock have been incorrectly set, so that the clock reads 4:30 instead of 3:30, etc.

Many players complain that the flag fell prematurely. The arbiter can hardly allow himself to judge whether the flag did indeed fall a few seconds or even half a minute ahead of time; he should abide by the principle that the fall of the flag is conclusive. The player does have the possibility of discovering any defect prior to the time-control, for the functioning of the clock can be seen when the minute-hand crosses the figure 12 for the first time.

In addition to disputes over the correct functioning of the flag, there are also frequent disputes over the correct functioning of the clock. This may include several possible situations, some of which can be corrected, while others cannot.

a) *Both clocks running at the same time.* The arbiter will determine for how long both clocks have been running at the same time. This is the difference between the sum total of expended time shown on the defective clocks of both players, and the time which has elapsed since the commencement of play. For example, the sum total of both players' time reads 3 hours and 20 minutes on the defective clock while 3 hours and 10 minutes have elapsed since the beginning of play. In other words, both clocks ran simultaneously for ten minutes. Here the arbiter will replace the defective clock and will give five more minutes on the clock to each player.

b) *One clock is constantly running and the other is correct.* As in the first case, the arbiter will first establish the surplus of time shown on the defective clock, then will replace that clock with another one on which he will set the actual expended time of the player with the defective clock. The time of the other player remains the same, as his clock was in good working order.

c) *Both clocks (or one) run fast.* The arbiter can establish the surplus of time shown on the clocks in the same way. The surplus for both players will be subtracted from the defective clocks' display of time expended, so that both players will be given this 'benefit' equally if both clocks are running fast. However, it is far more difficult for the arbiter to establish that one clock was fast while the other worked normally, which is why these cases are usually resolved by reducing the 'unjustified surplus' equally for both after replacing the defective clocks with working ones.

d) *Both clocks run slow.* Here, again, it is difficult to establish which clock ran slower. If both players agree, then the established time difference is added equally to both and the new time is set on a new clock. This, however, should not be allowed to bring one of the players into a hopeless situation or to make one of them overstep the time limit. If agreement is not reached, the arbiter will do best to reset the new clock according to the time indicated on the defective clock. The arbiter will proceed in the same manner if both clocks stopped working for a time.

e) *The clock of one player does not work.* According to the FIDE interpretation of 1971, that player receives the difference between the time which has elapsed since the beginning of the session and the total time shown on both clocks.

f) *Both clocks do not work.* This, too, is a situation envisaged by the aforementioned FIDE interpretation. The difference should be divided by the two players and their new clocks advanced accordingly (the difference is calculated in the same way as in the preceding example).

Here again, it should be stressed that according to FIDE's interpretation for e) and f), the arbiter is given the freedom to use his best judgement in determining the time of the players and should ensure that these corrections do not lead to disastrous results for either player. A defective clock is something beyond the control of the players and they are not to be blamed for such defects; consequently, understanding and flexibility should be shown in settling such cases.

One should add that there are cases (such as when several adjourned games resume one after the other) in which it is difficult to follow the guidelines. That is why, here again, the arbiter is given the freedom to decide the issue.

Note to Art. 14.6.:

The Laws provide for several situations in which the clock can be stopped: to find a new piece to replace a promoted pawn (Art. 6.6.c.), to complete both scoresheets according to Art. 13.2, to correct illegal positions, to replace a defective clock, to establish whether the time limit has been overstepped after the fall of the flag. Of course, there are exceptional situations (when the lights go out in the hall, sudden and unforeseen situations which prevent play, etc.) in which the arbiter may stop the clocks. In principle, the arbiter has the right to stop the clock when he deems that this is essential in order to correct some irregularity. It should be stressed, however, that it is the arbiter and not the players who has the right to stop the clock. The players may do so only upon approval from the arbiter (for instance, when the light goes out in the hall the arbiter may signal the players immediately to stop the clock, etc.). Otherwise, players may not stop the clock or make any corrections on it, nor may they pick it up and move it, etc. Some countries have extremely strict laws: stopping a clock is taken as a sign of resigning the game, and the player may stop the clock himself only after having sealed a move.

Note to Art. 14.7.:
In some situations, calculating the time according to this formula can lead to one player overstepping the time limit. In such situations, even if the player who would overstep the time limit is the player who is responsible for the irregularity, the arbiter should find a solution in which that player can have at least as many minutes as there are moves until the time-control.

Article 15. The Adjournment of the Game

15.1. If a game is not finished upon conclusion of the time prescribed for play, the player having the move must write his move in unambiguous notation on his scoresheet, put this scoresheet and that of his opponent in an envelope, seal the envelope, and then stop the clocks. If the player makes the said move on the chessboard, he must seal this same move on his scoresheet.

15.2. Upon the envelope shall be indicated –
   (a) the names of the players,
   (b) the position immediately before the sealed move,
   (c) the time used by each player, and
   (d) the name of the player who has sealed the move and the number of that move.

15.3. Custody of the envelope must be assured.

FIDE INTERPRETATION ART. 15.1 (1966). In adjourning a game, the player having the move made a note of the adjourning move, placed the paper in an envelope, sealed it, and put it on the table; however, the clocks were not stopped. When the arbiter took the envelope, the player asked him to return it, since he was still thinking over his move. The arbiter refused to do so, stating that in that phase of the game it was not possible to permit modification of an adjourning move.

The Commission declares that an adjourning move had not been definitely made and therefore the decision of the arbiter was not correct.

FIDE INTERPRETATION ART. 15.1 (1973). The Commission declares that it should be left to the discretion of the arbiter whether no game should be adjourned more than an hour before the end of the time fixed for adjourning.

FIDE INTERPRETATION ART. 15.1 (1978). Question: Article 15.1 of th Rules tells that a player who has the move must put his next move under envelope if the required number of moves is played on both sides and if the time prescribed for play is over. The following example which happened in an Open Tournament could perhaps need a new Interpretation.

The speed of play was 50 moves in $2\frac{1}{2}$ hours with end of play after five hours; the next control was at move 70 with the speed of play of 20 moves in 1 hour. At the end of the first playing session the situations were as follows: Player A, having the move: 63 moves played in 3 h 28 minutes; Player B: 63 moves played in 1 h 32 minutes. If arbiter had applied the FIDE Rules, A had had to put his move in the envelope with practically 99% chances to lose on time since he had still 7 moves to play in 2 minutes to reach the second time control. So, arbiter has asked this player to play and ordered his opponent to put the move in the envelope. What is opinion of the Rules Commission on this matter?

Answer: The Rules Commission decided that 'A' had to seal the move. As he was extremely short of time he could use his right to make his move on the board and let this move stand as the sealed move. The envelope would then be prepared and sealed.

FIDE INTERPRETATION ART.15 (1979). Question: What should be the duration of an adjourned game session?

Answer: The adjourned game session shall be controlled by the wall clock with the time to start and finish announced in advance. The chess clock can be used for control in exceptional cases when clearly stated by the regulations of a competition.

Note to Art. 15.1.:

When the number of moves prescribed for the given session has been made and when the time determined for play has expired, a game still in progress is adjourned. The arbiter announces the time for adjourning the game or sounds a gong. At that moment, the players who have the move will not make their move on the board, but instead will write it down secretly and place it in an envelope.

The arbiter, however, may give the sign that the time for play has expired (based on the wall clock), while some of the players' chess clocks show that the time for the session has not yet expired: it may happen that one of the chess clocks is slow and that the players still have another minute or so until the time-control. In such cases these games are extended until such time as these chess clocks (the sum total of the time expended by both players) show that the time for the given session has expired.

Apart from the gong, there are also other ways to show that the game is being adjourned. This is done by the arbiter who goes from table to table, gives each player an envelope and announces that the game is being adjourned. He will wait only if there is a game where the time on the chess clock has not yet run out nor the prescribed number of moves made.

The gong is usually used at large competitions, such as olympiads. The good side of this is that the games are adjourned simultaneously, but the bad side is that some games may not yet at that moment have reached the time-control. If the arbiter goes from table to table, however, he cannot reach all the games at once. Hence, it is ideal in major competitions for the arbiter to signal the adjournment, but for a controller to stand by each board and verify whether this applies to the given game.

When the signal for adjournment is given, the player must seal his move unless he is at that very moment in the act of executing a move. He cannot shift the obligation of sealing to his opponent. If, after the given sign, a player makes a move, it shall be considered as a sealed move.

A move may be sealed only after the player with the black pieces has made his last move prescribed for a given period of time. If, for example, the rate of play at a tournament is 40 moves in two hours, then both players must make 40 moves each in the first four hours of play, and only then can the 41st move of either Black or White be sealed. Under no conditions may the 40th move be sealed, for this move had already to be executed within the time prescribed for the first session.

A move is considered to be sealed only when the player who is to seal it (and no-one else) has stopped his clock. Until that actual moment, he may change the move he has written down, since his clock is still in motion.

If a player executes the move on the board, he must still write it down on the scoresheet (this is considered to be 'public sealing'). Here, it is best to call the arbiter who will note on the envelope that such and such a move has been sealed publically. If the players do not call the arbiter, a dispute may arise subsequently if a player made one move but wrote another down on his scoresheet. If there are no witnesses for the executed move, then the move written down on the scoresheet is the one considered to be valid.

Usually while one player is contemplating the move he will seal, his partner writes down the position and other particulars on the envelope.

As a rule, the player who is sealing a move should place both scoresheets in the envelope and seal it. The player often gives the envelope to the arbiter to seal, which is incorrect, but the sealing should in any case be done in the presence of both players or at least of the one who is sealing the move. It is customary, but not obligatory, for both players to sign their names on the envelope once it has been sealed.

It is the duty of the arbiter to verify all the particulars on the envelope and especially the time of the player who has sealed the move.

There have been cases at tournaments when players have not placed the scoresheet in the envelope. At the 1972 Olympiad in Skopje, grandmaster Tringov sealed a move, but on resumption it emerged that his scoresheet was not in the envelope, so that his opponent Korchnoi won the game automatically. At the Soviet Ladies' Championship in 1971, Marta Shul wrote down her sealed move, but instead of putting her scoresheet in the envelope, she absent-mindedly put it in her purse. Of course, on resumption the arbiter gave the point to her opponent.

In another game, the player sealed his move with the approval of the arbiter, since although the playing time had not yet expired, the scoresheets of both players had the prescribed number of moves written down for that session. Before the continuation of the game, however, it emerged that the set number of moves had not, in fact, been made, for the players had incorrectly written down an extra move: the sealed move should be made in the first session. The player who sealed the move had to lose the game, since he had not executed the prescribed number of moves in the first session. The arbiter cannot be expected to verify the number of executed moves in each game; this can be asked of him only in games where disagreement arises and where doubt exists as to the validity of the registered moves.

When the playing time expires, the arbiter should not permit the time to be extended 'for just a bit' at the request of a player. There are known cases in which a player went from a winning to a losing position and then questioned the regularity of the extension.

Sometimes a player asks the arbiter to verify that the sealed move has been properly written down. The arbiter should decline as this is not his responsibility, and, in any case, the sealed move should remain secret.

From the above we see that the basic conditions for adjourning a game are that the prescribed number of moves have been made publicly on the board, and that the time prescribed for play has expired. If, for instance, the rules of a competition prescribe 40 moves for the first five hours of play, then only after an executed 40 moves and five hours of overall play may the game be adjourned.

The game may be adjourned at the request of a player before the arbiter indicates that the playing time has expired only if the prescribed number of moves has already been made and if the player who wishes to seal a move takes on all the time left until the end of the given session. The additional time is calculated by adding the time expended up to this point by the two players, and then subtracting this total from the duration time of the session.

The arbiter must especially ensure that by taking on the remaining time, the player does not find himself in a situation where he loses the game because of overstepping the time limit; the arbiter should also caution the player if he will be facing time-pressure.

The arbiter must give his approval for a player to seal a move before the end of the session. The remaining time is always taken on by that player. No player can force his opponent to seal a move ahead of time.

To the question of whether a move can be sealed before the control move, in principle the answer is no. However, some objective disturbance may arise in play, for instance, there may be an extended period in which the lights go out. Here, the arbiter can decide to adjourn all games and to seal moves by candle-light, regardless of the number of moves made.

And there is yet another question: how should the length of individual sessions in a chess game be determined, by the wall clock or by the chess clocks? Let us presume that the first session is due to last five hours (it is played from 16:00 to 21:00), and the adjournment session six hours (from 16:00 to 22:00).

Here, too, there are different opinions and different methods used in various countries. There was even a difference between the Regulations for FIDE Candidates' Matches and an interpretation given by the Rules Commission (which was later withdrawn).

Let us illustrate this with an example from a match. After five hours of play, a player considered his sealed move for 45 minutes. The first session therefore lasted 5 hours and 45 minutes. According to the programme, the adjournment session was played from 16:00 to 22:00. After 5 hours and 15 minutes of play in the adjournment session (i.e. at 21:45), one of the players asked to seal a move, since the time prescribed for the first and second sessions had expired (i.e. the chess clock registered a total of 11 hours of play) and the given number of moves had been made (88). The question is whether the player had the right to seal a move at this point or whether play should have continued until 22:00 according to the wall clock). The arbiter judged that the player did have the right to seal his move, in keeping with the regulations of that competition. The regulations stipulated that the first session must last five hours, and the second six hours 'on the chess clocks'. On the basis of these explicit provisions of the regulations the player had the right to adjourn the game.

This method of calculating the time of playing sessions was also applied in the Final Candidates' Match between Spassky and Korchnoi in 1977. The Supplementary Protocol of the match stated that agreement on this had been reached by the two sides (with the participation of the arbiter, representatives of both players, the president of FIDE, etc.).

This, however, is an exception and not general practice, especially not at tournaments. The rule in the Soviet Union for example is that the length of the first session is determined according to the chess clock, while the length of the subsequent sessions is determined according to the wall clock. This seems justified, especially at tournaments. What can happen here, however, is that the players may execute the prescribed number of moves (let us say 88) and use up the prescribed time for thought (let us say 11 hours, the total time on both clocks), and then they must still continue to play. Thus, one of the players (at, say, 22:00 local time) may have to seal a move when he is pressed for time! It is for this reason that the participants in the match preferred the first alternative so as not to have a situation in which a player must seal a move under time-pressure. Such a solution, however, must be stipulated in advance.

It is to be expected that the Rules Commission will give an interpretation on this matter which will dovetail the diverse practice we witness today.
Note to Art. 15.2. and 15.3.:
The arbiter must carefully verify that all the particulars have been properly written on the envelope. Any oversight when sealing a move may be fatal for the further regularity of the game.

When recording the time, it is best to write down the time indicated on the face on the clock; it is not necessary to work out the time spent.

In big tournaments and matches, sealed moves are often kept in a safe, the key is held by the arbiter and its duplicate by his deputy. At the Petrosian-Korchnoi match in 1977, the envelope was first placed in small strongbox to which only the chief arbiter had the key, and then this was placed in the large hotel safe.

Article 16. The Resumption of the Adjourned Game

16.1. When the game is resumed, the position immediately before the sealed move shall be set up on the chessboard, and the time used by each player when the game was adjourned shall be indicated on the clocks.

16.2. The envelope shall be opened only when the player having the move (the player who must reply to the sealed move) is present. That player's clock shall be started after the sealed move has been made on the chessboard.

16.3. If the player having the move is absent, his clock shall be started, but the envelope shall be opened only at the time of his arrival.

16.4. If the player who has sealed the move is absent, the player having the move is not obliged to reply to the sealed move on the chessboard. He has the right to record his move in reply on his scoresheet, to put the scoresheet in an envelope, to stop his clock, and to start his opponent's clock. The envelope should then be put into safekeeping and opened on the opponent's arrival.

16.5. If the envelope containing the move recorded in accordance with Article 16.4 has disappeared, the game shall be resumed from the position at the time of adjournment and with the clock times recorded at the time of adjournment.

If the envelope containing the move sealed on adjournment has disappeared without it being possible to restablish the position and the times used for the adjourned game, or if for any other reason the said position and the said times cannot be reestablsihed, the game is annulled, and a new game must be played instead of the adjourned game.

16.6. If, upon resumption of the game, the time used has been incorrectly indicated on either clock, and if either player points this out before making his first move, the error must be corrected. If the error is not so established, the game continues without correction.

FIDE INTERPRETATION ART. 16.1 (1973A). The Commission accepts the proposal that before the last round starts all adjourned games should be finished, as a recommendation.

FIDE INTERPRETATION ART. 16.1 (1973B). The Commission declares that it should be left to the discretion of the arbiter whether, in order to finish the adjourned games as quickly as possible, the arbiter has the right, on the day reserved for adjourned games, to interrupt a game of presumed long duration in favor of one or more adjourned games which might be finished more quickly.

FIDE INTERPRETATION ART. 16.1 (1973C). The Commission declares that it should be left to the discretion of the arbiter (provided that in FIDE tournaments no player should be forced to play more than seven hours a day) whether the duration of the time fixed for the playing off of adjourned games may be prolonged, if necessary, but not by more than two hours, provided that the players concerned have been warned in advance.

FIDE INTERPRETATION ART. 16.2 (1974). *Question: What happens –*

(a) if two players agree on a draw and announce their decision to the arbiter and then find, when the envelope is opened, that an illegal move has been recorded, or

(b) when one of the players in an adjourned game notifies the arbiter in writing that he resigns and then finds, when the envelope is opened, that his opponent has recorded an illegal move?

Answer: In case (a) the draw is still valid. In case (b) the resignation is still valid.

FIDE INTERPRETATION ART. 16.4 (1958). *Question: What happens in the case when, in the situation described in Article 16.4, a player has sealed a move, the real significance of which it is impossible to establish?*

Answer: The Commission declares that this case is governed by Article 17.3.

FIDE INTERPRETATION ART. 16.5 (1970). *Question: What measures should be taken when the conditions indicated in Article 16.5 are only partially fulfilled, in that the envelope containing the sealed move has disappeared, but it is still possible to establish by an agreement between the players the position at the adjournment and the times used until that moment?*

Answer: The Commission decides that the game under such circumstances has to be continued.

FIDE INTERPRETATION ART. 16.6 (1976). *The Commission points out that checking the times on the clocks before play (at the beginning of the game as well as upon resumption) is a responsibility of the players. If they neglect to check the times indicated on the clock, they must bear the consequences of their negligence, unless the arbiter feels that, in a particular case, these consequences would be too severe.*

Note to Art. 16.1.:

While the Laws do not explicitly say so, it can be implied from this article that the players may, in the resumption session, use the time saved in the first session. This means that if the rate of play was 2 hours for the first 40 moves and 20 moves for every subsequent hour of play, then the player who used up only, say, 1 hour and 30 minutes for the first 40 moves, will be able to add on those saved 30 minutes to his regular one hour limit for making the next 20 moves.

The schedule for games and for resumption of adjourned games is precisely defined in advance by the regulations and programme of the tournament. All participants should be informed of this so as to avoid any subsequent misunderstanding. It is best to have regular rounds played at the same time (for instance, from 16:00 to 21:00, etc.), and after every three or four rounds to have a day reserved for adjourned games. But there are also other methods, such as playing the games in the afternoon, so that after a two-hour break 'for dinner', continuations are played for another two hours. The advantage of this method is that the games usually end in one day and the players do not suffer from sleepless nights as they analyse the adjourned games. On the other hand, opponents of this method say that this in fact means that one plays nine hours without a break, since the players will use the two-hour recess to analyse the game all the same.

At smaller competitions, the round is played in the afternoon, and then the next morning (from, say, 10:00 to 12:00) the adjourned games are resumed. But morning play is becoming less and less popular, although in some instances it is unavoidable (such as at olympiads). At FIDE competitions, six rounds are played in nine days, with a day reserved for adjourned games at the end of each three rounds, and the ninth day entirely free.

The arbiter usually draws up the schedule for playing adjourned games in the case of several such games. It is best to draw up a schedule which will wind up as many games as possible (first those which will probably be shorter in duration, then those of the leaders, etc.). In FIDE matches adjournments are played off in chronological order.

All players with adjourned games must be in the tournament hall at the time designated for resumption. This is necessary as some games can be completed without play, and then the arbiter can immediately set up the next game for continuation.

Note to Art. 16.2.:

If the envelope does not show who sealed the move, and if both players are absent, then the arbiter will not set the clock into motion and will wait for one of the players to arrive. Once he learns who sealed the move, the arbiter will start the clock of the player who has the move and will advance his time by the difference between the hour scheduled by the programme for the resumption, and the arrival of the player.

Note to Art. 16.3.:

If the player who did not seal is absent for more than one hour for the resumption, as a rule, he loses the game by default. The arbiter should not open the envelope, but rather simply write on it that the said player was absent for more than one hour for the continuation and that he loses the game. It may transpire before the next round, however, that the player had a justified reason for being absent (illness, an accident, etc.), in which case his reason may be accepted by the arbiter or the Appeals Committee. If the arbiter has not opened the envelope, the secrecy of the sealed move is then preserved.

The envelope should in any case be preserved, even after it has been opened, as proof in the case of an appeal.

Note to Art. 16.4.:

The player is not obliged to place his reply in the envelope; he may also execute it on the board. If, however, he opts for this 'publicly sealed' move, he must make sure to write down a correct move, or else he loses the game according to Article 17.

Note to Art. 16.5.:

The disappearance of the envelope reflects badly upon the arbiter. According to earlier FIDE Laws, if the envelope disappeared, the game could be continued only if both players agreed on the position and the expended times. At FIDE's 1976 Congress, however, an important change was introduced and agreement by both players was eliminated as a condition. The Congress, however, forgot to eliminate FIDE's 1975 interpretation to Art. 15.1., which pertained to the former text of this article, and which no longer applies. Hence, it is left up to the arbiter to determine the actual situation on the basis of evidence and witnesses. If the lost envelope is found during play in the continuation, and it is established that a different move had been sealed, then the game is resumed from the sealed move.

Note to Art. 16.6.:

This urges both the players and the arbiter to be extremely careful and to check the times on the clock before the continuation, since an error cannot be corrected. Usually, what happens is that the clock is set either an hour ahead or an hour behind. However, an illegal position can be claimed as long as the game is still in progress.

At the end of this article let us add that a sealed move is considered to be an already executed move, which is important for the provision on claiming a draw by threefold repetition (Art. 12.3.).

When the time prescribed for the first resumption session has expired, then the game shall again be adjourned, according to the same procedure as for the first adjournment. This means that if six hours were prescribed for the continuation of the game, at the end of those six hours (on the wall clock), the arbiter will declare the end of the session and the player who has the move must seal it.

As we have already observed in the Note to Art. 15.1., the player may ask to seal a move even before the time for the session expires, provided that he has made the prescribed number of moves for that session and that he can take on the time difference left until the end of the session.

It may happen that the player must seal his move under time-pressure (i.e. when the next time control is imminent). Some federations have adopted the rule that a move cannot be sealed if less than five minutes remains until the next time control and if the prescribed number of moves for this control has not been played.

Article 17. The Loss of the Game

A game is lost by a player –
    1. who has not played the prescribed number of moves in the given time,
    2. who arrives at the chessboard more than one hour late,
    3. who has sealed a move the real significance of which it is impossible to establish, or
    4. who during the game refuses to comply with the Laws of Chess.

If both players refuse to comply with the Laws of Chess or if both players arrive at the chessboard more than one hour late, the game shall be declared lost by both players.

FIDE INTERPRETATION ART. 17.1 (1970). With reference to the General Observations (FIDE Interpretation Art. 1 [1959]), the Commission expresses the opinion that special regulations should be allowed insofar as they are required for conducting tournaments in which the number of players is large and the number of officials is rather small, so that the procedure to determine whether a player has lost a game under Article 17.1 cannot be observed.

FIDE INTERPRETATION ART. 17.1 (1979). Question: Player A had almost no time for several moves. He moved and inadvertently knocked over several pieces. He pressed his clock. Player B immediately pressed his side of the clock, stating that A had made an illegal move. 'A's' clock fell. Was A correct in pressing his clock before correcting the position?

Answer: A was wrong, and properly lost on time. B acted correctly.

FIDE INTERPRETATION ART. 17.1 (1979). Question: Both players were in a time scramble. Player A's flag fell. They could not agree on how many moves were made, or on how to reconstruct the game. A offered a set of moves ending in 40, but B had another set that meant A would lose on time. The Arbiter ruled, since there was no clear reconstruction, that the game should be continued. Was he correct?

Answer: The Arbiter must make every effort to determine all the facts, including questioning of witnesses. If he is then not certain whether the time control has been passed, then, as an exception and only in tournaments played according to the Swiss System, the Arbiter can allow the game to continue.

FIDE INTERPRETATION ART. 17.2 (1958). In the case where a player or team of players arrives late for a competition, the Commission deems that it should stand by the principles of the General Observations (FIDE Interpretation Art. 1 [1958]). If the delay is due to a cause for which the players are not responsible, then it must follow from the principle of sportsmanship in chess, at least in international tournaments, that concessions should be granted as far as it is possible to do so without creating eventual difficulties to other players or to the organizers.

FIDE INTERPRETATION ART. 17.2 (1962). The Commission declares that the stipulations of Article 17.2 and 17.4 of the Laws of Chess, stating that a game is lost for players arriving at the chessboard more than one hour late, are applicable as much at the commencement of a game as on resumption of play after an adjournment. In the opinion of the Commission, there cannot be any difficulty in applying this rule in the situation in which, on resumption of an adjourned game, the player who has sealed a move is absent while his opponent presents himself at the chessboard. If the former is still absent after the lapse of one hour, the game is lost for him unless it has been decided previously by one of three circumstances, viz. –

(a) the absent player has won the game by virtue of the fact that the sealed move is checkmate,

(b) the absent player has produced a drawn game by virtue of the fact that the sealed move entails stalemate, or

(c) the player present at the chessboard has lost the game according to Article 17.1 by exceeding his time-limit.

Basically, this declaration by the Commission implies a mere substantiation of the evident fact that what happens in consequence of an action or of an omission after the termination of a game is without importance.

FIDE INTERPRETATION ART. 17.2 (1966). Question: If in adjourning a game, a player has some remaining time in his favor (more than one hour), should his opponent, when the game is continued, wait an hour or wait until the full time which the player has in his favor has elapsed before claiming a win in case of the player's nonappearance?

Answer: This case has already been solved by FIDE Interpretation Art. 17.2 (1962).

FIDE INTERPRETATION ART. 17.3 (1958). Having been asked for a more precise formulation of Article 17.3, the Commission once again refers to the General Observations (FIDE Interpretation Art. 1 [1959]). It is the duty of the arbiter to make the necessary decision in accordance with the circumstances of each particular case.

FIDE INTERPRETATION ART. 17.3 (1965). According to the opinion of the Commission, it ought to be clearly established by the wording of this Article that not only when the notation is inexact but also when a clear notation indicates an irregular move, it is incumbent on the arbiter to judge whether there exists any reasonable doubt as to the move which the player has intended to indicate.

FIDE INTERPRETATION ART. 17.3 (1975). Question: In a recent tournament Player A was asked to seal a move of adjournment. Player A subsequently handed his sealed-move envelope to the arbiter, who kept it in his custody. When the adjourned game was resumed, the envelope was opened, but only the scoresheet of Player B was found in the envelope. The arbiter ruled that Player A's failure to seal his move automatically entailed the loss of the game under Article 17.3. Was the arbiter's ruling correct?

Answer: Yes. It should be remarked, however, that the arbiter (or one of his assistants) should be blamed, as he did not make sure that the scoresheet of Player A was in the envelope, even though it was his duty to do so.

FIDE INTERPRETATION ART. 17.3 (1976). Question: According to FIDE Interpretation Article 17.3 (1958), the arbiter has the duty of deciding the real significance of a sealed move. This is undesirable, as the arbiter should interfere as little as possible in the game and should serve only to see that neither player gains an unfair advantage of his mistakes. What is the opinion of the Commission?

Answer: The player sealing a move should be aware that the responsibility for sealing a correct move is entirely his and that if he seals an illegal or ambiguous move, he may lose the game.

Note to Art. 17.:
This article discusses the loss of the game by forfeit. Article 11 of the Laws discusses the won game.
Note to Art. 17.1.:
When a player oversteps the time limit, then the arbiter declares the game ended, which means that the players can no longer agree to draw or to go on playing, etc.

As has already been said, the fall of the flag is conclusive when observed. When a player's flag falls, the arbiter should verify whether the prescribed number of moves has been made. If necessary, he will stop the clock, and if there is any doubt as to the number of moves, he will, together with the players, undertake the necessary reconstruction of the game.

If the arbiter is absent, then the player will summon and point out to him that the opponent has overstepped the time limit. The arbiter will then make the necessary verification and will declare the loss of the game if the claim was correct.

Consequently, both the players and the arbiter are responsible for seeing the flag drop (and not the spectators, etc.). Overstepping the time limit, therefore, must be either observed by the arbiter or claimed by one of the players.

Both players may be greatly pressed for time and one may press the clock only for both flags to fall, virtually at the same time. If both players have not made the prescribed number of moves, then the game is lost by the player whose clock is not in motion. This is logical since it is to be presumed that the last player to press the clock had his flag fall earlier, i.e. he did not manage to completely execute his move and instead the flag fell, after which he put his opponent's clock in motion, the flag of which most likely fell only then.

Some federations (such as the US) have a provision that when the flag falls, the other player may claim a win, provided that at that moment he has accurately written down the moves on his scoresheet (up to three incomplete move lines are tolerated), and that recorded moves show that the time limit has been overstepped. The reason for this provision is that a player should not win a game on the basis of one paragraph (the fall of the flag), when that same player is violating the second paragraph of the Rules (the provision on keeping a scoresheet of the game). Despite the possible logic of this, the FIDE Laws do not include such provisions and conditions.

Any move made after overstepping the time limit is not valid and is not counted as part of the game.

Note to Art. 17.2.:

The player must arrive for the game not more than one hour later than the time set for the commencement. He is not obliged to execute a move during this period, but he must be in the tournament hall. One hour is counted from the actual beginning of play according to the wall clock and not the chess clock of that player. The player with the white pieces may be half an hour late while his clock was in motion all that time. Once he executes a move, the clock of the player with the black pieces is started. If the latter was absent from the beginning of the game, then only a half-hour wait will ensue, and not a further hour.

On the resumption of a game, the player is considered late as of the moment when the said adjourned game has been set up for play and the arbiter has put the chess clock in motion. The arbiter will then note on the envelope the time of the game's resumption and will register which player is absent. The absent player loses the game at the end of one hour (barring the exceptions enumerated in FIDE's 1962 Interpretation). Of course, the absent player may lose the game even before the one hour period expires, if he oversteps the time limit.

Even if, in the adjournment session, the absent player has more than one hour for thought, he still loses the game one hour after the resumption.

The following situations may occur during the adjournment session:

a) Both players are absent for over one hour. The chess clock of that player who has not sealed a move is put in motion. If that player's time limit runs out less than an hour after the commencement of the session, then he loses the game, and his opponent is recorded a win. If the player whose clock is running does not exceed the time limit at the end of one hour after the commencement of the session, then both players lose the game, even if according to the chess clock they have not overstepped the time limit. The exception here, of course, is if the sealed move is mate or stalemate.

b) The player who has sealed a move is absent, but his opponent is present. The envelope is opened and, upon execution of the sealed move, the clock of the player who did not seal a move is put into motion.

If the player who sealed the move does not appear within a period of one hour or if his time limit expires before that, then he loses the game. There are three exceptions, mentioned in the FIDE interpretation, in which the absent player does not lose the game: if the sealed move is mate (whereby he wins the game), if the sealed move produces immediate stalemate (whereby the game is a draw) and if the present player has exceeded the time limit before the end of one hour from the resumption of the game (whereby the absent player wins the game).

c) The player who did not seal a move is absent, and his opponent is present. The envelope is *not* opened, and the clock of the absent player is put in motion. He loses the game if he arrives more than one hour late, and even earlier if his chess clock shows that the prescribed time limit has been exceeded.

Note to Art. 17.3.:

Here, the decisions of the arbiter greatly vary: some make strictly formalistic decisions, while others are more liberal. It is better, however, for the arbiter to avoid a purely formalistic approach to an unclear move. A player should not lose a game because of an obvious slip of the pen, provided that the meaning of his move can be unravelled on the basis of logical judgement and interpretation.

In making his decision the arbiter should abide by the following principle: if the sealed move can be interpreted in two ways, then the player who sealed such an ambiguous move loses the game; if the sealed move can be interpreted in one way only, then the arbiter should acknowledge that interpretation. A few examples may illustrate this.

If, for instance, the player wrote Se2-f5 (instead of Se2-f4), then the arbiter should accept the move as correct, provided that another knight of the same colour cannot occupy the same square.

Ambiguity sometimes arises, depending on the piece, since it is not the same thing if the move is one with, say, a bishop (which moves along an established diagonal) or one with a queen (which has a far greater radius of movement and more possible moves).

Hence, it is extremely difficult to resolve what is meant if a player seals De4-f6 (instead of De4-f5), since he may have meant De6, Dg6, Df5, and even Df3! Tc4-e3 is equally ambiguous, since this can also mean Te4 and Tc3.

The move Lb2-c2 however, admits of fewer interpretations. Although Lc3 was not what was written down, this may be accepted as a correct move, provided that the bishop cannot occupy c1. If both moves are possible, then the sealed move is ambiguous and the player loses the game.

The player may seal a move without the name of the piece, for instance e2-d4 (instead of Se2-d4). The move can be accepted provided there is no possibility for the pawn move d2-d4 or other ambiguity.

The player may seal a move by taking the reverse position of the chess board, and write b2-b4 or g2-g4 instead of b7-b5, or write Kb7 instead of Kg2, or seal f5-f7 instead of f7-f5, etc. Once again, in such cases of inversion, what should be considered is whether several interpretations of the move exist.

One must admit that liberal interpretations are difficult and that it is simpler to be a formalist. Nonetheless, the arbiter should endeavour to find a just solution whenever possible. In any case, the player who did not seal a clear and correct move bears the responsibility for any consequences.

A move may be sealed with full or with abbreviated notation, provided that it is correctly written down. In the latter instance, the player should be sure to specify and distinguish between pieces of the same kind, if they can occupy the same square, so that it is clear which piece is in question. If, for instance, the sealed move is Sd5, and both knights can be moved to this square, then the player will lose the game. The same holds true for rooks.

To recapitulate: the player is obliged to seal a clear and unambiguous move. In certain exceptional cases, the arbiter may accept a move as correct if the sealed move can be interpreted in only one way. In principle, it is difficult to systematize such cases, for a great deal depends on the position itself. We might mention the following cases: a move may be accepted as correct if the piece and the square of arrival are correctly indicated (even if the square of departure is not correctly indicated); if the square of departure and the square of arrival are correctly written (but the name of the piece has been omitted), unless there is some ambiguity; if the name of the piece and the arriving file are correctly written, but there is an error in the number indicating the rank (provided that that same piece cannot come to some other square along the same file); and finally, when it is clearly a case of inversion in designating the ranks and files, the arbiter may by tolerant, if he concludes that this was an obvious slip.

In all the above cases, however, the arbiter must operate with extreme caution.

Note to Art. 17.4.:
Both players may lose the game if they violate the Laws and ethical principles of chess (by 'fixing' a game, etc.).

Article 18. The Drawn Game

18.1. A proposal of a draw under the provisions of Article 12.2 may be made by a player only at the moment when he has just made a move. On then proposing a draw, he starts the clock of his opponent. The latter may accept the proposal or, either orally or by making a move, he may reject it; in the interval the player who has made the proposal cannot withdraw it.

18.2. If a player claims a draw under the provisisions of Article 12.3 the Arbiter must first stop the clock while the claim is being investigated. If the claim is found to be correct, the game shall be declared drawn. If the claim is found to be incorrect, the arbiter shall then add five minutes to the claimant's time. If this means that the claimant has overstepped the time limit, his game will be declared lost. Otherwise the game will be continued.

FIDE INTERPRETATION ART. 18.1 (1974A). A proposal to draw not made in accordance with Article 18.1 is treated as follows –

(a) if a player proposes a draw while his opponent's clock is running, the opponent may agree to the draw or reject the offer; or

(b) if a player proposes a draw while his own clock is running, the opponent may accept or reject the offer, or he may postpone his decision until after the player has completed a move.

In these situations the opponent may reject the proposal orally or by completing a move at his first opportunity. In the interval between the offer of a draw and the opponent's acceptance of it, the player who made the proposal cannot withdraw it.

FIDE INTERPRETATION ART. 18.1 (1974B). A player proposed a draw and made his move on the board before his opponent had replied to the offer. The opponent, after some minutes' consideration, accepted the offer. The arbiter rendered the player's proposal valid and thus proclaimed the game drawn. One of the arguments for this decision was that the proposal maintained its validity since the proposal itself is more important than the form.

The Commission disagrees with the last-mentioned argument, since here the way the draw is offered is the thing that matters. In spite of the reasoning offered, the Commission approves the actual decision taken in this particular case.

The Commission thinks that this matter has adequately been covered by FIDE Interpretation Art. 18.1 (1974A).

FIDE INTERPRETATION ART. 18.1 (1959, 1960, 1963, 1964). THE QUESTION OF PREMATURE DRAWS.

FIDE INTERPRETATION ART. 18.1 (1959). From a sporting point of view, it is quite inappropriate that a game be finished before a real fight has commenced; competition ought to imply that every player should try to fight in order to win his game until the moment when the situation does not afford any further hope of victory.

Attention is drawn in particular to the fact that in this respect the Internaional Grandmasters and the International Masters of FIDE ought to serve as

178/The Laws, their Interpretation and Author's Comments

examples to the other players. Players who repeatedly act without respecting their duty to the organizers and to the chess public may be subject to disciplinary measures taken by the arbiter.

FIDE INTERPRETATION ART. 18.1 (1960). It is hardly possible to establish prescriptions sufficiently detailed to be directly applicable to each particular case. On the basis of the general principle that the players may not ignore the necessity of an honest fight, the examination of each particular case ought, according to the opinion of the Commission, to devolve upon the person who is in charge of the tournament in which the game in question has been played. At this examination it must not be forgotten that a player may have quite legitimate reasons – his actual situation in the tournament table, his state of health, etc. – for desisting from whatever prospects he has in a given situation for continuing the game to a victory and that he may therefore be considered entitled to make or accept an offer of a draw.

FIDE INTERPRETATION ART. 18.1 (1963). It seems necessary to stipulate clearly and in writing certain moral principles which should guide the game, but are not incorporated in the Laws of Chess, in order to enable the arbiter to secure as far as possible a fair, sportsmanlike contest.

The Commission emphasizes the following points.

(a) Every agreement to draw should, as a matter of principle, be based on a position on the chessboard which, in the opinion of each of the two players, offers no tangible possibility of pursuing the game to a victorious conclusion without running an obvious risk of defeat.

(b) Particular circumstances may exist, however, which should authorize a player to propose or accept a draw in cases differing from those mentioned in (a). It is not possible to define these particular circumstances in a complete manner, just as in the official regulations the stipulations governing agreements to draw should, in the opinion of the Commission, be so conceived as to comprise only basic principles and goals, as competent arbiters must be presumed to know how to apply them to concrete cases in an equitable manner.

The principles so formulated relate to a basic principle, according to which each player should conduct his whole game as a fight for the best possible result. Voluntary measures to evade the fight or to favor the opponent or a third player should be held contemptible for reasons of sport and be judged accordingly.

It is easy to establish that it is difficult, in certain cases even impossible, to judge correctly the measures to be taken in situations varying in character, and the arbiter should impose penalties only in cases which clearly constitute contraventions of the moral principles involved.

FIDE INTERPRETATION ART. 18.1 (1964). An agreement to draw a game before the 30th move in many cases involves an act which rightly could be deemed contradictory to the stated principles on premature draws. Tournament arbiters are requested to impose, in cases where clear contraventions of the moral principles of the game are demonstrated, penalties as severe as loss of the game.

FIDE INTERPRETATION ART. 18.2 (1974). Question: What happens when an arbiter –

(a) accepts a claim of a draw, but then is proved to have made a mistake;

or

  (b) *turns down a claim of a draw which afterwards proves to have been correct?*

  Answer: If a claim of a draw has been mistakenly accepted by the arbiter and a higher authority subsequently rejects the claim, then the player who has not claimed the draw is entitled to resume the game.

  If a claim of a draw has been mistakenly refused by the arbiter, then the player who has made the claim is entitled to stop playing and appeal to a higher authority. If then the player's claim is proved to be incorrect, the game shall be declared lost for the player who stopped playing.

  FIDE INTERPRETATION ART. 18.2. See FIDE Interpretation Art. 12.3 (1960).

  FIDE INTERPRETATION ART. 18.2 (1979). Question: A player claims a draw under the provisions of 12.3. Can he withdraw his claim before it is verified?

  Answer: After the Arbiter has stopped the clock to prepare to verify the claim, the player cannot withdraw the claim.

Note to Art. 18.1.:

This article prescribes the strict procedure to be followed by the player offering a draw. This is so as to avoid situations in which a player disturbs his opponent by making frequent peace offers. Nevertheless, players agree to a draw without following the prescribed procedure. Here, the arbiter must accept the agreement. According to the Laws, the offer of a draw must follow a strict procedure: first the player must execute a move, then offer a draw and then start the clock of his opponent. In practice, however, a draw is often offered without having first executed a move. Here, the opponent has the right to ask the player offering the draw to execute a move and only then will he receive a reply. The latter cannot withdraw his offered draw.

  The player who is due to seal a move, or has already placed the scoresheet in the envelope, may offer a draw. At one tournament, the opponent asked the proposer of the draw to execute the move, but he was not entitled to insist on this. The above procedure of offering a draw cannot apply to a sealed move or a move about to be sealed, since this is a secret move: consequently, the Laws' provisions do not apply to the sealed move, nor is any procedure envisaged for such an exceptional case. The players are free to agree according to their inclination, and the arbiter will accept their agreement. The procedure of offering a draw was established so as not to disturb the opponent during play, but such a danger does not exist when a move is sealed. During the adjournment, the players may try to agree to draw the adjourned game without resumption, 'provided' that the player has not sealed an impossible move or 'provided' that he has sealed such and such a move, etc. The arbiter should not accept such 'conditional' agreements. He can accept an agreement made 'without any strings attached', and if the players agree to a draw, then it is irrelevant which move was sealed. According to the interpretation of Art. 16.2. (FIDE General Assembly 1974) an agreement is valid even if an impossible move has been sealed. Here, priority is given to the agreement of the players, even if one of the players resigns the game to an opponent who sealed an impossible move.

  When the players agree to a draw (or to resign) when play is not in progress, it is best for the arbiter to get their statements in writing.

  It may happen that a player offers a draw, and that the flag falls on the opponent's clock in the interim (while he is consulting his captain, for example). The arbiter must register a loss for the player who exceeded his time limit.

There used to be a rule that a game could not be drawn before the 30th move. First, as its 1962 General Assembly, FIDE said that this could be done but only with the approval of the arbiter. At its next General Assembly, FIDE gave a more rigid formulation, i.e. under no circumstances could a draw be made before the 30th move, except in the case of perpetual check and threefold repetition. But by its 1964 General Assembly, this clause banning draws before the 30th move was virtually eliminated, since it has proved easy to evade by simply formally repeating positions, etc.

Nevertheless, the present regulations include a clause which gives arbiters the right to oppose any attempt to evade battle. Several interpretations exist on premature draws and the arbiter may apply them in such cases. Of course, he must appraise the situation realistically and show understanding for it, bearing in mind the situation on the board, and in the competition itself.

The Hübner–Rogoff game at the 1972 Student Olympiad is often mentioned in this connection. Hübner proposed a draw after his first move, and his opponent accepted. The arbiter, however, rejected their peace offering, and they continued the game. But they played a kind of giveaway chess, ultimately leaving king against king on the board. The arbiter refused to accept this kind of draw either, and scheduled a new game. Hübner did not show up for the game, and (unfairly) only he was registered a loss.

There has been considerable discussion at FIDE meetings (especially in 1964) on proposing draws without a fight. What was stressed were the moral obligations of the players, the responsibility of the arbiter to penalize any evasion of the moral principles of chess, and the fact that organizers should not invite players who respect neither these principles nor the chess public.

The arbiter must carefully weigh whether it is a matter of evading the principles and must be sure that his intervention is fitting and justified. He cannot be the 'regulator' of the game, order the players to play, and, when it is not his job, assess who has the better position and on the basis of this uncertain evaluation demand a fight.

Note to Art. 18.2.:
The new text of this article introduces an entirely new element in that it stipulates that the player who claims a draw by threefold repetition of position has his chess clock advanced by exactly five minutes. It is felt that this is sufficient time to verify whether or not the claim is correct. This is good because the player will not be the victim of overly slow verification, and the arbiter will not have to rush. Sometimes the verification process can be completed more rapidly, but the player still has the five minutes added on. Real complications arise, however, when it emerges that the five-minute advancement on his clock will make the player exceed his time limit, i.e. when the player has approximately five minutes left until the time-control and the arbiter must precisely calculate the new time. The player may be left with only a few seconds until the time control, and this is bound to lead to polemics.

The 1979 FIDE Congress amended the article in line with the 1976 FIDE interpretation. In order to add the five minutes, the arbiter will first have to register the exact time and stop the clock and only then tell the players what the time will be with the five-minute addition (which he can add immediately or at the end of the verification). The article used to read that 'his clock must continue to run' which was technically impossible.

Verification of a claim for a draw based on the same position appearing three times is done in the presence of both players. At a ladies' tournament in the Soviet Union, the player who had sealed the move was absent from the resumption. The envelope was opened and the opponent who was present claimed that the move she was about to play would give rise to a threefold repetition of position and so she claimed a draw. The arbiter accepted this, after having completed the necessary verification. The arbiter, however, acted incorrectly; he should have waited for the other player, added on the time difference between the commencement and her arrival, and then carried out the verification at the time-expense of the player who had claimed a draw. If the player was still absent at the end of one hour after the commencement of the session, then she would lose the game by forfeit.

The FIDE Laws say nothing about whether a player who has claimed a draw by threefold repetition can withdraw his claim during the verification process. According to the laws of some federations, this is possible: at a Soviet championship, Spassky withdrew a claim since seven minutes had elapsed and the arbiter had still not begun the verification, and he feared he might lose the game by overstepping the time limit should the claim be incorrect. FIDE's Laws, however, do not provide for the possibility of a player withdrawing a claim.

Article 19. The Conduct of the Players

19.1. (a) During play the players are forbidden to make use of handwritten or printed notes or to analyze the game on another chessboard; they are also forbidden to have recourse to the advice or opinion of a third party, whether solicited or not.

(b) No analysis is permitted in the playing rooms during play or during adjourned sessions.

(c) It is forbidden to distract or annoy the opponent in any manner whatsoever.

19.2. Infractions of the rules indicated in Article 19.1 may incur penalties even to the extent of loss of the game.

FIDE INTERPRETATION ART. 19.1a (1960). The Commission shares the opinion that the result of a game of chess ought to depend exclusively on the actual strength of each player and that consequently the collaboration of others ought to be allowed no more after an adjournment than in the course of the game at the chessboard. It must, however, be observed that whereas in the playing rooms perfect control can be upheld, this is not possible during the time the game is adjourned. It must therefore be held in mind that a general prohibition of the use of seconds would probably not be respected by all players and that in practice it might be disadvantageous for those players who would loyally respect the prohibition.

Thus, the only effective and just means of eliminating, as far as possible, the use of seconds probably consists in a change of the system for the organisation of tournaments.

FIDE INTERPRETATION ART. 19.1a (1975). Question: In a time-trouble game the captain of one side informed (without being asked to do so) the player of his side (White) that his opponent had just completed the last move of the prescribed series of moves. As a consequence of this, White had now enough time to think his position over. He found the winning continuation in the rather complicated position.

Black felt that his chances had been damaged by the action of the captain of the opposite side, particularly as in the time-trouble phase of the game the chances for a win changed continuously. In this phase of the game both players did not write down their moves and did not even mark the number of moves they played.

The appeals committee did not accept the protest of Black and gave the motives for its decision by referring to many international tournaments where the players, the arbiter, and other persons present in the tournament hall can see continuously the position and the number of moves made on the big wall boards. The committee said that everyone had the right to inform the players at any time about the number of moves completed, as long as there is no infringement of Article 19.1a.

Here follow three specific questions:

(a) When may a player be informed about the number of moves he has made (before or after the time-control)?

(b) Who has the right (or is obliged) to give that information (the arbiter, the team captain, other persons)?

(c) What kind of penalty should be given in connection with the above-mentioned parties for incorrect behaviour?

Answers:

(a) Never.

(b) Nobody.

(c) This is left to the discretion of the arbiter.

[But see FIDE INTERPRETATION ART. 13.2 (1976) for the procedure at the time-control.]

FIDE INTERPRETATION ART. 19.1a (1976A). The prohibition against handwritten or printed notes applies not only to notes brought in from the outside but also to notes made during play which could in any way serve as an aid to memory. Aside from the actual recording of the moves, only the addition of an objective fact such as the time on the clocks is permitted.

FIDE INTERPRETATION ART. 19.1a (1976B). Question: How is Article 19.1a to be applied in the case of a team competition and more specifically, what actions are permissible for a team captain while play is in progress?

Answer: The role of the team captain is basically an administrative one. According to the regulations of the competition, the captain may be required to do such things as deliver to a tournament official a written list giving the players of his team who will participate in each round, see that those of his players who are not taking part in the current match or those who have finished their games are not present in the space reserved for the players, report the results of a match to a tournament official at the end of play, etc. In principle, the captain must abstain from any intervention during play. He should not, by virtue of his own playing strength, give information to a player concerning the position on the chessboard of that or any other player, since the captain would then be giving information to a member of his team on the play of the game which the team member's own abilities might not have allowed him to discover for himself. The captain is, by the weight of practice, entitled to advise the players of his team to make or to accept an offer of a draw or to resign a game, on condition that he does not make any comments concerning the actual position on the chessboard.

He must confine himself to giving only brief information which can in no way be interpreted by the player as an opinion on the game, but might instead be interpreted as based on any number of circumstances pertaining to the match.

In addition to the captain's being prohibited from expressing an opinion on the state of the game to any other person, he is also prohibited from consulting any other person as to the state of the game, just as players are subject to the same prohibitions.

The captain may say to a player, 'Offer a draw', 'Accept the draw', or 'Resign the game', but this brief information should be given in a general way and not in any way that may be interpreted as an opinion on the state of the game. For example, if asked by a player whether he should accept an offer of a draw, the captain should not begin to analyze for himself any board in such a way that his reply could be interpreted as an opinion on the position.

Even though in a team competition there is a certain team loyalty which goes beyond a player's individual game, a game of chess is, at base, a competition between two players. Therefore, the player must have the final say over the play of his own game. Although the advice of the captain should weigh heavily with the player, the player is not absolutely compelled to abide by that advice. Likewise, the captain cannot act on behalf of a player and his game without the knowledge and consent of the player.

FIDE INTERPRETATION ART. 19.1c (1958). Article 19.1c should be applied in the case where a player who has proposed a draw reiterates his proposal without reasons that are clearly well-founded before the opponent has, in his turn, made use of his right to propose a draw.

Article 19.1c protects the players sufficiently, and the application of this Article can always be requested from the arbiter against a player who proposes a draw too frequently to his opponent.

Note to Art. 19.1.:
During play players must neither receive nor give advice. It is also prohibited for the spectators to give advice. The arbiter may remove undisciplined spectators from the playing room, and if he has reason to believe that advice from the audience is part of an agreement with the player, he may take sanctions against the player as well.

During play, players are forbidden recourse to book and pocket sets or other such aids, nor may they receive assistance from third parties, especially seconds. At one time, FIDE wanted to find a way to eliminate seconds, but finally refrained from the idea, so that they are now mentioned in regulations.

In principle, participants in a tournament are not permitted to converse, and this also applies to participants in team competitions (at least such conversation should be kept to a minimum and must not relate to the game itself). Conversation between the players often evokes the suspicion among others that they are analysing the game in progress. After the 1962 Candidates' Tournament, Fischer accused others of having spoken during the game and having agreed to play collectively against him.

There are various ways to 'prompt' moves (at a ladies' tournament the demonstrator allegedly suggested moves by 'adjusting' the pieces on the demonstration board).

During the game the player must not leave the tournament premises without the explicit approval of the arbiter. While the game is in progress, the arbiter must be in a position to keep an eye on the movements of the players, so as to dispel any doubt that they are analysing the game or having recourse to books, etc. There have been instances at tournaments when a player was out of the room for some time, only to return and find that the arbiter had registered a zero for that game. At important competitions, especially world title matches, the players are separated from the audience and must not in any way contact their seconds.

The arbiter should not permit players who have finished their game to analyse it in the playing room. This is especially important if two or more games have begun with the same opening variation! An analysis room should always be provided, to avoid accidental advice as well as distraction for the players whose games are still in progress.

Article 19.1c is extremely broad and embraces all cases of distraction not mentioned in the Laws. Recently, the regulations for FIDE competitions, and especially the Rules for the Candidates' Matches and for the World Title Match, have codified many details which had previously been considered insignificant. Fischer deserves credit for the fact that many playing conditions have been improved, something which was severely neglected in the past. There was an interesting situation in his match with Taimanov, in Vancouver in 1971. Without meaning to disturb his opponent, Taimanov used to walk around the stage after having made his move. This is 'standard procedure' at many tournaments. Fischer complained that Taimanov's walking distracted him. Taimanov pointed out, however, that this was customary at all tournaments and that he could not be expected to stand rivetted to one place, and anyway, the regulations did not prohibit walking. One should add that what is not distracting in a tournament may be so in a match! Faced with an unpleasant situation, the arbiter called over the two sides' representatives and persuaded them to settle this minor problem like gentlemen. Taimanov promised that he would try not to walk around the stage, but he asked Fischer's representative (E. Edmondson) that Fischer refrain from tapping his feet while his opponent had the move. Taimanov admitted that this is a difficult habit to shake, and he doubted whether Fischer would be able to rid himself of this 'incurable disease'. Indeed, Fischer did tap his feet under the table at many tournaments, and it was noticeable. Hence it was all the more surprising when, after the arbiter's talk with the two sides' representatives, Fischer was seen quietly sitting at his table that same afternoon, without a single tapping of the foot. But Taimanov, too, respected the agreement, and did not take one of his customary strolls. It is worth noting that Fischer did not resume his old habit in any of the subsequent matches either; a well-meaning talk had been enough to settle the entire matter.

Present match regulations provide that players may walk behind the stage, where they may drink non-alcoholic beverages and eat without disturbing their opponents. All the particulars of this possibility, however, should be regulated by agreement before the competition, for sometimes players agree to have beverages and coffee at the table on the stage, but food behind the scenes.

Picture-taking is another problem for players at major competitions which attract the interest of both journalists and photographers. Flashlights may blind the players to such an extent that it takes them some time to see properly again. It was agreed at the Final Candidates' Match between Korchnoi and Spassky in Belgrade in 1977, to permit photographing and filming, but only during the first five minutes of each game, and without flashlights. This could also be done during the game, provided that it was 'silent' and 'invisible' to the players, while the possibility was left open for agreement on other cases.

This article discusses the conduct of the players, but it does not even begin to embrace the 'rich repertoire' of some players who want to seize a point at any cost. One should start by saying that there are very few great chessplayers who resort to tricks at the chess board. 'Tournament practice', however, has produced a number of examples which should be known to the arbiter so that he may cope better at competitions.

One should distinguish between tricks and legitimate psychology, which is an integral part of chess. Grandmaster Bronstein wrote an article entitled *Honest Deception* (published in *Shakhmaty v SSSR* in 1971) in which he described his thoughts and psychological battle in a game with Korchnoi, when he saw a lovely combination, but wondered how to draw his opponent into it and 'take him off his guard'. Bronstein writes in great detail about how he seemed to overlook it, only to outwit his opponent. Korchnoi spoke in a similar vein in 1974, when discussing the psychological battle in chess. 'Chess is not only a kind of sport, science, and art, it is also a kind of psychological battle', said Korchnoi about the 13th game in the 1974 match with Mecking. 'I saw that Mecking was winning, but I remained completely calm. He thought that I might have some defence hidden up my sleeve. He deliberated 45 minutes and finally he made the wrong choice, because I had been calm!'.

On the other hand, there are many tricks which are unethical. Some players, for instance, become profoundly absorbed in thought when the opponent forgets to press his clock. Others are not gentlemen enough to admit defeat, and instead adjourn completely lost positions or even seal 'resigns'. There have been cases at tournaments when a player would write down an extra move on the scoresheet so as to disorient the opponent in time trouble and make him overstep the time limit, or else omit a move so as to frighten the opponent into making an extra move. There are those who 'circle' the pieces with their hand before executing a move, who do not place the pieces properly on the squares but leave it to their opponents to align them, who make a 'wreck' of the chess clock, are deliberately late for the commencement of a game so as to annoy the opponent at the very outset, who 'shake' the clock, bang the pieces, etc. A counter-gambit exists for many of these tricks and the arbiter can use it, but the Laws themselves are not explicit. For chess is nevertheless an art and a game whose purity should be safeguarded.

And finally, let us note that the spectators can also distract the players. There are some players who are highly sensitive to this. Fischer always demanded that the spectators be at least 40 feet from the stage, and Fischer's ideal would seem to be to play without an audience at all. Chess competitions, like all sport competitions, are public and are played before spectators. In the twelfth game of his match with Alekhine, Capablanca asked that the spectators be removed because of undue noise, and the third game of the 1972 Spassy–Fischer match was played behind the scenes. Only in exceptional cases, when it is judged that there is no other way to avoid the din of the spectators, can the arbiter transfer the game to an alternative room or remove the spectators from the playing room.

Article 20. The Arbiter of the Competition

An arbiter should be designed to control the competition. His duties are: –

1. to see that these Laws of Chess are strictly observed;

2. to supervise the progress of the competition, to establish that the prescribed time-limit has not been exceeded by the players, to arrange the order of resumption of play in adjourned games, to see that the arrangements contained in Article 15 are observed (above all to see that the information on the envelope is correct), to keep the sealed-move envelope until the time when the adjourned game is resumed, etc.;

3. to enforce the decisions he may make in disputes that have arisen during the course of the competition; and

4. to act in the best interest of the match or tournament to ensure that a good playing environment is maintained and that the players are not disturbed by each other or by the audience.

5. to impose penalties on the players for any fault or infraction of these Laws of Chess.

FIDE INTERPRETATION ART. 20.3 (1958). The Commission considers that there is no need to include in the Laws of Chess prescriptions concerning appeals against the decision of an arbiter. However, when it is a question of international tournaments, it is doubtless appropriate to have a committee at the place where the competition takes place entrusted with the task of resolving disputes in the event of appeals against an arbiter's decision.

Note to Art. 20.:
This article lists the principle duties of the arbiter of a competition, but he also has many other obligations to fulfill in order for the competition to run smoothly. More is said about this in the section devoted to the organization of competetitions.

In some countries, the arbiter is called the director. In many European countries, the arbiter of the competition sees to the normal course of the game, the application of the Laws of Chess and the regulations of the competition, while the director of the competition deals with the organizational and technical problems of the competition. In some cases, these duties overlap. The director of a tournament, for instance, sees to it that a suitable playing room for the competition is found, but the arbiter must verify whether the playing room is suitable for play, whether the lighting is what it should be, whether the playing conditions are good, etc. Usually, the arbiter draws up the regulations of the competition, but for this he must be in consultation with the organizers who are holding, financing and running the competition. In any case, it is the duty of the arbiter to be acquainted in detail, and before the competition, with all the rules and regulations concerning the competition and to suggest the clarification of all other questions not encompassed by the regulations (by drawing up a supplementary protocol, etc.). The work of the arbiter begins with establishing the proper conditions in the tournament room (the lighting, arrangement on the stage, suitable equipment, etc.), participation in drawing up the regulations, drawing of lots, etc., and includes all other matters concerning the normal course of the game.

Note to Art. 20.3.:
The Laws do not so stipulate, but it is regular procedure to form appeals committee for the competition, which, in the event of an appeal, rules on the decisions of the arbiter. The decision of this committee is usually final, since there is not enough time to wait for a decision by a higher body which is not on the spot.

Note to Art. 20.4.:
The penalties which may be imposed by the arbiter range from a formal warning to forfeiting a player, and even to disqualification from the tournament. The arbiter has an extremely broad range of authority as stated in the Introduction to the Laws of Chess of FIDE. It is superfluous to underline that he must be objective and entirely unbiased.

Article 21. The Interpretation of the Laws

In case of doubt as to the application or interpretation of these Laws, FIDE will examine the evidence and render official decisions. Rulings published are binding on all affiliated federations.

FIDE INTERPRETATION ART. 21 (1957). INDIVIDUAL PRIZES IN TEAM TOURNAMENTS. When, in a team chess competition, special prizes are instituted for the best percentage results arrived at by individual players, only the results of participants who have played a number of rounds at least two-thirds of the total number of rounds are to be counted.

FIDE INTERPRETATION ART. 21 (1967). APPLICATION OF THE SONNEBORN–BERGER SYSTEM IN THE CASE OF A TIE IN A TEAM TOURNAMENT. Question: How is the Sonneborn–Berger System to be applied in the case of a tie in a team tournament?

Answer: In the application of the Sonneborn–Berger (Tie-Breaking) System to an individual tournament, every player is assigned a number of points calculated by a special rule. Specifically, each player is given the total number of points scored by each opponent he defeated and half the total number of points scored by each opponent with whom he drew. Three alternatives, then, are possible: a win giving the total number of points scored in the tournament by the opponent, a draw giving half that number of points, and a loss giving no points.

In a team tournament, when game points are being used, the number of alternatives possible depends upon the number of players on each team. For example, in a tournament where the number of players on each team is four, there are nine possible alternatives: $4, 3\frac{1}{2}, 3, 2\frac{1}{2}, 2, 1\frac{1}{2}, 1, \frac{1}{2}, 0$. If, in a tournament of this kind, two participating teams, A and B, have the same number of game points, whereas a third team, C, has 16 points, the Sonneborn–Berger totals which Team A and Team B each obtained in their match with Team C are calculated as follows:

If the team scored 4 points (100 %), its S–B total is 16.
"   "   "   " $3\frac{1}{2}$ "   ($87\frac{1}{2}$%), "   "   "   " 14.
"   "   "   "   3   "   (75 %), "   "   "   " 12.
"   "   "   " $2\frac{1}{2}$ "   ($62\frac{1}{2}$%), "   "   "   " 10.
"   "   "   "   2   "   (50 %), "   "   "   " 8.
"   "   "   " $1\frac{1}{2}$ "   (37 %), "   "   "   " 6.
"   "   "   "   1   "   (25 %), "   "   "   " 4.
"   "   "   " $\frac{1}{2}$ "   ($12\frac{1}{2}$%), "   "   "   " 2.
"   "   "   "   0   "   (0 %), "   "   "   " 0.

FIDE INTERPRETATION ART. 21 (1970, 1973). CONSEQUENCES WHEN A PLAYER OR A TEAM WITHDRAWS OR IS EXPELLED FROM A TOURNAMENT.

FIDE INTERPRETATION ART. 21 (1970). Question: What are the consequences when a player or team withdraws or is expelled from a round-robin tournament?

Answer: If a player has not completed at least 50% of his games when he leaves the tournament, his score remains in the tournament table (for rating and historical purposes), but the points scored by him or against him are not counted in the final standings. For the games not played or finished, the player, as well as his opponent, gets /–/ in the tournament table.

If a player has completed at least 50% of his games when he leaves the tournament, his score remains in the tournament table and will be counted in the final standings. For the games not played the opponents will get a /1/ and the player himself will get a /0/.

The same rules apply equally when a team is concerned instead of a player.

FIDE INTERPRETATION ART. 21 (1973). Relating to a player's retirement from a tournament, chroniclers of events are at liberty to indicate in the tournament table whether the defeats of such a player were 'actual' or 'declared' (defaulted).

FIDE INTERPRETATION ART. 21 (1971). AWARDING OF PRIZES IN CASE OF WITHDRAWAL. The question of whether or not a player who withdraws from a match is still entitled to receive the loser's prize was not decided.

FIDE INTERPRETATION ART. 21 (1976). Upon an inquiry by the Hungarian Chess Federation, the Commission recommends that tie-breaking be avoided if possible. For the purposes of published crosstables, tied players should be indicated as such and arranged in a convenient way, e.g., alphabetically. In those cases when tie-breaking must be used, such as to qualify players to a subsequent competition or to award a single trophy, the organizers should announce in advance which methods will be used for breaking the ties, and these methods should be included in the regulations for the tournament.

FIDE INTERPRETATIONS ART. 21 (1957, 1975). STANDARDS OF CHESS EQUIPMENT FOR FIDE TOURNAMENTS.

FIDE INTERPRETATION ART. 21 (1957). In a competition of FIDE, or one under FIDE auspices, it is recommended that the pieces be of the Staunton pattern or a similar pattern in order that the participants may recognize the pieces without confusion.

If the pieces would be different from those prescribed in the preceding paragraph and if one of the players or the captain of a team demands that the prescribed pattern be used, the utilization of that pattern is obligatory.

FIDE INTERPRETATION ART. 21 (1975). These regulations define the general standards for chess equipment to be used in FIDE competitions and apply only to the equipment used in FIDE competitions. Manufacturers of equipment and organizers are completely free to make and use equipment for all other competitions. Manufacturing is encouraged of all sets of artistic value, regardless of the practical possibilities of their use.

(a) Used in matches of two players shall be the chess pieces agreed upon by both. Their agreement shall also be observed concerning other equipment – chess table, board, and clock. In case the players disagree, the equipment to be used shall be decided by the chief arbiter of the match, who shall bear in mind the following standards for size and form.

(b) Used in the tournaments, Olympiads, and other competitions within the FIDE system shall be the chess equipment offered by the organizers (hosts) of a particular competition, provided that it conforms to the following standards and has been approved by the chief arbiter.

Chess Pieces.

Material. Chess pieces should be made of wood, plastic, or an imitation of these materials.

Height, Weight, Proportions. The king's height should be 8.5 to 10.5 cm (3.3 to 4.1 in.). The diameter of the king's base should measure 40 to 50% of the height. The size of the other pieces should be proportionate to their height and form. Other elements, such as stability, aesthetic considerations, etc., may also be taken into account. The weight of the pieces should be suitable for comfortable moving and stability.

Form, Style of Make. Recommended for use in FIDE competitions are those types of chess sets and equipment which have already been used in Men's Olympiads, Interzonal Tournaments, Candidates' Matches and Tournaments, and World Championship Matches. The pieces should be shaped so as to be clearly distinguishable from one another. In particular, the top of the king should differ distinctly from that of the queen. The top of the bishop may bear a notch or be of a special color clearly distinguishing it from a pawn.

Color of Chess Pieces. The dark pieces should be brown or black in color or dark shades of these colors. The light pieces may be white or cream or other light colors. The natural color of wood (walnut, maple, etc.) may also be used for this purpose. The pieces should not be shiny and should be pleasing to the eye.

Chessboards.

Material. Wood, plastic, cardboard, or cloth are recommended as material for chessboards. The board may also be of stone (marble) with appropriate light and dark colors, provided that the chief arbiter has found it acceptable. Natural wood with sufficient contrast, such as birch, maple, or European ash against walnut, teak, beech, etc., may also be used for boards, which must have a dull or neutral finish, never shiny.

Color of Chessboards. Combinations of colors, such as brown, green, or very light tan and white, cream, off-white ivory, buff, etc., may be used for the squares in addition to natural colors.

Proportions. The board size should be such that the pieces appear neither too crowded nor too lonely on the squares. It is recommended that the side of a square measure 5 to 6.5 cm (2.0 to 2.6 in).

Tables. A table, comfortable and of suitable height, may be fitted with a chessboard. If the table and board are separate from one another, the latter must be fastened and thus prevented from moving during play.

Chess Clocks.

Chess clocks should have a device signaling precisely when the hour hand indicates full hours. They should have the flag fixed at the figure 12 or at some other figure, but always so that its fall can be clearly seen, helping the arbiters and players to check the time. The clock should have no shine making the flag poorly visible. It should work as silently as possible, in order not to disturb the players during play.

Note to Art. 21.

The Laws and FIDE's interpretations do not embrace all situations in tournament practice. The growing number of competitions in the world and the growing number of those now studying the Laws will provide fresh material for improving the Laws. Special regulations should be drawn up for each competition, and should precisely define the details and particulars relating to that competition. This has been discussed in the section on organizing tournaments. Not all competitions are of the same importance or level, nor are the conditions the same, so that the regulations must be adapted to the given situation.

National federations have their own rules and supplementary provisions which are of internal significance. For international competitions, of course, FIDE's Laws and official Interpretations are conclusive. The authors have endeavoured in these notes to ensure that the advice and interpretations are in conformity and in full accordance with the official Laws and Interpretations of FIDE.

SUPPLEMENT NO. 1 TO THE LAWS OF CHESS

The Notation of Chess Games

Approved by the 1977 Central Committee Meeting.

FIDE recognizes for its own tournaments and matches only one system of notation, the algebraic system, and recommends the use of this uniform chess notation also for chess literature and periodicals. (*)

Description of the Algberaic system
1. Each piece is indicated by the first letter, a capital letter, of its name. Examples: K = king, Q = queen, R = rook, B = bishop, N = knight. (**)
2. For the first letter of the name of a piece, each player is free to use the first letter of the name which is commonly used in his country. Examples: F = fou (French for bishop), L = loper (Dutch for bishop). In printed publications, the use of figurines for the pieces is recommended.

3. Pawns are not indicated by their first letter, but are recognized by the absence of such a letter. Examples: e5, d4, a5.
4. The eight files (from left to right for White and from right to left for Black) are indicated by the small letters *a, b, c, d, e, f, g,* and *h,* respectively.
5. The eight ranks (from bottom to top for White and from top to bottom for Black) are numbered *1, 2, 3, 4, 5, 6, 7,* and *8,* respectively. Consequently, in the initial position the white pieces and pawns are placed on the first and second ranks; the black pieces and pawns on the eighth and seventh ranks.

(*) The provisions of this paragraph become effective on January 1, 1981. Until that date the descriptive system (and the long form of the algebraic system) are recognized, mainly to give those federations in which the descriptive notation is customary, ample opportunity to introduce the algebraic notation within the realm of their federation. Each federation should do its utmost to promote the algebraic notation, the simple rules of which are given in detail in this Supplement. Furthermore, each federation should do its utmost to urge the organizers of tournaments and matches other than those of FIDE within its realm to follow the provisions of this Supplement.
(**) In the case of the knight, for convenience's sake, N is used.

6. As a consequence of the previous rules, each of the sixty-four squares is invariably indicated by a unique combination of a letter and a number.

BLACK

8	a8	b8	c8	d8	e8	f8	g8	h8
7	a7	b7	c7	d7	e7	f7	g7	h7
6	a6	b6	c6	d6	e6	f6	g6	h6
5	a5	b5	c5	d5	e5	f5	g5	h5
4	a4	b4	c4	d4	e4	f4	g4	h4
3	a3	b3	c3	d3	e3	f3	g3	h3
2	a2	b2	c2	d2	e2	f2	g2	h2
1	a1	b1	c1	d1	e1	f1	g1	h1
	a	b	c	d	e	f	g	h

WHITE

7. Each move of a piece is indicated by (a) the first letter of the piece in question and (b) the square of arrival. There is no hyphen between (a) and (b). Examples: Be5, Nf3, Rd1. In the case of pawns, only the square of arrival is indicated. Examples: e5, d4, a5.

8. When a piece makes a capture, an *x* is inserted between (a) the first letter of the piece in question and (b) the square of arrival. Examples: Bxe5, Nxf3, Rxd1.

When a pawn makes a capture, not only the square of arrival but also the file of departure must be indicated, followed by an *x*. Examples: dxe5, gxf3, axb5. In the case of an en passant, the square of arrival is given as the square on which the capturing pawn finally rests and 'e.p.' is appended to the notation.

9. If two identical pieces can move to the same square, the piece that is moved is indicated as follows:

(1) If both pieces are on the same rank: by (a) the first letter of the name of the piece, (b) the file of departure, and (c) the square of arrival.

(2) If both pieces are on the same file: by (a) the first letter of the name of the piece, (b) the number of the square of departure, and (c) the square of arrival.

(3) If the pieces are on different ranks and files, method (1 is preferred. In case of a capture, an *x* must be inserted between (b) and (c). Examples:

(1) There are two knights, on the squares g1 and d2, and one of them moves to the square f3: either Ngf3 or Ndf3, as the case may be.

(2) There are two knights, on the squares g5 and g1, and one of them moves to the square f3: either N5f3 or N1f3, as the case may be.

(3) There are two knights, on the squares h2 and d4, and one of them moves to the square f3: either Nhf3 or Ndf3, as the case may be.

If a capture takes place on the square f3, the previous examples are changed by the insertion of an *x:* (1) either Ngxf3 or Ndxf3, (2) either N5xf3 or N1xf3, (3) either Nhxf3 or Ndxf3, as the case may be.

10. If two pawns can capture the same piece or pawn of the opponent, the pawn that is moved is indicated by (1) the letter of the file of departure, (b) an *x*, and (c) the square of arrival. Example: If there are white pawns on the squares c4 and e4, and a black pawn or piece on the square d5, the notation for White's move is either cxd5 or exd5, as the case may be.

11. In the case of the promotion of a pawn, the actual pawn move is indicated, followed immediately by the first letter of the new piece. Examples: d8Q, f8N, b1B, g1R.

Essential abbreviations

0-0	=	castling with rook h1 or rook h8 (king-side castling)
0-0-0	=	castling with rook a1 or rook a8 (queen-side castling)
x	=	captures
+	=	check
++	=	mate
e.p.	=	captures 'en passant'.

Sample game

1. d4, Nf6 2. c4, e6 3. Nc3, Bb4 4. Bd2, 0-0 5. e4, d5 6. exd5, exd5 7. cxd5, Bxc3 8. Bxc3, Nxd5 9. Nf3, b6 10. Qb3, Nxc3 11. bxc3, c5 12. Be2, cxd4 13. Nxd4, Re8 14. 0-0, Nd7 15.a4, Nc5 16. Qb4, Bb7 17. a5, etc.

N.B. There is a variation in the indication of a capture which is used by a number of chess players, consisting in the use of a colon (:) instead of an *x*. From January 1, 1981 on, this variation will no longer be recognized in the interest of uniformity and clarity.

Other Systems Recognized until January 1, 1981

Algebraic System: Long Form

1. Each move in the long form is indicated by (a) the first letter of the piece in question, (b) the square of departure, and (c) the square of arrival. Pawns are not indicated by their first letter, but are recognized by the absence of such a letter. The squares of departure and of arrival are joined by a hyphen. Examples: Bd4–e5, Ng1–f3, Ra1–d1, e4–e5, d2–d4.

2. When a piece of pawn makes a capture, the hyphen is replaced by an *x*. Examples: Bd4xe5, Ng1xf3, Ra1xd1, e4xf5, d2xe3.

Sample game

1. d2–d4, Ng8–f6 2. c2–c4, e7–e6 3. Nb1–c3, Bf8–b4 4. Bc1–d2, 0-0 5. e2–e4, d7–d5 6. e4xd5, e6xd5 7. c4xd5, Bb4xc3 8. Bd2xc3, Nf6xd5 9. Ng1–f3, b7–b6 10. Qd1–b3, Nd5xc3 11. b2xc3, c7–c5 12. Bf1–e2, c5xd4 13. Nf3xd4, Rf8–e8 14. 0-0, Nb8–d7 15. a2–a4, Nd7–c5 16. Qb3–b4, Bc8–b7 17. a4–a5, etc.

Descriptive System

1. Each piece and pawn is indicated by the first letter, a capital letter, of its name. The pieces on the queen's side of the board in the initial position are indicated by a Q preceding to distinguish them from the similar pieces on the

BLACK

QR8	QN8	QB8	Q8	K8	KB8	KN8	KR8
QR7	QN7	QB7	Q7	K7	KB7	KN7	KR7
QR6	QN6	QB6	Q6	K6	KB6	KN6	KR6
QR5	QN5	QB5	Q5	K5	KB5	KN5	KR5
QR4	QN4	QB4	Q4	K4	KB4	KN4	KR4
QR3	QN3	QB3	Q3	K3	KB3	KN3	KR3
QR2	QN2	QB2	Q2	K2	KB2	KN2	KR2
QR1	QN1	QB1	Q1	K1	KB1	KN1	KR1

WHITE

king's side of the board in the initial position, indicated by a Ǩ preceding. Examples: R, N (or Kt), B, WR, KN.

2. For the first letter of the name of a piece, each player is free to use the first letter of the name which is commonly used in his country. Examples: F = fou (French for bishop), L = loper (Dutch for bishop).

3. The eight files (from left to right for White and from right to left for Black) are indicated by the pieces which occupy them in their initial position: QR, QN, QB, Q, K, KB, KN and KR, respectively.

4. The eight ranks (each player counting from bottom to top from his side) are indicated by 1, 2, 3, 4, 5, 6, 7 and 8, respectively. Consequently, in the initial position the white pieces and pawns are placed on the first and second ranks, the black pieces and pawns on the seventh and eight ranks from White's side and vice versa from Black's side.

5. As a consequence of the preceding rules, each of the sixty-four squares is indicated by two combinations of letters and numbers, depending upon whether White's or Black's move is being recorded.

6. Each pawn is indicated by the file on which it stands: QRP, QNP, QBP, QP, KP, KBP, KNP, KRP.

7. A move to a vacant square is indicated by (a) the first letter(s) of the piece or pawn in question and (b) the square of arrival, joined by a hyphen. When a move is written down, the basic forms R, N, B, and P (additionally, in the case of a pawn, the semi-condensed forms RP, NP, and BP), are used when only one piece or pawn of the specified type can move as indicated or if a recorded check identifies the move or capture. Examples: R-N3, B-B5, P-B4ch.

8. A capture is indicated by the first letter(s) of the capturing and captured pieces or pawns, joined by an *x*. Examples: BxB, QxR, PxP, PxBP.

9. When a basic form would be ambiguous at any point in the indicated move,

(1) a king-side or queen-side piece or pawn is specified if the piece or pawn can easily be so identified.

(2) the basic form is used, followed by a stroke (/) and the rank (preferably) or the file on which the piece or pawn stands, whichever will unambiguously identify the piece or pawn.

Examples: (1) There are two knights, on the squares KN1 and Q2, and one of them moves to the square KB3: either KN-B3 or QN-B3, as the case may be.

(2) There are two knights, on the squares KN5 and KN1, and one of them moves to the square KB3: either N/5-B3 or N/1-B3, as the case may be.

If a capture takes place on the square KB3, the previous examples are changed by the substitution of an *x* for the hyphen and of the first letter(s) of the captured piece or pawn for the square on which the capture takes place: (1) either KNxR or QNxR, (2) either N/5xR or N/1xR, as the case may be.

10. In the case of the promotion of a pawn, the actual pawn move is indicated, followed by a stroke or an equal sign and the first letter(s) of a new piece. Examples: PxR/Q or PxR=Q.

N.B. In a slightly different form of the descriptive system used in non-English-speaking countries, the rank precedes the square of arrival without a hyphen. Examples (in Spanish): P4AD, C3AR, P4D.

Essential abbreviations

0-0	=	castling with the king's rook
0-0-0	=	castling with the queen's rook
x	=	captures
ch.	=	check (or, in Spanish, +)
e.p.	=	captures 'en passant'.

Sample game

1. P-Q4, N-KB3 2. P-QB4, P-K3 3. N-QB3, B-N5 4. B-Q2, 0-0 5. P-K4, P-Q4 6. KPxP, PxP 7. PxP, BxN 8. BxB, NxP 9. N-B3, P-QN3 10. Q-N3, NxB 11. PxN, P-QB4 12. B-K2, PxP 13. NxP, R-K1 14. 0-0, N-Q2 15. P-QR4, N-B4 16. Q-N4, B-N2 17. P-QR5, etc.

SUPPLEMENT NO. 3.

A. Correspondence Notation

1. Each square of the chessboard is designated by a two-digit number as shown in the diagram below:

BLACK

1 2 3 4 5 6 7 8

WHITE

2. A move (including a capture) is indicated by stating the number of the square of departure and the number of the square of arrival, thus forming one four-figure number. Castling is expressed simply as a king's move. Thus, e2–e4 = 5254, and 0–0 = 5171 (king-side castling for White) or 5878 (king-side castling for Black).

B. Telecommunications Notation (Uedemann Code)

1. Each square of the chessboard is designated by two letters as shown in the diagram below:

BLACK

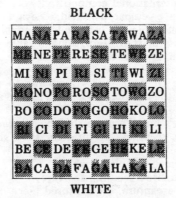

WHITE

2. A move (including a capture) is indicated by stating the two letters of the square of departure and the two letters of the square of arrival, thus forming one group of four letters. Castling is expressed simply as a king's move. Thus, e2–e4 = GEGO, and 0–0 = GAKA (king-side castling for White) or SAWA (king-side castling for Black).

SUPPLEMENT NO. 4.

Rules for Playing Chess Between Sighted and Blind Players

Advice:

In competitive chess between sighted and blind players (but also between blind players) the use of two chess-boards shall be obligatory, the sighted player using a normal chess-board, while the blind player (if two blind players each of them do so) uses an adapted chess-board (one with securing apertures). The special chess-board for the blind player is: a board with a minimum form of 20 X 20 cm . . . Each square of this special board has a securing aperture, in which the special chess pieces, placed on that field, will be secured. The squares must be distinguishable by touch; with the black squares somewhat higher than the white squares. The chess pieces are of Staunton pattern and the black pieces have a mark (for instance a small knob on the head.) Other forms of pieces are not allowed.

The following regulations shall govern play:

1. The moves shall be announced clearly and in the order in which they are played, repeated by the opponent and executed by each player on his board, in principle by himself.

Advice:

The announcements can be clearer, if names are used instead of the letters etc. In that case, in international competitions, one can use for the vertical lines: a - anna, b - bella, c - caspar, d - david, e - eva, f - felix, g - gustav and h - hector. Pieces and numbers in the best understandable language for the two players. In tournaments of the International Braille Chess Association (the world chess federation for the blind) they use the german numbers: eins, zwei, drei, vier, fünf, sechs, sieben, acht, and the pieces Turm, Springer, Läufer, Dame, König. Of course it is advisable to agree the international announcements before the competitive game with the arbiter.

2. On the blind player's board a piece shall be deemed 'touched' when it has been taken out of the securing aperture; for the sighted player the normal laws of chess apply.
3. A move shall be deemed completed when:
   (a) a piece is placed into a securing aperture;
   (b) in the case of a capture, the captured piece has been removed from the board of the player, who has the move;
   (c) the move has been announced.
Only after this (after the move has been announced) shall the opponent's clock be started.
4. A chess clock with a flag, accessible to touch, made specially for the blind, shall be admissible, if the blind player will use it. If such a clock is not used, the blind player has the right to ask for the consumed time at every moment.

5. If a clock is used, the blind player must record the moves in braille or in a tape/cassette recorder. In any case the sighted player must record the moves. If the blind player doesn't record the game, he has the right to ask for the exact number of moves made. The sighted player must give this information no later than completing his next move.

6. A slip of the tongue in announcing a move must be corrected immediately and before starting the clock of the opponent.

7. If, during a game, different positions should arise on the two boards, such differences have to be corrected with the assistance of the controller and by consulting both players' game scores. In resolving such differences, the player who has written down the correct move, but executed the wrong one, has to accept certain disadvantages, as the play has to be resumed from the point in which the game scores are the same (the current position).

8. If, when such discrepancies occur, the two game scores are also found to differ, the moves shall be retraced up to the point where the two scores agree, and the arbiter shall readjust the clocks accordingly. The controller should always correct the positions on the boards of the players until they correspond to the current position according to the game scores.

9. The blind player shall have to right to make use of an assistant who shall have the following duties:

    (a) to make the moves of the blind player on the board of the opponent;

    (b) to announce the moves of the sighted player;

    (c) to keep the score for the blind player and start his opponent's clock;

    (d) to inform the blind player, at his request, of the number of moves made and the time consumed by both players;

    (e) to claim the game in cases where the time-limit has been exceeded; and

    (f) to carry out the necessary formalities in cases where the game is adjourned.

10. If the blind player does not require any assistance, the sighted player may make use of an assistant who shall announce the moves of the sighted and after that he may start the clock of the blind player, and make the blind player's moves on the board of the sighted player. If it is necessary, the sighted player may also use this article, if the blind player also has use of an assistant, so that the sighted player and the blind player do not lose time on their clocks.

20 Equipment

The chess pieces began to be standardised in the mid-19th century through Howard Staunton's adoption of a set designed by Nathaniel Cook in 1849. 'Staunton' pieces were used in the Spassky–Fischer and Karpov–Korchnoi world championship matches.

Slight variations on the Staunton patterns have sprung up in many countries. See for instance the photo of the plastic pieces manufactured in Hong Kong and used widely in English-speaking countries.

Yugoslavia designed a special variant for the Dubrovnik 1950 Olympiad.

My wife, Olga Kažić, designed the pieces for the Skopje 1972 Olympiad . . .

. . . and the chess table that went with them.

The height of the king in the Staunton set is usually about 9.5 cm (3¾ inches). Such sets require boards with about 5.5 cm (2¼ inches) squares.

Boards are made from numerous materials. In early days in India, cloth boards were used. Nowadays wooden, rigid and roll-up plastic, and even paper boards are common. Folding boards are a convenient type.

There are many other types of sets, e.g. large ones for public parks . . . and pocket portable ones . . .

Demonstration boards (demoboards) are used for exhibiting the games of important competitions or lectures to large audiences.

Old-fashioned demoboards used hooks or ledges to support the pieces. The photograph shows a magnetic set on a metal board.

Modern boards for teachers include flockpaper on flannelograph boards, special sets for use on overhead projectors and videorecorder by which positions are transmitted onto television screens.

Chess Clocks

Clocks for controlling time-limits are becoming very sophisticated. A common club clock is the German BHB model.

The photo shows a more advanced model with a special scale to show in greater detail the last few minutes.

Digital clocks which clearly show the exact time including seconds are almost certain to become standard in the 1980's.

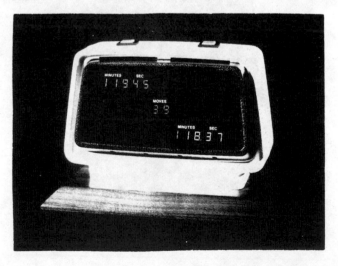

Timing devices for 5, 10 and/or 15 seconds per move have their markets. Special sets are available for blind players.

Stationery

In addition to the above equipment, chess also has its own special stationery. The illustrations below show the scoresheet used in the Fischer-Taimanov match, Vancouver 1971 and also a scoresheet in use in the United Kingdom.

These scoresheets often include a diagram which can be used to record the position at adjournment. An example is given on the next page.

BLACK .... pieces (RINGED)

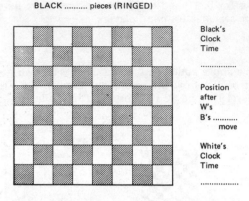

Black's
Clock
Time

....

Position
after
W's ....
B's ....
move

White's
Clock
Time

....

WHITE .... pieces

A similar form which incorporates further details is also available for submitting a position for adjudication.

Adjournment envelopes, in which the sealed move is placed, have space for all necessary information but can vary in actual format. The one used in the Spassky-Korchnoi match, Belgrade 1977, and another in common use in England, are shown below.

Correspondence (postal) chess also has a special scoresheet on which the dates of receipt and despatch of moves are recorded. This can take the form of the illustration, where the complete score of the game is transmitted on each occasion using an ordinary window envelope or of the illustration opposite, more popular for international events, where only the latest moves are shown. This latter type usually contains further information in more than one language, as the illustration shows.

DATES R | S	WHITE	BLACK	DATES R | S	DATES R | S	WHITE	BLACK	DATES R | S
		1				1	
		2				2	
		3				3	
		4				4	
		5				5	
		6				6	
		7				7	
		8				8	
		9				9	
		10				10	
		11				11	

GAME No.:   GAME No.

		12				12	
		13				13	
		14				14	
		15				15	
		16				16	
		17				17	
		18				18	
		19				19	
		20				20	
		21				21	
		22				22	
		23				23	
		24				24	
		25				25	
		26				26	
		27				27	

BRIAN ELEY & CO Dearne Road Bolton-on-Dearne Rotherham S63 8JR

		28				28	
		29				29	
		30				30	
		31				31	
		32				32	
		33				33	
		34				34	
		35				35	
		36				36	
		37				37	
		38				38	
		39				39	
		40				40	
		41				41	
		42				42	

You moved	I move												My total time	days
Vous avez joué	Je joue		**A**	**B**	**C**	**D**	**E**	**F**	**G**	**H**		Mon temps total	jours
Sie zogen	Ich ziehe	8	18	28	38	48	58	68	78	88	8	Meine Gesamtzeit	Tage
На Ваш ход	отвечаю	7	17	27	37	47	57	67	77	87	7	Мое полное время	дней
Ha jugado usted	Yo juego	6	16	26	36	46	56	66	76	86	6	Mi tiempo total es de	dias
		5	15	25	35	45	55	65	75	85	5		
		4	14	24	34	44	54	64	74	84	4	Your total time	days
		3	13	23	33	43	53	63	73	83	3	Votre temps total	jours
		2	12	22	32	42	52	62	72	82	2	Ihre Gesamtzeit	Tage
		1	11	21	31	41	51	61	71	81	1	Ваше полное время	дней
			A	**B**	**C**	**D**	**E**	**F**	**G**	**H**		Su tiempo total es de	dias

I propose a draw;	I accept;	I refuse;	I resign	Holidays from:	to:
Je propose nulle;	J'accepte;	je refuse;	J'abandonne.	Les vacances de:	a
Ich biete Remis;	ich nehme an;	Ich lehne ab;	Ich gebe auf.	Urlaub von	bis
Предлагаю ничью	принимаю	отклоняю	сдаюсь	Отпуск от	до
Propongo tablas;	acepto;	rebuso;	abandono	Las vacaciones desde el	al

Received	sent	Time employed by me:	days	Yours sincerely
Reçu	expédié	Mon temps de réflexion:	jours	Votre devoué
An	ab	Bedenkzeit	Tage	Mit Gruss
Получено	отослано	Время на обдумывание	дней	С приветом
Recibido	remitido	Tiempo empleado por mi	dias	Saludos

Your move is impossible. Votre coup est impossible. Ihr Zug ist unmöglich.
Ваш ход не возможен   Su jugada es imposible

Appendix

BERGER INTERNATIONAL TABLES OF ROUNDS

3 or 4 Players

Round	Pairings	
1	1:4	2:3
2	4:3	1:2
3	2:4	3:1

5 or 6 Players

Round	Pairings		
1	1:6	2:5	3:4
2	6:4	5:3	1:2
3	2:6	3:1	4:5
4	6:5	1:4	2:3
5	3:6	4:2	5:1

7 or 8 Players

Round	Pairings			
1	1:8	2:7	3:6	4:5
2	8:5	6:4	7:3	1:2
3	2:8	3:1	4:7	5:6
4	8:6	7:5	1:4	2:3
5	3:8	4:2	5:1	6:7
6	8:7	1:6	2:5	3:4
7	4:8	5:3	6:2	7:1

9 or 10 Players

Round	Pairings				
1	1:10	2:9	3:8	4:7	5:6
2	10:6	7:5	8:4	9:3	1:2
3	2:10	3:1	4:9	5:8	6:7
4	10:7	8:6	9:5	1:4	2:3
5	3:10	4:2	5:1	6:9	7:8
6	10:8	9:7	1:6	2:5	3:4
7	4:10	5:3	6:2	7:1	8:9
8	10:9	1:8	2:7	3:6	4:5
9	5:10	6:4	7:3	8:2	9:1

NOTE: where there are an odd number of players the highest number represents the bye.

11 or 12 Players

Round	Pairings					
1	1:12	2:11	3:10	4:9	5:8	6:7
2	12:7	8:6	9:5	10:4	11:3	1:2
3	2:12	3:1	4:11	5:10	6:9	7:8
4	12:8	9:7	10:6	11:5	1:4	2:3
5	3:12	4:2	5:1	6:11	7:10	8:9
6	12:9	10:8	11:7	1:6	2:5	3:4
7	4:12	5:3	6:2	7:1	8:11	9:10
8	12:10	11:9	1:8	2:7	3:6	4:5
9	5:12	6:4	7:3	8:2	9:1	10:11
10	12:11	1:10	2:9	3:8	4:7	5:6
11	6:12	7:5	8:4	9:3	10:2	11:1

13 or 14 Players

Round	Pairings						
1	1:14	2:13	3:12	4:11	5:10	6:9	7:8
2	14:8	9:7	10:6	11:5	12:4	13:3	1:2
3	2:14	3:1	4:13	5:12	6:11	7:10	8:9
4	14:9	10:8	11:7	12:6	13:5	1:4	2:3
5	3:14	4:2	5:1	6:13	7:12	8:11	9:10
6	14:10	11:9	12:8	13:7	1:6	2:5	3:4
7	4:14	5:3	6:2	7:1	8:13	9:12	10:11
8	14:11	12:10	13:9	1:8	2:7	3:6	4:5
9	5:14	6:4	7:3	8:2	9:1	10:13	11:12
10	14:12	13:11	1:10	2:9	3:8	4:7	5:6
11	6:14	7:5	8:4	9:3	10:2	11:1	12:13
12	14:13	1:12	2:11	3:10	4:9	5:8	6:7
13	7:14	8:6	9:5	10:4	11:3	12:2	13:1

15 or 16 Players

Round				Pairings				
1	1:16	2:15	3:14	4:13	5:12	6:11	7:10	8:9
2	16:9	10:8	11:7	12:6	13:5	14:4	15:3	1:2
3	2:16	3:1	4:15	5:14	6:13	7:12	8:11	9:10
4	16:10	11:9	12:8	13:7	14:6	15:5	1:4	2:3
5	3:16	4:2	5:1	6:15	7:14	8:13	9:12	10:11
6	16:11	12:10	13:9	14:8	15:7	1:6	2:5	3:4
7	4:16	5:3	6:2	7:1	8:15	9:14	10:13	11:12
8	16:12	13:11	14:10	15:9	1:8	2:7	3:6	4:5
9	5:16	6:4	7:3	8:2	9:1	10:15	11:14	12:13
10	16:13	14:12	15:11	1:10	2:9	3:8	4:7	5:6
11	6:16	7:5	8:4	9:3	10:2	11:1	12:15	13:14
12	16:14	15:13	1:12	2:11	3:10	4:9	5:8	6:7
13	7:16	8:6	9:5	10:4	11:3	12:2	13:1	14:15
14	16:15	1:14	2:13	3:12	4:11	5:10	6:9	7:8
15	8:16	9:7	10:6	11:5	12:4	13:3	14:2	15:1

17 or 18 Players

Round	Pairings								
1	1:18	2:17	3:16	4:15	5:14	6:13	7:12	8:11	9:10
2	18:10	11:9	12:8	13:7	14:6	15:5	16:4	17:3	1:2
3	2:18	3:1	4:17	5:16	6:15	7:14	8:13	9:12	10:11
4	18:11	12:10	13:9	14:8	15:7	16:6	17:5	1:4	2:3
5	3:18	4:2	5:1	6:17	7:16	8:15	9:14	10:13	11:12
6	18:12	13:11	14:10	15:9	16:8	17:7	1:6	2:5	3:4
7	4:18	5:3	6:2	7:1	8:17	9:16	10:15	11:14	12:13
8	18:13	14:12	15:11	16:10	17:9	1:8	2:7	3:6	4:5
9	5:18	6:4	7:3	8:2	9:1	10:17	11:16	12:15	13:14
10	18:14	15:13	16:12	17:11	1:10	2:9	3:8	4:7	5:6
11	6:18	7:5	8:4	9:3	10:2	11:1	12:17	13:16	14:15
12	18:15	16:14	17:13	1:12	2:11	3:10	4:9	5:8	6:7
13	7:18	8:6	9:5	10:4	11:3	12:2	13:1	14:17	15:16
14	18:16	17:15	1:14	2:13	3:12	4:11	5:10	6:9	7:8
15	8:18	9:7	10:6	11:5	12:4	13:3	14:2	15:1	16:17
16	18:17	1:16	2:15	3:14	4:13	5:12	6:11	7:10	8:9
17	9:18	10:8	11:7	12:6	13:5	14:4	15:3	16:2	17:1

19 or 20 Players

Round	Pairings									
1	1:20	2:19	3:18	4:17	5:16	6:15	7:14	8:13	9:12	10:11
2	20:11	12:10	13:9	14:8	15:7	16:6	17:5	18:4	19:3	1:2
3	2:20	3:1	4:19	5:18	6:17	7:16	8:15	9:14	10:13	11:12
4	20:12	13:11	14:10	15:9	16:8	17:7	18:6	19:5	1:4	2:3
5	3:20	4:2	5:1	6:19	7:18	8:17	9:16	10:15	11:14	12:13
6	20:13	14:12	15:11	16:10	17:9	18:8	19:7	1:6	2:5	3:4
7	4:20	5:3	6:2	7:1	8:19	9:18	10:17	11:16	12:15	13:14
8	20:14	15:13	16:12	17:11	18:10	19:9	1:8	2:7	3:6	4:5
9	5:20	6:4	7:3	8:2	9:1	10:19	11:18	12:17	13:16	14:15
10	20:15	16:14	17:13	18:12	19:11	1:10	2:9	3:8	4:7	5:6
11	6:20	7:5	8:4	9:3	10:2	11:1	12:19	13:18	14:17	15:16
12	20:16	17:15	18:14	19:13	1:12	2:11	3:10	4:9	5:8	6:7
13	7:20	8:6	9:5	10:4	11:3	12:2	13:1	14:19	15:18	16:17
14	20:17	18:16	19:15	1:14	2:13	3:12	4:11	5:10	6:9	7:8
15	8:20	9:7	10:6	11:5	12:4	13:3	14:2	15:1	16:19	17:18
16	20:18	19:17	1:16	2:15	3:14	4:13	5:12	6:11	7:10	8:9
17	9:20	10:8	11:7	12:6	13:5	14:4	15:3	16:2	17:1	18:19
18	20:19	1:18	2:17	3:16	4:15	5:14	6:13	7:12	8:11	9:10
19	10:20	11:9	12:8	13:7	14:6	15:5	16:4	17:3	18:2	19:1

21 or 22 Players

Round					Pairings					
1	1:22	2:21	3:20	4:19	5:18	6:17	7:16	8:15	9:14	10:13	11:12
2	22:12	13:11	14:10	15:9	16:8	17:7	18:6	19:5	20:4	21:3	1:2
3	2:22	3:1	4:21	5:20	6:19	7:18	8:17	9:16	10:15	11:14	12:13
4	22:13	14:12	15:11	16:10	17:9	18:8	19:7	20:6	21:5	1:4	2:3
5	3:22	4:2	5:1	6:21	7:20	8:19	9:18	10:17	11:16	12:15	13:14
6	22:14	15:13	16:12	17:11	18:10	19:9	20:8	21:7	1:6	2:5	3:4
7	4:22	5:3	6:2	7:1	8:21	9:20	10:19	11:18	12:17	13:16	14:15
8	22:15	16:14	17:13	18:12	19:11	20:10	21:9	1:8	2:7	3:6	4:5
9	5:22	6:4	7:3	8:2	9:1	10:21	11:20	12:19	13:18	14:17	15:16
10	22:16	17:15	18:14	19:13	20:12	21:11	1:10	2:9	3:8	4:7	5:6
11	6:22	7:5	8:4	9:3	10:2	11:1	12:21	13:20	14:19	15:18	16:17
12	22:17	18:16	19:15	20:14	21:13	1:12	2:11	3:10	4:9	5:8	6:7
13	7:22	8:6	9:5	10:4	11:3	12:2	13:1	14:21	15:20	16:19	17:18
14	22:18	19:17	20:16	21:15	1:14	2:13	3:12	4:11	5:10	6:9	7:8
15	8:22	9:7	10:6	11:5	12:4	13:3	14:2	15:1	16:21	17:20	18:19
16	22:19	20:18	21:17	1:16	2:15	3:14	4:13	5:12	6:11	7:10	8:9
17	9:22	10:8	11:7	12:6	13:5	14:4	15:3	16:2	17:1	18:21	19:20
18	22:20	21:19	1:18	2:17	3:16	4:15	5:14	6:13	7:12	8:11	9:10
19	10:22	11:9	12:8	13:7	14:6	15:5	16:4	17:3	18:2	19:1	20:21
20	22:21	1:20	2:19	3:18	4:17	5:16	6:15	7:14	8:13	9:12	10:11
21	11:22	12:10	13:9	14:8	15:7	16:6	17:5	18:4	19:3	20:2	21:1

23 or 24 Players

Round	Pairings											
1	1:24	2:33	3:22	4:21	5:20	6:19	7:18	8:17	9:16	10:15	11:14	12:13
2	24:13	14:12	15:11	16:10	17:9	18:8	19:7	20:6	21:5	22:4	23:3	1:2
3	2:24	3:1	4:23	5:22	6:21	7:20	8:19	9:18	10:17	11:16	12:15	13:14
4	24:14	15:13	16:12	17:11	18:10	19:9	20:8	21:7	22:6	23:5	1:4	2:3
5	3:24	4:2	5:1	6:23	7:22	8:21	9:20	10:19	11:18	12:17	13:16	14:15
6	24:15	16:14	17:13	18:12	19:11	20:10	21:9	22:8	23:7	1:6	2:5	3:4
7	4:24	5:3	6:2	7:1	8:23	9:22	10:21	11:20	12:19	13:18	14:17	15:16
8	24:16	17:15	18:14	19:13	20:12	21:11	22:10	23:9	1:8	2:7	3:6	4:5
9	5:24	6:4	7:3	8:2	9:1	10:23	11:22	12:21	13:20	14:19	15:18	16:17
10	24:17	18:16	19:15	20:14	21:13	22:12	23:11	1:10	2:9	3:8	4:7	5:6
11	6:24	7:5	8:4	9:3	10:2	11:1	12:23	13:22	14:21	15:20	16:19	17:18
12	24:18	19:17	20:16	21:15	22:14	23:13	1:12	2:11	3:10	4:9	5:8	6:7
13	7:24	8:6	9:5	10:4	11:3	12:2	13:1	14:23	15:22	16:21	17:20	18:19
14	24:19	20:18	21:17	22:16	23:15	1:14	2:13	3:12	4:11	5:10	6:9	7:8
15	8:24	9:7	10:6	11:5	12:4	13:3	14:2	15:1	16:23	17:22	18:21	19:20
16	24:20	21:19	22:18	23:17	1:16	2:15	3:14	4:13	5:12	6:11	7:10	8:9
17	9:24	10:8	11:7	12:6	13:5	14:4	15:3	16:2	17:1	18:23	19:22	20:21
18	24:21	22:20	23:19	1:18	2:17	3:16	4:15	5:14	6:13	7:12	8:11	9:10
19	10:24	11:9	12:8	13:7	14:6	15:5	16:4	17:3	18:2	19:1	20:23	21:22
20	24:22	23:21	1:20	2:19	3:18	4:17	5:16	6:15	7:14	8:13	9:12	10:11
21	11:24	12:10	13:9	14:8	15:7	16:6	17:5	18:4	19:3	20:2	21:1	22:23
22	24:23	1:22	2:21	3:20	4:19	5:18	6:17	7:16	8:15	9:14	10:13	11:12
23	12:24	13:11	14:10	15:9	16:8	17:7	18:6	19:5	20:4	21:3	22:2	23:1

TABLES FOR THE SCHEVENINGEN SYSTEM

Match on 4 boards

round 1	round 2	round 3	round 4
A_1–B_1	B_2–A_1	A_1–B_3	B_4–A_1
A_2–B_2	B_1–A_2	A_2–B_4	B_3–A_2
B_3–A_3	A_3–B_4	B_1–A_3	A_3–B_2
B_4–A_4	A_4–B_3	B_2–A_4	A_4–B_1

Match on 6 boards

round 1	round 2	round 3	round 4	round 5	round 6
B_1-A_1	B_2-A_1	A_1-B_3	A_1-B_4	B_5-A_1	A_1-B_6
B_5-A_2	A_2-B_1	A_2-B_2	B_6-A_2	B_4-A_2	A_2-B_3
A_3-B_4	B_3-A_3	B_1-A_3	A_3-B_5	A_3-B_6	B_2-A_3
A_4-B_2	B_4-A_4	B_6-A_4	A_4-B_1	B_3-A_4	A_4-B_5
A_5-B_3	A_5-B_6	B_5-A_5	B_2-A_5	A_5-B_1	B_4-A_5
B_6-A_6	A_6-B_5	A_6-B_4	B_3-A_6	A_6-B_2	B_1-A_6

Match on 8 boards

round 1	round 2	round 3	round 4	round 5	round 6	round 7	round 8
A_1-B_1	B_2-A_1	A_1-B_3	B_1-A_1	A_1-B_5	B_6-A_1	A_1-B_7	B_8-A_1
A_2-B_2	B_3-A_2	A_2-B_4	B_1-A_2	A_2-B_6	B_7-A_2	A_2-B_8	B_5-A_2
A_3-B_3	B_4-A_3	A_3-B_1	B_2-A_3	A_3-B_7	B_8-A_3	A_3-B_5	B_6-A_3
A_4-B_4	B_1-A_4	A_4-B_2	B_3-A_4	A_4-B_8	B_5-A_4	A_4-B_6	B_7-A_4
B_5-A_5	A_5-B_6	B_7-A_5	A_5-B_8	B_1-A_5	A_5-B_2	B_3-A_5	A_5-B_4
B_6-A_6	A_6-B_7	B_8-A_6	A_6-B_5	B_2-A_6	A_6-B_3	B_4-A_6	A_6-B_1
B_7-A_7	A_7-B_8	B_5-A_7	A_7-B_6	B_3-A_7	A_7-B_4	B_1-A_7	A_7-B_2
B_8-A_8	A_8-B_5	B_6-A_8	A_8-B_7	B_4-A_8	A_8-B_1	B_2-A_8	A_8-B_3

HUTTON PAIRING SYSTEM

Bd. 1 B v C means that Board 1 of each B and C team play each other, with the first named having White.

Where there is an odd number of teams the last column shows where one team plays against another one, not on the same board number.

At the end of each sequence of pairings, extra boards should be played in the same order as given, starting again with the top pairings.

Teams should be allocated Team letters by lot before play commences.

3 Teams

Bd.	1	B—C;	
"	2	A—B;	C2—A1
"	3	B—A;	
"	4	C—B;	A4—C3

4 Teams

Bd.	1	A—B;	C—D;
"	2	B—C;	D—A;
"	3	A—C;	B—D;
"	4	D—B;	C—A;
"	5	C—B;	A—D
"	6	B—A;	D—C

5 Teams

Bd.				
1	B—E;	D—C;		
2	A—D;	C—B;	E2—A1	
3	A—C;	E—D;		
4	B—A;	C—E;	D4—B3	
5	B—C;	D—A;		
6	C—D;	E—B;	A6—E5	
7	A—B;	E—C;		
8	C—A;	D—E;	B8—D7	

6 Teams

Bd.			
1	A—E;	B—D;	F—C;
2	C—B;	D—A;	E—F
3	A—C;	E—D;	F—B
4	B—A;	C—E;	D—F
5	A—F;	B—E;	C—D
6	D—C;	E—B;	F—A
7	C—F;	D—B;	F—A
8	A—D;	B—C;	F—E
9	B—F;	C—A;	D—E
10	A—B;	E—C;	E—D

7 Teams

Bd.				
1	B—G;	D—E;	F—C;	
2	A—F;	C—D;	E—B;	G2—A1
3	C—A;	D—G;	E—F;	
4	A—D;	B—C;	G—E;	F4—B3
5	A—E;	D—B;	G—F;	
6	B—A;	C—G;	F—D;	E6—C5
7	B—E;	D—C;	F—A;	
8	C—F;	E—D;	G—B;	A8—G7
9	C—B;	D—A;	E—G;	
10	A—C;	F—E;	G—D;	B10—F9
11	A—B;	D—F;	G—C;	
12	B—D;	E—A;	F—G;	C12—E11

8 Teams

Bd.				
1	A—H;	B—G;	C—F;	D—E
2	E—C;	F—B;	G—A;	H—D
3	A—F;	B—E;	C—D;	G—H
4	D—B;	E—A;	F—G;	H—C
5	A—D;	B—C;	F—H;	G—E
6	C—A;	D—G;	E—F;	H—B
7	A—B;	E—H;	F—D;	G—C
8	B—A;	C—G;	D—F;	H—E
9	E—D;	F—C;	G—B;	H—A
10	A—G;	B—F;	C—E;	D—H
11	D—C;	E—B;	F—A;	H—G
12	A—E;	B—D;	C—H;	G—F
13	C—B;	D—A;	E—G;	H—F
14	A—C;	B—H;	F—E;	G—D

9 Teams

Bd.					
1	B—I:	D—G;	F—E;	H—C;	
2	A—H;	C—F;	E—D;	G—B;	I2—A1
3	C—A;	E—H;	F—G;	I—D;	
4	A—F;	B—E;	D—C;	G—I;	H4—B3
5	A—E;	B—D;	H—G;	I—F;	
6	C—B;	D—A;	E—I;	F—H;	G6—C5
7	B—F;	C—E;	G—A;	H—I;	
8	A—B;	D—H;	E—G;	I—C;	F8—D7
9	B—G;	D—E;	F—C;	H—A;	
10	C—H;	E—F;	G—D;	I—B;	A10—I9
11	C—D;	E—B;	F—A;	I—G;	
12	A—C;	D—I;	G—F;	H—E;	B12—H11
13	A—D;	B—C;	H—F;	I—E;	
14	D—B;	E—A;	F—I;	G—H;	C14—G13
15	B—A;	C—I;	G—E;	H—D;	
16	A—G;	E—C;	F—B;	I—H;	D16—F15

10 Teams

Bd.					
1	A—J;	B—I;	C—H;	D—G;	E—F
2	F—D;	G—C;	H—B;	I—A;	J—E
3	A—H;	B—G	C—F;	D—E;	I—J
4	E—C;	F—B;	G—A;	H—I;	J—D
5	A—F;	B—E;	C—D;	H—J;	I—G
6	D—B;	E—A;	F—I;	G—H;	J—C
7	A—D;	B—C;	G—J;	H—F;	I—E
8	C—A;	D—I;	E—H;	F—G;	J—B
9	A—B;	F—J;	G—E;	H—D;	I—C
10	B—A;	C—I;	D—H;	E—G;	J—F
11	F—E;	G—D;	H—C;	I—B;	J—A
12	A—I;	B—H;	C—G;	D—F;	E—J
13	E—D;	F—C;	G—B;	H—A;	J—I
14	A—G;	B—F;	C—E;	D—J;	I—H
15	D—C;	E—B;	F—A;	G—I;	J—H
16	A—E;	B—D;	C—J;	H—G;	I—F
17	C—B;	D—A;	E—I;	F—H;	J—G
18	A—C;	B—J;	G—F;	H—E;	I—D

11 Teams

Bd.						
1	B—K;	D—I;	F—G;	H—E;	J—C;	K2—A1
" 2	A—J;	C—H;	E—F;	G—D;	I—B;	
" 3	A—C;	E—J;	F—I;	G—H;	K—D;	J4—B3
" 4	B—G;	C—F;	D—E;	H—A;	I—K;	
" 5	D—B;	E—A;	F—K;	G—J;	H—I;	I6—C5
" 6	A—F;	B—E;	C—D;	J—H;	K—G;	
" 7	A—G;	C—E;	F—B;	I—J;	K—H;	H8—D7
" 8	B—C;	D—A;	E—K;	G—I;	J—F;	
" 9	B—H;	C—G;	F—D;	I—A;	J—K;	G10—E9
" 10	A—B;	D—J;	E—I;	H—F;	K—C;	
" 11	B—I;	D—G;	F—E;	H—C;	J—A;	A12—K11
" 12	C—J;	E—H;	G—F;	I—D;	K—B;	
" 13	A—H;	E—D;	F—C;	G—B;	K—I;	B14—J13
" 14	C—A;	D—K;	H—G;	I—F;	J—E;	
" 15	D—C;	E—B;	F—A;	G—K;	H—J;	C16—I15
" 16	A—E;	B—D;	I—H;	J—G;	K—F;	
" 17	A—D;	C—B;	F—J;	I—G;	K—E;	D18—H17
" 18	B—F;	E—C;	G—A;	H—K;	J—I;	
" 19	B—A;	C—K;	F—H;	I—E;	J—D;	E20—G19
" 20	A—I;	D—F;	G—C;	H—B;	K—J;	

12 Teams

Bd.						
1	A—K;	B—J;	C—I;	D—H;	E—G;	I—F
" 2	F—E;	G—D;	H—C;	I—B;	J—A;	K—L
" 3	A—I;	B—H;	C—G;	D—F;	K—J;	L—E
" 4	E—D;	F—C;	G—B;	H—A;	I—K;	J—L
" 5	A—G;	B—F;	C—E;	J—I;	K—H;	L—D
" 6	D—C;	E—B;	F—A;	G—K;	H—J;	I—L
" 7	A—E;	B—D;	I—H;	J—G;	K—F;	L—C
" 8	C—B;	D—A;	E—K;	F—J;	G—I;	H—L
" 9	A—C;	H—G;	I—F;	J—E;	K—D;	L—B
" 10	B—A;	C—K;	D—J;	E—I;	F—H;	G—L
" 11	G—F;	H—E;	I—D;	J—C;	K—B;	L—A
" 12	A—L;	B—K;	C—J;	D—I;	E—H;	F—G
" 13	F—L;	G—E;	H—D;	I—C;	J—B;	K—A
" 14	A—J;	B—I;	C—H;	D—G;	E—F;	L—K
" 15	E—L;	F—D;	G—C;	H—B;	I—A;	J—K
" 16	A—H;	B—G;	C—F;	D—E;	K—I;	L—J
" 17	D—L;	E—C;	F—B;	G—A;	H—K;	I—J
" 18	A—F;	B—E;	C—D;	J—H;	K—G;	L—I
" 19	C—L;	D—B;	E—A;	F—K;	G—J;	H—I
" 20	A—D;	B—C;	I—G;	J—F;	K—E;	L—H

13 Teams

Bd.							
1	B—M;	D—K;	F—I;	H—G;	J—E;	L—C;	M2—A1
" 2	A—L;	C—J;	E—H;	G—F;	I—D;	K—B;	
" 3	C—A;	D—M;	E—L;	I—H;	J—G;	K—F;	L4—B3
" 4	A—J;	B—I;	F—E;	G—D;	H—C;	M—K;	
" 5	B—D;	E—A;	F—M;	H—K;	I—J;	L—G;	K6—C5
" 6	A—H;	C—F;	D—E;	G—B;	J—L;	M—I;	
" 7	A—G;	B—F;	C—E;	K—J;	L—I;	M—H;	J8—D7
" 8	D—C;	E—B;	F—A;	G—M;	H—L;	I—K;	
" 9	A—I;	C—G;	F—D;	H—B;	K—L;	M—J;	I10—E9
" 10	B—C;	D—A;	E—M;	G—K;	J—H;	L—F;	
" 11	A—K;	D—H;	E—G;	I—C;	J—B;	M—L;	H12—F11
" 12	B—A;	C—M;	F—J;	G—I;	K—E;	L—D;	
" 13	B—K;	D—I;	F—G;	H—E;	J—C;	L—A;	A14—M13
" 14	C—L;	E—J;	G—H;	I—F;	K—D;	M—B;	
" 15	C—H;	D—G;	E—F;	I—B;	J—A;	K—M;	B16—L15
" 16	A—F;	C—K;	G—J;	H—I;	L—E;	M—D;	
" 17	B—G;	E—D;	F—C;	H—A;	I—M;	L—J;	C18—K17
" 18	A—E;	D—B;	G—L;	J—I;	K—H;	M—F;	
" 19	A—F;	B—E;	C—D;	K—I;	L—H;	M—G;	D20—J19
" 20	E—C;	F—B;	G—A;	H—M;	I—L;	J—K;	

14 Teams

Bd.	1	A—M;	B—L;	C—K;	D—J;	E—I;	F—H;	N—G
"	2	G—F;	H—E;	I—D;	J—C;	K—B;	L—A;	M—N
"	3	A—K;	B—J;	C—I;	D—H;	E—G;	M—L;	N—F
"	4	F—E;	G—D;	H—C;	I—B;	J—A;	K—M;	L—N
"	5	A—I;	B—H;	C—G;	D—F;	L—K;	M—J;	N—E
"	6	E—D;	F—C;	G—B;	H—A;	I—M;	J—L;	K—N
"	7	A—G;	B—F;	C—E;	K—J;	L—I;	M—H;	N—D
"	8	D—C;	E—B;	F—A;	G—M;	H—L;	I—K;	J—N
"	9	A—E;	B—D;	J—I;	K—H;	L—G;	M—F;	N—C
"	10	C—B;	D—A;	E—M;	F—L;	G—K;	H—J;	I—N
"	11	A—C;	I—H;	J—G;	K—F;	L—E;	M—D;	N—B
"	12	B—A;	C—M;	D—L;	E—K;	F—J;	G—I;	H—N
"	13	H—G;	I—F;	J—E;	K—D;	L—C;	M—B;	N—A
"	14	A—N;	B—M;	C—L;	D—K;	E—J;	F—I;	G—H
"	15	G—N;	H—F;	I—E;	J—D;	K—C;	L—B;	M—A
"	16	A—L;	B—K;	C—J;	D—I;	E—H;	F—G;	N—M
"	17	F—N;	G—E;	H—D;	I—C;	J—B;	K—A;	L—M
"	18	A—J;	B—I;	C—H;	D—G;	E—F;	M—K;	N—L
"	19	E—N;	F—D;	G—C;	H—B;	I—A;	J—M;	K—L
"	20	A—H;	B—G;	C—F;	D—E;	L—J;	M—I;	N—K

15 Teams

Bd.	1	B—O;	D—M;	F—K;	H—I;	J—G;	L—E;	N—C;	O1—A2
"	2	A—N;	C—L;	E—J;	G—H;	I—F;	K—D;	M—B;	
"	3	C—A;	E—N;	F—M;	I—J;	K—H;	L—G;	O—D;	N4—B3
"	4	A—L;	B—K;	D—I;	G—F;	H—E;	J—C;	M—O;	
"	5	B—D;	E—A;	G—N;	H—M;	J—K;	L—I;	O—F;	M6—C5
"	6	A—J;	C—H;	D—G;	F—E;	I—B;	K—O;	N—L;	
"	7	E—C;	F—B;	G—A;	H—O;	I—N;	J—M;	K—L;	L8—D7
"	8	A—H;	B—G;	C—F;	D—E;	M—K;	N—J;	O—I;	
"	9	B—H;	C—G;	F—D;	I—A;	L—M;	N—K;	O—J;	K10—E9
"	10	A—F;	D—C;	E—B;	G—O;	H—N;	J—L;	M—I;	
"	11	A—K;	B—J;	G—E;	H—D;	I—C;	N—M;	O—L;	J12—F11
"	12	C—B;	D—A;	E—O;	F—N;	K—I;	L—H;	M—G;	
"	13	A—M;	D—J;	E—I;	H—F;	K—C;	L—B;	O—N;	I14—G13
"	14	B—A;	C—O;	F—L;	G—K;	J—H;	M—E;	N—D;	
"	15	B—M;	D—K;	F—I;	H—G;	J—E;	L—C;	N—A;	A16—O15
"	16	C—N;	E—L;	G—J;	I—H;	K—F;	M—D;	O—B;	
"	17	C—J;	E—H;	F—G;	I—D;	K—B;	L—A;	O—M;	B18—N17
"	18	A—C;	D—O;	G—L;	H—K;	J—I;	M—F;	N—E;	
"	19	B—I;	E—F;	G—D;	H—C;	J—A;	L—N;	O—K;	C20—M19
"	20	A—E;	D—B;	F—O;	I—L;	K—J;	M—H;	N—G;	

16 Teams

Bd.	1	A—O;	B—N;	C—M;	D—L;	E—K;	F—J;	G—I;	P—H
"	2	H—G;	I—F;	J—E;	K—D;	L—C;	M—B;	N—A;	O—P
"	3	A—M;	B—L;	C—K;	D—J;	E—I;	F—H;	O—N;	P—G
"	4	G—F;	H—E;	I—D;	J—C;	K—B;	L—A;	M—O;	N—P
"	5	A—K;	B—J;	C—I;	D—H;	E—G;	N—M;	O—L;	P—F
"	6	F—E;	G—D;	H—C;	I—B;	J—A;	K—O;	L—N;	M—P
"	7	A—I;	B—H;	C—G;	D—F;	M—L;	N—K;	O—J;	P—E
"	8	E—D;	F—C;	G—B;	H—A;	I—O;	J—N;	K—M;	L—P
"	9	A—G;	B—F;	C—E;	L—K;	M—J;	N—I;	O—H;	P—D
"	10	D—C;	E—B;	F—A;	G—O;	H—N;	I—M;	J—L;	K—P
"	11	A—E;	B—D;	K—J;	L—I;	M—H;	N—G;	O—F;	P—C
"	12	C—B;	D—A;	E—O;	F—N;	G—M;	H—L;	I—K;	J—P
"	13	A—C;	J—I;	K—H;	L—G;	M—F;	N—E;	O—D;	P—B
"	14	B—A;	C—O;	D—N;	E—M;	F—L;	G)K;	H—J;	I—P
"	15	A—P;	I—H;	J—G;	K—F;	L—E;	M—D;	N—C;	O—B
"	16	B—O;	C—N;	D—M;	E—L;	F—K;	G—J;	H—I;	P—A
"	17	H—P;	I—G;	J—F;	K—E;	L—D;	M—C;	N—B;	O—A
"	18	A—N;	B—M;	C—L;	D—K;	E—J;	F—I;	G—H;	P—O
"	19	G—P;	H—F;	I—E;	J—D;	K—C;	L—B;	M—A;	N—O
"	20	A—L;	B—K;	C—J;	D—I;	E—H;	F—G;	O—M;	P—N

RECORD OF TEAM MATCH

_____

(team)   (team)

(place, date) _ _ _ _ _ _ _   _(Competition, round)_ _ _ _

No. Board	Team	Result		Team	Note
	(names)			(names)	
	Total				

On odd boards the team . . . had the white pieces.

(captain) _____   Arbiter _____   (captain) _____

(Notes)

The above is a typical result form for a team match. See p. 13.

ARBITER'S RECORD OF CHESS COMPETITION

(name of competition) _____

(Date) _ _ _ _ _ _ _   (Round) _ _ _ _ _

                    (Place and hours of play) _ _ _

No.	Players White Black	Result	Opening	No. of moves	Time of finish	Note

Arbiter,

Some arbiters refer to the above chart as a daysheet. See p. 70.

CROSSTABLE FORM FOR TEAM COMPETITION

(This method of Soviet arbiter I. Alekseyev shows at the same time team and individual results.)

		CYPRUS		YUGOSLAVIA		BRAZIL		JAPAN		TOTAL	PLACE
CYPRUS	KLEOPAS CONSTANTINOU AVGOUSTI MARTIDES VASSIADES HADJITOFI	— — 0 0 0 0	0		0	0 — 1 0 0	1	0 — 0 ½ ½	1	2	IV
YUGOSLAVIA	GLIGORIC IVKOV LJUBOJEVIĆ MATANOVIC MATULOVIC RUKAVINA	— 1 — 1 1 1	4			1 ½ 1 — — ½	3	— 1 1 1 1 —	4	11	I
BRAZIL	GERMAN TROIS NOBREGA TOTH VAN RIEMSDYK SANTOS	1 0 — 1 1 —	3	0 ½ 0 ½ — —	1			1 1 ½ 1 — —	3½	7½	II
JAPAN	MIYASAKA MATSUMOTO HONDA TAKAHASHI OTANI NAKAMORI	1 1 — ½ ½	3	0 — 0 0 — 0	0	0 0 ½ 0 — —	½			3½	III

The above chart is used for round-robin team tournaments. See p. 13 & 121.

CHART OF POINTS REQUIRED FOR INTERNATIONAL TITLES

%	Categories					Number of Games												
	GM	IM	FM	WGM	IWM	9	10	11	12	13	14	15	16	17	18	19	20	21
76	7	1		5W	1W	$7\frac{1}{2}$	8	$8\frac{1}{2}$	$9\frac{1}{2}$	10	11	$11\frac{1}{2}$	$12\frac{1}{2}$	13	14	$14\frac{1}{2}$	$15\frac{1}{2}$	16
73	8	2		6W	2W	7	$7\frac{1}{2}$	$8\frac{1}{2}$	9	$9\frac{1}{2}$	$10\frac{1}{2}$	11	12	$12\frac{1}{2}$	$13\frac{1}{2}$	14	15	$15\frac{1}{2}$
70	9	3		7W	3W	$6\frac{1}{2}$	7	8	$8\frac{1}{2}$	$9\frac{1}{2}$	10	$10\frac{1}{2}$	$11\frac{1}{2}$	12	13	$13\frac{1}{2}$	14	15
67	10	4		8W	4W	$6\frac{1}{2}$	7	$7\frac{1}{2}$	$8\frac{1}{2}$	9	$9\frac{1}{2}$	$10\frac{1}{2}$	11	$11\frac{1}{2}$	$12\frac{1}{2}$	13	$13\frac{1}{2}$	$14\frac{1}{2}$
64	11	5	1	1	5W	6	$6\frac{1}{2}$	$7\frac{1}{2}$	8	$8\frac{1}{2}$	9	10	$10\frac{1}{2}$	11	12	$12\frac{1}{2}$	13	$13\frac{1}{2}$
60	12	6	2	2	6W	$5\frac{1}{2}$	6	7	$7\frac{1}{2}$	8	$8\frac{1}{2}$	9	10	$10\frac{1}{2}$	11	$11\frac{1}{2}$	12	13
57	13	7	3	3	7W	$5\frac{1}{2}$	6	$6\frac{1}{2}$	7	$7\frac{1}{2}$	8	9	$9\frac{1}{2}$	10	$10\frac{1}{2}$	11	$11\frac{1}{2}$	12
53	14	8	4	4	8W	5	$5\frac{1}{2}$	6	$6\frac{1}{2}$	7	$7\frac{1}{2}$	8	$8\frac{1}{2}$	$9\frac{1}{2}$	10	$10\frac{1}{2}$	11	$11\frac{1}{2}$
50	15	9	5	5	1	$4\frac{1}{2}$	5	$5\frac{1}{2}$	6	$6\frac{1}{2}$	7	$7\frac{1}{2}$	8	$8\frac{1}{2}$	9	$9\frac{1}{2}$	10	$10\frac{1}{2}$
47	16	10	6	6	2	$4\frac{1}{2}$	5	$5\frac{1}{2}$	6	$6\frac{1}{2}$	7	$7\frac{1}{2}$	8	8	$8\frac{1}{2}$	9	$9\frac{1}{2}$	10
43		11	7	7	3	4	$4\frac{1}{2}$	5	$5\frac{1}{2}$	6	$6\frac{1}{2}$	$6\frac{1}{2}$	7	$7\frac{1}{2}$	8	$8\frac{1}{2}$	9	$9\frac{1}{2}$
40		12	8	8	4	4	4	$4\frac{1}{2}$	5	$5\frac{1}{2}$	6	6	$6\frac{1}{2}$	7	$7\frac{1}{2}$	8	8	$8\frac{1}{2}$
36		13	9	9	5	$3\frac{1}{2}$	4	4	$4\frac{1}{2}$	5	$5\frac{1}{2}$	$5\frac{1}{2}$	6	$6\frac{1}{2}$	$6\frac{1}{2}$	7	$7\frac{1}{2}$	8
33		14	10	10	6	3	$3\frac{1}{2}$	4	4	$4\frac{1}{2}$	5	5	$5\frac{1}{2}$	6	6	$6\frac{1}{2}$	7	7
30		15	11	11	7	3	3	$3\frac{1}{2}$	4	4	$4\frac{1}{2}$	$4\frac{1}{2}$	5	$5\frac{1}{2}$	$5\frac{1}{2}$	6	6	$6\frac{1}{2}$

CATEGORIES

WOMEN
1W	2051–2075
2W	2076–2160
3W	2101–2125
4W	2126–2150

5W	2151–2175
6W	2176–2200
7W	2201–2225
8W	2226–2250

STANDARD
1	2251–2275
2	2276–2300
3	2301–2325
4	2326–2350

5	2351–2375
6	2376–2400
7	2401–2425
8	2425–2450

9	2451–2475
10	2476–2500
11	2501–2525
12	2526–2550

13	2551–2575
14	2576–2600
15	2601–2625
16	2626–2650

A CROSSTABLE OF A SWISS-SYSTEM TOURNAMENT

Louis D. Statham Masters-Plus Tournament
Lone Pine, California, March 20–30, 1977

Player	FIDE Rating	USCF Rating	1	2	3	4	5	6	7	8	9	Sc.	USCF Perf. Rating
1 Yuri Balashov (USR), GM	2565	—	W14	D7	W18	W8	D5	W20	L2	D10	W9	6½	2633
2 Oscar Panno (ARG), GM	2550	2558	W41	D18	D15	W29	D7	W4	W1	D9	D3	6½	2642
3 Dragutin Sahovic (YUG), IM	2460	—	L8	W27	W24	D4	D15	W30	W6	W7	D2	6½	2590
4 Nona Gaprindashvili (USR), IM	2430	—	W48	W17	L5	D3	W13	L2	W12	W20	W7	6½	2647
5 William Lombardy (USA), GM	2530	2534	D36	W39	W4	W23	D1	L7	D20	D11	W16	6	2570
6 Larry Christiansen (USA), GM	2460	2470	W25	D8	D30	L20	W34	W32	L3	W14	W15	6	2503
7 John Peters (USA)	2370	2413	W43	D1	W42	W13	D2	W5	D9	L3	L4	5½	2515
8 Roy Ervin (USA)	2360	2356	W3	D6	W10	L1	D16	D11	D21	D27	W20	5½	2564
9 Pal Benko (USA), GM	2455	2513	D22	D40	W38	D30	W23	D29	D7	D2	L1	5½	2497
10 Walter S. Browne (USA), GM	2545	2547	D15	D31	L8	W43	W33	D16	W23	D1	D11	5½	2498
11 Samuel Reshevsky (USA), GM	2490	2459	D42	D22	W46	D15	W33	D8	W29	D5	D10	5½	2479
12 Leonid Shamkovich (USA), GM	2485	2485	D24	D38	D22	W40	D32	D14	L4	W29	W27	5½	2457
13 Anatoly Lein (USA), GM	2525	2524	D38	W36	W33	L7	L4	W26	L14	W39	W24	5½	2473
14 Kenneth Regan (USA)	2375	2394	L1	W48	D34	D42	W35	D12	W13	L6	W21	5½	2502
15 Julio Kaplan (USA), IM	2445	2379	D10	W19	D2	D11	D3	D37	D16	W25	L6	5	2534
16 Norman Weinstein (USA), IM	2475	2455	D46	D24	D40	W18	D8	D10	D15	W22	L5	5	2446
17 James Tarjan (USA), GM	2495	2535	W27	L4	W31	D32	L20	D22	D18	D23	W30	5	2441
18 Michael Rohde (USA), IM	2380	2377	W21	D2	L1	L16	D47	W28	D17	W37	D19	5	2546
19 Miguel Quinteros (ARG), GM	2555	2531	D31	L15	W25	D33	L29	W46	D39	W26	D18	5	2403
20 Peter Blylasas (CAN), IM	2435	2409	D35	D24	W45	W6	W17	L1	D5	L4	L8	4½	2419
21 Laszio Szabo (HUN), GM	2530	—	L18	D45	W36	D22	D42	W38	W33	D24	L14	4½	2353
22 Yasser Selrawin (USA)	—	2362	D9	D11	D12	D21	D26	D17	W33	L16	D23	4½	2462
23 John Grefe (USA), IM	2425	2445	W47	W34	D29	L5	L9	W42	L10	D17	D22	4½	2403

	Player	FIDE Rating	USCF Rating	1	2	3	4	5	6	7	8	9	Sc.	USCF Perf. Rating
24	Edward Formanek (USA)	2410	2361	D12	D16	L3	D31	D39	W35	W32	D21	L13	4½	2437
25	Eugene Meyer (USA)	2345	2360	L6	D26	L19	W44	D28	W31	W30	L15	D32	4½	2405
26	Mark Diesen (USA), IM	2360	2399	L29	D25	W44	D34	D22	L13	W42	L19	W38	4½	2356
27	Peter Cleghorn (USA)	—	2378	L17	L3	W48	L35	W41	W45	W37	D8	L12	4½	2403
28	William Martz (USA), IM	2410	2446	D40	L42	D35	D46	D25	L18	D38	W47	W39	4½	2350
29	Jaime Sunye (BRA)	2565	—	W26	W37	D23	L2	W19	L9	L11	L12	D31	4	2438
30	Helgi Olafsson (ICE)	2385	2362	D37	W44	D6	D9	D11	L3	L25	W35	L17	4	2391
31	Arnold Denker (USA), IM	2335	2385	D19	L10	L17	D24	D46	L25	W40	W42	D29	4	2360
32	Arthur Bisguier (USA), GM	2440	2417	L34	W47	W43	D17	D12	L6	L24	D38	D25	4	2332
33	Kenneth Frey (MEX), IM	2390	2338	D44	W35	L13	D19	L10	W47	L22	D34	D36	4	2335
34	Denis Verduga (ECU), IM	2300	2186	W32	L23	D14	D26	L6	L39	W41	D33	D37	4	2377
35	Jonathan Tisdall (USA)	2375	2297	D20	L33	D28	W27	L14	L24	W48	L30	W43	4	2322
36	John Fedorowicz (USA)	2440	2327	D5	L13	L21	L45	D43	W48	D47	W46	D33	4	2340
37	Larry Evans (USA), GM	2555	2565	D30	L29	D39	D38	W45	D15	L27	L18	D34	3½	2237
38	Curt Brasket (USA)	—	2364	D13	D12	L9	D37	W40	L21	D28	D32	L26	3½	2380
39	Carlos Garcia-Palermo (ARG)	2380	—	D45	L5	D37	D47	D24	W34	L19	D13	L28	3½	2324
40	David Goodman (ENG)	2340	—	D28	D9	D16	D12	L38	D43	L31	L41	W48	3½	2315
41	David Strauss (USA)	2260	2381	L2	L43	L47	W48	L27	D44	L34	W40	W46	3½	2245
42	Lawrence Day (CAN), IM	2355	—	D11	W28	L7	D14	D21	L23	L26	L31	D44	3	2281
43	Bryon Nickoloff (CAN)	—	2300	L7	W41	L32	L10	D36	D40	D46	D44	L35	3	2242
44	Vincent McCambridge (USA)	—	2260	D33	L30	L26	L25	L48	D41	W45	D43	D42	3	2204
45	Jay Whitehead (USA)	—	2239	D39	D21	L20	W36	L37	L27	L44	L48	W47	3	2260
46	Arthur Dake (USA), IM	2365	2348	D16	D20	L11	D28	D31	L19	D43	L36	L41	2½	2238
47	Ronald Henley (USA)	—	2331	L23	L32	W41	D39	D18	L33	D36	L28	L45	2½	2200
48	Eugene Martinovsky (USA)	—	2306	L4	L14	L27	L41	W44	L36	L35	W45	L40	2	2122

Index

The following index lists terms which are likely to be required, except that some expressions are grouped under a general title, e.g. Laws of Chess, with the most significant of these being cross-referenced. Page numbers are italicised.